Black

Legacy Of African Diaspora

Brian A. Belton

C000156508

Black Routes

Legacy Of African Diaspora

Brian A. Belton

HANSIB PUBLICATIONS

London and Hertfordshire UK

First published 2007 in Great Britain
by Hansib Publications Limited
London and Hertfordshire, UK
Website: www.hansib-books.com
Email: info@hansib-books.com

ISBN 978-1-870518-92-5

© Brian A. Belton
The right of Brian A. Belton to be identified as the author of this work has been asserted
in accordance with sections 77 and 78 of the Copyright, Designs and Patents Act 1988.

All rights reserved. No part of this publication may be reproduced, stored in or
introduced into a retrieval system, or transmitted in any form, or by any means,
electronic, mechanical, photocopying, recording, or otherwise, without the prior
permission of the publishers.

Design and production by Print Resources, Hertfordshire, England

Typeset in Baskerville 11/13pt.

Cover design by Shareef Ali, Graphic Resolutions, Hertfordshire, England

Printed by The Alden Press, Oxford, UK

"To Sofia and Israel Belton...the Slave and the Quaker, who by marriage unshackled each other and bequeathed me African genes and freedom's dreams."

The Author

DR. BRIAN BELTON was born and bred in the West Ham/Canning Town area of London. Brian's father, the son of a Gypsy mother and a gas works stoker father, was a stall holder (costermonger); his mother, a former school dinner lady, is the daughter of an East London socialist councillor who played an active role in the radical Popularism movement of the 1920s.

After finishing his initial education at Burke Secondary Modern School in Plaistow, Brian started his working life alongside his father. He graduated from the East End youth gang culture of the late 1960s and early 1970s, to take up professional training in youth and community work. After practicing as a youth worker in Bethnal Green he attended City University to gain his BSc. Working with some of the most challenging young people in locations as diverse as Glasgow and the Falkland Islands, Brian completed his Masters degree at Essex University and was awarded his Doctorate by the University of Kent in 2000 (his thesis focused on the nature of identity, race and ethnicity).

Brian is now a Senior Lecture at the YMCA George Williams College in Canning Town and an experienced author, sociologist, critical anthropologist and social historian. He has taught all over the world and has written more than twenty books (several focusing on his beloved West Ham United football club), including: *Questioning Gypsy Identity: Ethnic Narratives in Britain and America*, AltaMira (2004): *Gypsy and Traveller Ethnicity: The Social Generation of an Ethnic Phenomenon*, Routledge,an imprint of Taylor & Francis Books Ltd (2004): *Black Hammers: The Voices of West Ham's Ebony Heroes*, Pennant Books Ltd. (2006): *A Dream Come True: Lewis Hamilton, Black Lightening*, Pennant Books Ltd. (2007): *Fay Taylour: Queen of Speedway*, Panther Publishing Ltd (2006)

Contents

Introduction

BLACK ROUTES is published at a moment when British society celebrates its two hundred year march away from slavery and its abandonment of that malevolent institution that betrayed shackled black people and utterly demeaned and dehumanised the whites who profited from that shameful trade. The book has been published at this time to draw attention to representatives of those who have made the great journey of black people over those two centuries and exemplify the beautiful black blossoms of humanity that have bloomed out of the barbarity of bondage; to demonstrate how far we have come, 'Up From Slavery', but also to remind us that our passage is not yet done.

However, '*Black Routes*' has had an expedition of its own. The book was motivated by the response to a series of lunch-time lectures held at the YMCA George Williams College, in Canning Town, East London. I started giving these talks as many students had commented on the lack of appreciation for the contribution of black thinkers to the modern world. But my own study of these figures had started many years previously. These people had inspired me to move from the gang and street life of the East End, where I was born and brought up, through a range of sparking vistas. They were the individuals I had read about in Plaistow library or heard talking or being talked about on late night Radio Four programmes that I thought only I was listening to, stereotypically under the bedclothes, at first with a torch, but after threats from my grandfather, in the suffocating darkness, with my transistor at its lowest possible volume, pressed hard to my ear until it went numb.

Before I reached the age of twenty figures like Malcolm X, Gwendolyn Brooks and Kwame Ture (aka Stokely Carmichael) had made me want to change the world. These glorious minds and intelligent yet exciting activists taught me what injustice was and something of the means to address it. Like me, many of them were from hard neighbourhoods, where education was distrusted and/or a rare, not altogether understood process.

So, if they could do it, so could I. From the educational basis of Burke Secondary Modern School, where the hapless and hopeless of the East End were assigned, I both amazed and alienated my peers, and signed up to take a couple of 'O' levels at night school at West Ham College of Further Education. It was the start of a long road fraught with obstacles and difficulties, but sprinters with arms held high, with fists clenched in black gloves, Ali dancing, shouting poetry at a stunned world and always, the words of Malcolm, "by any means necessary" kept me focused.

Over two decades later I received my PhD in a very white Canterbury Cathedral. I had studied the nature of race and ethnicity and found them to be, as Ashley Montague would have it "Man's Most Dangerous Myth". Then I raised my fist too. Not for me, but in recognition of those who had accompanied me from the educational dustbin of one of the worst educational authorities in Britain, at a time when the UK had the poorest record of secondary education in Western Europe.

As such, it is perhaps not surprising, when my time came to lecture to others, I talked about these people. Politics, Panthers, people, power, pulsating, pumping, pandemonium. Critique, cringing calamity, crisis, change, charging charismatic chimera. But when people approached me, often young black men and women, and told me they had never heard of Michael Akintaro, that they had not a clue who Clive Charles or Ericka Huggins were, when fellow academics, who never even attended the lectures, dismissed the Black Panthers as no more than a "bunch of trouble makers", I knew more was needed and thus the idea of this book was born - out of wisdom, ignorance, knowledge and prejudice. What a dangerous child it might be.

At all the lectures the notes were sold for a very small fee to raise funds to help fight sickle cell anaemia. In a small way, fighting suffering on another front. By reading this book you will join the great human struggle that all the people included in the pages that follow have been part of. It is this struggle that is their legacy, part of the contribution of the African Diaspora to the development, the route, the path of humanity. The subjects were not included for any particular reason; there are many others that could have doubled the words between these covers. Perhaps everyone who looks at the names could add many more. In fact I hope you might do this and that someone will write a book about those not included here. It will be a massive volume indeed. That is what this book is meant to do, to introduce to or remind the reader of the intellectual contribution of people bound together by oppression and love, liberation and a constant resistance to hatred. As such it is not altogether an academic book, but a work that contains the sum of lives and the wisdom of those existences. Please read it gently and with care...but remember, as Panther Eldridge Cleaver would have it, too much agreement kills the chat, so feel the power of these lives and do it... "by any means necessary".

Brian A. Belton

CHAPTER 1

Gwendolyn Brooks
The Poet who called to black people everywhere

The literary career of Gwendolyn Brooks was distinguished enough to be coveted by any writer but it is also axiomatic that, being black and a woman, she achieved more than her fair share of 'firsts' in a vocation that spanned eight decades. Amongst other things she was the first African-American to win the Pulitzer Prize (1950) and to be appointed to the American Academy of Arts and Letters (1976).

A woman of many literary achievements and perhaps the most beloved ambassador for poetry in America during the second half of the 20th century, Gwendolyn was born on 7th. June, 1917 in her grandmother's home of Topeka, Kansas, the first child of David Anderson Brooks, a janitor - son of a runaway slave - and school teacher Keziah Corinne Wims Brooks. The one month-old Gwendolyn was taken by her parents to Champlain Avenue, Chicago and remained a 'Chicagoan' all her life. The city was to inspire much of her finest work, just as it had done for Carl Sandburg fifty years earlier, the person she followed as Poet Laureate of Illinois in 1968.

Brooks described her upbringing as being based on duty, decency, dignity, industry and, tellingly, kindness. A shy, bookish child, she developed an early passion for poetry and in 1930 her first published verse appeared in *American Childhood* magazine. By the age of 17 Gwendolyn was submitting work to the weekly poetry column of the *Chicago Defender*, a newspaper primarily for Chicago's black community in which she published almost a hundred poems.

Graduating from college during the Depression, Brooks was obliged to take up domestic and secretarial work to make a living. However, at the age of twenty she was publicity director of the Youth Council of the National Association for the Advancement of Coloured People. In 1939 she married Henry Blakely, also an aspiring writer. They divorced in 1969 but were reunited four years later. Her first collection of poetry, *A Street in Bronzeville* appeared in 1945. It depicted everyday life of black people on Chicago's South Side, an area peopled with memorable and impressive characters.

In 1946 Gwendolyn won a Guggenheim fellowship, and a $1,000 award from the American Academy of Arts and Letters. Three years later she was awarded the Pulitzer Prize for her second collection, *Annie Allen*. She was 33 years of age and the first black American to win a Pulitzer.

Annie Allen was a sequence of poems about a black girl growing up in Chicago; it won particular praise for Brooks' innovation in poetic technique, the sonnet-ballad. Her poetic oeuvre grew to include more than a dozen books, including *Bronzeville Boys and Girls* (1956) and *The Bean Eaters* (1960), that was typical of her work in that it was strikingly forthright, rejecting the exclusive poetics that became so common in academic poetry in Britain and America. It provided an original study of the lives of mainly poor urban blacks, taking in the heroism of early civil-rights workers and events of particular outrage. She dealt directly, for example, with the 1955 Emmett Till lynching and the 1957 school desegregation crisis in Little Rock, Arkansas, placing "the evil that men do" within the commonplaces of the perpetrators', and the victims', everyday lives.

Selected Poems was published in 1963, the memorable year of the March on Washington, a time when the civil rights movement was in full swing across America. More and more black writers were increasingly outspoken in attacking racism and insisting on full political, economic, and social equality for all black Americans. The rest of the sixties would be an eventful decade for black civil-rights in America and Brooks. She was nominated for a National Book Award in 1968 for *In the Mecca*.

Throughout her career Brooks travelled incessantly, giving thousands of readings around the world. Her reputation as a poet somewhat overshadowed her only novel, *Maud Martha* published in1953, which is, in many ways, a significant precursor of more recent fiction by African-American women. Written with an affecting precision that details the process by which the young woman protagonist gradually matures, Brooks acknowledged its similarities to the trajectory, if not the specifics, of her own life, reflecting "There's fact-meat in the soup, among the chunks of fancy."

More specific autobiography was included in her 1972 book, *Report From Part One*. This book marks a point at which her work was becoming more outspoken and militant. It is a medley of reminiscences, interviews, photographs and vignettes, in which Brooks tellingly writes:-

> "Are you aware of the fact-that-should-be startling about the High Days of my youth? All were Europe-rooted or America-rooted. Not one celebration in my black household or in any black household that I knew featured any black glory, greatness or grandeur. A capricious bunch of entries and responses has brought me to my present understanding of fertile facts. Know-nows: I know now that I am essentially an essential African, in occupancy here because of an indeed 'peculiar' institution. I know that the

black emphasis must be, not against white, but FOR black"

Respect

This is essentially a call for respect. John W. Gardner was one of America's greatest builders of ideas and institutions and a unifier of people and causes. He was a leader in many circles, from government and politics to civil rights, education, and philanthropy. John was a believer in the responsibility of government to create social change, as evidenced by his leadership in designing Medicare programs. According to him:-

> "If you have some respect for people as they are, you can be more effective in helping them to become better than they are."

Gwendolyn was able to engineer this type of process through her writing and her activity connected to the same. She continually described herself as a 'teacher'; she gave workshops on the craft of verse at numerous universities and throughout her work Brooks argues that one cannot hope to be respected by others unless one respects oneself. This is reminiscent of the thinking of Maurice Maeterlinck, the Belgium play-write and Nobel Prize winner who noted that if one lacks self-respect, one cannot properly respect others. He wrote:-

> "If you love yourself meanly, childishly, timidly, even so shall you love your neighbour."

For Maeterlinck, and also for Gwendolyn, respecting others matters, and because one's respect is worth little to others unless it is based on self-respect, one does well to cultivate it, based on all that one can thoughtfully and generously credit to oneself.

Inherent in Brooks' work is the contention that our first impulse on meeting someone for the first time should be to look to respect them. This is to say we should seek factors in their actions that warrant respect. To this extent respect is given but at the same time earned. We should approach people in this way for the sake of the innate dignity of humanity in general, and for the possibilities inherent in any individual in particular. The person we meet for the first time might turn out to be a new friend; they might turn out to be a person who, to the benefit of the world, has one or more human virtues or graces: for example talent, kindness, courage, integrity, warmth, humour or charm. They might turn out to be a person who suffers, which deserves respect in the form of sympathy (this is different to pity), or who dreams great dreams, which deserves the respect of indulgence. Grounds for respect are legion, and mostly familiar.

This view of human behaviour understands that virtues and graces deserve to be honoured because they add to the world's sum of good. The hope to find them in people, and to seek them in others, is an attitude that deserves respect. If the new acquaintance turns out to lack virtue or grace they might prove to be greedy, dishonest, unkind, selfish or worse; then one does not give respect, which, if the world were a better place, would be felt by people as the worst possible consequence of action.

Respect is an attitude that one free individual gives another, firstly in hope that one will find something to respect and secondly as the result of finding out that the other merits it. In short they earn the reward of continued respect.

Respect is not the same as admiration: "Fools admire", was the 17th century poet Alexander Pope's terse observation. How often are any of us guilty of salivating after the admiration of fools? And what fools we make of ourselves in the seeking adoration or prostrating ourselves in veneration. Maybe we would maintain more dignity or self-respect, perhaps gaining more respect in the process, if we were to give endorsement or agreement so following Popes contention that "...wise men approve".

We might also be wary of worship, which often seems to come too easily to people in these days of media idols and reverence for the poorest of actors propelled at us by way of the televised soap operas. Many of us appear to need to worship others or be worshiped. For the American Civil War poet and writer Oliver Wendell Holmes:-

"Men are idolaters, and want something to look at and kiss and hug, or throw themselves down before."

He went on to add that if the idol in question were made of wood, it could just as well be made of words.

Listening and being heard

Brooks maintained an unwavering commitment to reflect in her art lives actually lived. She related to the details of the day-to-day existence of 'ordinary' people. She examined the consequences of racial and ethnic identity and of prejudice, black pride and solidarity, family strengths and weaknesses, the experience of women, their capacity to love and the particulars of motherhood. Her efforts made Gwendolyn an established and respected talent, but she retained her steadfast fidelity to the community in which she lived, worked and taught from her earliest years.

After starting out as a 'literary integrationist', Brooks might have been marginalised by more strident black writings of the civil rights era, but she was open to change and always sought to develop her art. During the 1960s her career began to change under the influence of the civil rights movement. She was clear that through the movement that she rediscovered her blackness: it was in 1967 after a Fisk University writers' conference, following an address by an angry Leroi Jones (Amiri Baraka) the revolutionary black activist and poet. Brooks was startled by the younger writers she met of whom she was to say:

> "They seemed so proud, committed to their own people. They felt black poets should write…about blacks, and address themselves to blacks."

To her credit, Gwendolyn deftly rejected the insularity that such a position risks, but thereafter she was increasingly concerned with making her own and other writing accessible:

> "My aim, in the next future, is to write poems that will somehow successfully 'call' all black people: black people in taverns, black people in alleys, black people in gutters, schools, offices, prisons, the consulate; I wish to reach black people in pulpits, black people in mines. On farms, on thrones; not always to 'teach' – I shall wish often to entertain, to illume."

That phrase, to entertain and illume, was and is vitally important. It allowed Gwendolyn to transmit to her chosen audience the intricate messages found in the lives of the women, men, and children of America's black communities, the treasure she used to fill more than twenty books that provide a bountiful insight into humanity in general.

Gwendolyn's increasing concern for accessibility and affordable pricing led her to move publishers, and work with small local presses. Never forgetting the breath of experience within the human voice, she used her later work to support African American publishing houses, principally the black imprint Broadside Press, founded in Detroit by the poet Dudley Randall, with whom she published *Riot* (1969) and *Family Pictures* (1970). Brooks also established her own outlet, the David Company (named for her father). By turning her back on the far more commercial house of Harper & Row, her publisher for more than 20 years, no doubt Gwendolyn limited the distribution of her final books, and it cannot be a coincidence that her reputation in academic circles has waned in the past quarter of a century. But this was a professional decision based on conviction and ideals regardless of cost, and it was typical of the artistic choices that Brooks made. She was that rare being, a writer at once genuine and generous. She helped many younger poets through the maze of the American poetry industry to eventual publication, and was famous for accepting money from various literary awards and grants and then herself 'awarding' it to younger, unknown writers. These actions might be understood as being motivated by Gwendolyn's wish for others to hear the voice of black people, the voices she had listened to.

Brooks was singular talent in the modern world so obsessed with self rather than the needs of others. She never accepted a tenured post, keeping herself for her readership and the development of that constituency. For her, poetry was a public event, no matter how intimate the subject. She once said: "I believe that we all should know each other, if possible…and poetry is the best way to speak truth." According to Gwendolyn, poetry was an important voice in an elaborate conversation across time. Conversation relies on an exchange between listeners. Brooks' work was a product of her own listening that was at the same time an effort to facilitate the listening of others. In this she echoes Dietrich Bonhoeffer in *Life Together* (1949). Bonhoeffer was one of the few church leaders in Nazi Germany who stood in courageous opposition to Hitler and his policies. This 'resistance' led to Bonhoeffer's murder in the Flossenbürg concentration camp in 1945. In *Life Together* he writes about a 'Ministry of Listening' (p.87-89). I quote him at length because I feel he demonstrates how listening is linked to respect, of self and others, this being the kernel of Brooks' literary project.

As a Christian theologian Bonhoeffer makes his points in reference to 'God', but his position can also be grasped in more general terms; how the lack of an ability to listen in effect undermines the human integrity of the potential listener and those who wish to be heard. It puts into perspective our contemporary obsession with 'participation' that is often thought to be evidenced by 'talking'.

Please forgive the masculine pronouns, what follows was written long before our 'enlightened' times:-

"The first service that one owes to others in the fellowship consists in listening to them. Just as love of God begins with listening to His Word, so the beginning of love for the brethren is learning to listen to them. It is God's love for us that he not only gives us His Word but also lends us His ear. So it is his work that we do for our brother when we learn to listen to him. Christians, especially ministers, so often think they must always contribute something when they are in the company of others, that this is the one service they have to render. They forget that listening can be a greater service than speaking.

Many people are looking for an ear that will listen. They do not find it among Christians, because these Christians are talking where they should be listening. But he who can no longer listen to his brother will soon be no longer listening to God either; he will be doing nothing but prattle in the presences of God too. This is the beginning of the death of the spiritual life, and in the end there is nothing left but spiritual chatter and clerical condescension arrayed in pious words. One who cannot listen long and patiently will presently be talking beside the point and be never really speaking to others, albeit he be not conscious of it. Anyone who thinks that his time is too valuable to spend keeping quiet will eventually have not time for God and his brother, but only for himself and for his own follies.

Brotherly pastoral care is essentially distinguished from preaching by the fact that, added to the task of speaking the Word, there is the obligation of listening. There is a kind of listening with half an ear that presumes already to know what the other person has to say. It is an impatient, inattentive listening, that despises the brother and is only waiting for a chance to speak and thus get rid of the other person. This is no fulfilment of our obligation, and it is certain that here too our attitude toward our brother only reflects our relationship to God. It is little wonder that we are no longer capable of the greatest service of listening that God has committed to us, that of hearing our brother's confession, if we refuse to give ear to our bother on lesser subjects. Secular education today is aware that often a person can be helped merely by having someone who will listen to him seriously, and upon this insight it has constructed its own soul therapy, which has attracted great numbers of people, including Christians. But Christians have forgotten that the ministry of listening has been committed to them by Him who is Himself the great listener and whose work they should share. We should listen with the ears of God that we may speak the Word of God."

Particular truth

The colour of Gwendolyn's skin only added to the complexities of her public life. At various points in her career she was denounced by the political forces of the Left and Right, but she despised dogma and the propaganda that all too often tries to pass for verse. Her attention to detail, whether in colloquial speech patterns or the nuances of traditional prosody, allowed her poetry an admirable range of tone and subject. *We Real Cool* (from *The Bean Eaters*) shows both a fascination with rhythmic compression.

The novelist Richard Wright, who himself was born into a poor Mississippi sharecropping family, was a great admirer of Brooks. His father had deserted his family when Wright was just five years old five, but he was to become the first African-American novelist to reach a general audience, even though he had barely a ninth grade education. His harsh childhood is depicted in one of his best books, his autobiography, *Black Boy* (1945). He later said that his sense of deprivation, due to racism, was so great that only reading kept him alive. For him, *We Real Cool* captured "...the pathos of petty destinies, the whimper of the wounded, the tiny incidents that plague the lives of the desperately poor"

This poem is a voice of Chicago's South Side, the violent and demanding world that Brooks knew from childhood on and a background that she defended, celebrated and mourned through a lifetime of writing. In this we can see the listening that Bonhoeffer exalts. Such posturing, doomed ignorance was always a prime target of her work, but she was tough on charitable 'do-gooders'. In her often anthologised poem, *The Lovers of the Poor* she demonstrates her distaste for such individuals that she only just held in check. The concentration of satire demands its own hard-edged sympathies, a form of compassion that is the hallmark of Gwendolyn's best art.

Brooks gave us the opportunity to listen across a range of genre as she also produced many works of non-fiction, pieces for children, essays and reviews. Her idealism was untarnished by age; she was almost 80 when *Report From Part Two* appeared in 1995.

In addition to the graces and virtues, achievement, or at least endeavour, is among the principal things that command respect as does 'right intention'. Gwendolyn was rich in all these considerations. A person who respects others, as Gwendolyn did, can give them their due, and deal justly with them, with understanding and latitude. It is people such as her that deserve the respect of others. Imagine a society in which everyone could mutually respect each other in these ways. If you can manage this task of the imagination ask yourself if such a society would need laws and prisons.

Edgar Watson Howe was, from 1877 to 1911, editor and proprietor of the Atchison, Kansas, *Daily Globe*. In 1911 he established *E. W. Howe's Monthly*, which was published until 1937. His first and generally considered best book is *The Story of a Country Town* (1883). This was one of the first realistic novels of small-town life in the Midwest of America and a precursor of the naturalistic novel in American fiction. Howe was always a champion of the common people. He once wrote:

> "...man is still a savage to the extent that he has little respect for anything that can't hurt him."

In short, when we respect only that which can harm us we are no more than barbarians, it is in the respect we have for others, regardless of their influence over us, that we find the seed of our humanity. The opposite of respect is contempt. What Gwendolyn shows us, as did Martin Luther King and, in his last days Malcolm X would reiterate, is that it is our contempt for others that makes us contemptible. The end point of such a cycle is the concentration camp and the self-loathing that concludes in spiritual or actual suicide.

Summation

The commitment of Gwendolyn Brooks always remained steadfast. She asserted: "I am interested in telling my particular truth as I have seen it." It may well have been this commitment to veracity that inspired Robert Pinsky, translator, essayist and Poet Laureate of the United States (1997-2000) when he first heard of her death to respond:

> "Gwendolyn Brooks will be remembered as a brilliant, essential American writer and as a hero."

However, her tone was gently insistent, never degenerating into the kind of dogma she so detested. On 12th. December, 2000 Gwendolyn Elizabeth Brooks died in Chicago. She was 83 years of age. She was survived by a daughter and a son.

CHAPTER 2

Bernie Grant - African Rebel

Anti-Racist campaigner, freedom fighter, Pan-Africanist, humanitarian and
pioneering activist for racial equality

Bernard Alexander Montgomery Grant was born on17th. February, 1944 in Georgetown, British Guiana, now Guyana, the son of two schoolteachers, Eric and Lily, who named him after two British Generals who were then fighting the Second World War.

Bernie was a man who courageously walked a political road that many would never consider the challenge of traversing. As a Union shop-steward, council leader and valiant MP, Grant championed many campaigns.

A real militant and an enthusiastic advocate for the exploited and disenfranchised, Bernie always maintained that oppressed groups need to organise themselves into political alliance if they are to advance. For Grant, the unity of black people throughout the Diaspora was critical and he was regarded by many as a leading spokesperson, not only for black people, but also for women, the disabled, the elderly, the Irish, youth, the poor and deprived. Contrary to popular belief he fought not only for racial justice, but for oppressed people whoever they were. But he was also a wise counsellor, who was resolute in his efforts to demonstrate an alternative, enriched, more subtle and politically demanding model of justice than many of his peers; he was unique.

Although criticised vehemently for his views, Bernie always felt it was his duty to speak up for ethnic minorities. Grant's critical stance which brought attention to a range of social injustices in Britain was one aspect of living through the years of Thatcherism that was an education. It was his battle to comprehend and communicate the nature of reality and fight for the needs of those he represented to be met that will keep him dear to the hearts of many in Tottenham and well beyond, who his regard for generated enduring respect in return. Bernie's skill in understanding his constituents, those who for more thirteen years appreciated him, even if they didn't always agree with his more 'celebrated' positions. He was known to be a brave, insightful and honourable person, who offered a distinctly alternative programme born out of his faith, founded on a down-to-earth yet militant vision of an economically just Britain. His legacy is one of a consciousness of responsibility.

Grant made a huge contribution to Britain during the last part of the twentieth century. I hope that the short analysis of the same that follows will shed light on this and show him to be more than the usual caricature that portrays him as at best a mere dissenting voice and at worst no more than a mischievous trouble maker. Bernie was that rare individual, a politician that made a difference; he provided the means for people to change their lives for the better and in the process those same people are altering the world, hopefully creating a richer, more egalitarian and expansive existence for us all.

The young Grant was educated at St. Joseph's RC, Sacred Heart and Ituni Government Schools, and later at St. Stanislaus College (one of the finest schools in British Guiana). He started his working life as an analyst in the Demerara Bauxite Company, Guyana.

With his family, Bernie took up the British government's invitation to people from the colonies to emigrate to the United Kingdom in 1963. He worked as a British Rail clerk before studying at Tottenham Technical College between 1965 and 1967. Starting in 1967 he studied Mining Engineering at Heriot-Watt University in Edinburgh however, he left that institution in 1969 in protest against discrimination against black students. For the next nine years he worked as an International Telephonist, quickly becoming involved in the Union of Post Office Workers, fighting for the rights of fellow employees.

By 1978 Grant was a full-time union official with the National Union of Public Employees (NUPE) working as an Area Officer, responsible for local authority and health workers. He founded the Black Trades Unionists Solidarity Movement (BTUSM), and worked for it full time between 1981 and 1984.

Grant's early political leanings took him, briefly, into the Workers' Revolutionary Party and he was a member of the Socialist Labour League. However, having joined the Tottenham Labour Party in 1973 gaining experience in numerous positions within the local party, in 1978, with a reputation as a hard-left trade union leader, he moved into local politics and became a Labour councillor in the London Borough of Haringey. Bernie's dynamic character attracted a strong following among the unemployed, the black community and the left. His impact was immediate, and within a year he was Deputy Leader of the Council. He became known nationally for leading the fight against the Government's rate-capping of Haringey in 1984. This struggle split the local Labour Party, but Grant's political stance did not waver and his drive and enthusiasm took him to the leadership of the council in 1985. He was the first black head of a local authority in Europe, and was responsible for the well-being of a quarter of a million people, many of them from black and ethnic minorities.

Grant led Haringey to take control of the Alexandra Palace rebuilding project, but the financial burden was massive and the £15 million provided soon transformed into deficit and interest payments eventually took the debt to a total of £80 million.

From the beginning Grant's instincts and experience led him to court controversy as he freely aired his anti-establishment views. Bernie had a reputation for being anti-police, believing that they treated black people unfairly. In 1985 he had said that the police deserved a "bloody good kicking" after the collapse and death of a black Tottenham woman, Mrs Cynthia Jarrett, while police with a search warrant searched her home for stolen property. It was this tragedy that incited the Broadwater Farm Estate uprising following continued police harassment of that community subsequent to the arrest, during which a policeman, PC Blakelock was hacked to death in a face-to-face melee. Bernie came to national prominence after his defence of the youth that rioted against police harassment. His assertion that the police had been given "a bloody good hiding", together with his refusal to condemn the violence of black youths, led him to be denounced by the Labour Party leadership and the incumbent Tory Home Secretary, Douglas Hurd, called him "…the high Grant, Bernie priest of conflict" despite the local police chief in Tottenham describing him as a "caring, committed, hard-working and effective".

Grant argued that his remarks had been quoted out of context and was always to protest that he was only summing up people's point of view, making the remarks while attempting to persuade crowds of youths not to provoke further trouble. He subsequently apologised to PC Blakelock's family for the distress his remarks had caused them, but he was vilified throughout the media and he was generally labelled as being a belligerent opponent of the rule of law and nicknamed by the *The Sun* newspaper, as representative of the 'loony left', 'Barmy Bernie' (an epithet he found difficult to shake off).

Bernie was obliged to deal with the bile of the British press and media, but refused to compromise, even though his position as a Parliamentary candidate hung in the balance. With the support of a local black section, he won the nomination for a Parliamentary seat, ousting the sitting MP, the former Labour Party Treasurer on the NEC, Norman Atkinson (who had been 20 years in Tottenham). Bernie became an MP for Tottenham, in North London, in the 1987 election; he was the senior of the first three black MPs in the Commons, and made his mark almost immediately by shocking conventionalists and socialists alike, but gaining the respect of countless others, by wearing a traditional a dashiki at the State Opening of

Parliament; the figure of Bernie standing arrayed in the height of African glory remains one of the most powerfully enduring images in British black politics.

Tottenham

Tottenham has a grassroots intellectual tradition that has been nurtured on the margins of society. However, it is at such peripheries of society that have always provided some of the worst statistics on social exclusion. For all this, borders are also places where things happen, and it is at the margins where the most radical and exciting perspective on social thought can be generated.

Although Tottenham is a constituency with a great deal of poverty relative to the rest of London (even in the 'high employment era' of the first decade of the twenty-first century, the unemployment rate in Tottenham reached 11.6 percent, the third highest in England) it has never been impoverished in terms of its people. Across the centuries, the cultures of the world have traversed up and down Tottenham High Road: white English, Russians, Huguenots, Spaniards, Greek and Turkish Cypriots, Africans, Irish, Hasidic Jews, Asians, Caribbean islanders and, more latterly, Kosovans and other Eastern Europeans have made Tottenham their home. As such, it is a place of dynamic diversity; people from the far reaches of the earth are living side by side, following the widest range of religions imaginable and representing every race and cultural background. All contribute to the richness of life in the area.

Parliamentarian

Bernie Grant became an exceptional constituency MP and brought to parliament a long and distinguished campaigning record. He was a founder member of the Standing Conference of African-Caribbean and Asian Councillors and was a member of the Labour Party Black Sections. He convened major conferences of politicians, activists, researchers and academics to shape black agendas. Grant also helped tackle racism on a European wide level, in association with members of the European Parliament and anti-racist groups. A committed internationalist and pan-Africanist, he maintained a keen interest in Caribbean, Central American, Irish and Cypriot affairs and served on the National Executive of the Anti-Apartheid Movement in Britain. His forthright interventions in the House of Commons on issues of race, not least on racism within the police and the criminal justice system, made him one of the leading figures in the continuing agitation for racial equality and human rights in Britain.

Bernie was a 'natural' in terms of the Commons. An authentic and brutally honest voice, he walked a tightrope between street valour and government office. He made his maiden speech in July 1987 and demonstrated at once both his local knowledge and his confidence as a politician. He told the House:-

> "Unless the political system can offer some prospects, particularly to our young people and young black people, they will find other means of expressing their frustration."

He was referring to the Broadwater Farm Estate riots and went on to talk about the way in which that community and the local Council had worked together to harness the energies of the district and regenerate it. After the riots, the Tottenham MP had campaigned for the release of Winston Silcott who had been convicted for PC Blakelock's murder. Silcott's conviction was eventually quashed.

In Parliament Grant continually enhanced his reputation as a prime agitator, backing demands for black sections in the Labour Party, arguing for the exemption of Rastafarians from the poll tax, and flouting parliamentary tradition by interrupting the Chancellor's Budget speech in 1988, yelling "Shame! Shame!"

Bernie was perceived as a consistent embarrassment by his party leaders. He opposed holding the Vauxhall by-election in 1989 feeling that the Labour Party should not have nominated a white candidate in a constituency which encompassed Brixton that had a relatively high black population.

In that same year Grant co-founded the Parliamentary Black Caucus (a "natural focus for the political, economic and social advancement of black people in Britain") with Lord Pitt and his fellow 'first black parliamentarians' elected in 1987. Inspired by American Congressman Ron Dellums and the American Congressional Black Caucus, Grant told the PBC inaugural conference:-

> "For far too long the black community has had no voice in Britain and we are seeking to redress that."

Around the same time Grant helped launched the *Black Parliamentarian* magazine: "bringing parliament to the community".

As Chair of the All Party Group on Race and Community, and of the British Caribbean Group, Bernie took a leading role in establishing contacts with black people and politicians on a global basis, including the Congressional Black Caucus in the USA. He also attempted to bring together black business people, both in Britain and throughout the world and became the founder and (in 1995) Chair of the Global Trade Centre that looked to link local businesses with partners in Africa and the Caribbean. In these causes he travelled widely, especially to Africa and to his cherished Caribbean.

Grant was heavily involved in the anti-apartheid movement and in February 1990 he accompanied the Reverend Jesse Jackson on his mission to South Africa, greeting Nelson Mandela on the day of his release from Robyn Island (Bernie had a longstanding friendship with Mandela, whom he supported throughout the great man's imprisonment and subsequent release). Later, Grant established an Information Technology Centre amongst the townships in the Free State; it carries Bernie's name.

As member of the Committee of Eminent Persons on Reparations for Africa, it was also in 1990 that Bernie founded the Standing Conference on Racism in Europe. After the custodians of heritage sites and special collections were urged to do more to acknowledge slavery's legacy and Britain's past involvement in the transatlantic slave trade, in 1993, Grant founded the United Kingdom branch of the Africa Reparations Movement (ARM) and was prominent in bringing this issue to Britain as the Chair of this organisation. ARM called on the British and other Western governments to issue an apology for the enslavement and colonisation of Africans, for the return of cultural artefacts, as well as a more accurate portrayal of African history in order to restore dignity and self-respect to African people. One of the most widely reported events co-organised by ARM occurred in 1997, when Grant led a ceremony of remembrance on the Devon beach of Rapparee Cove, Ilfracombe, following the discovery of manacled human remains (presumed to been used on slaves) from the 1796 shipwreck of *The London*.

Bernie came close to trebling his majority in the 1992 General Election. Backed by the far left *Campaign* group, he stood (unsuccessfully) for the deputy leadership of the Labour Party.

Following years of being labelled anti-police in 1993 Grant played a major part in defusing a volatile situation after Joy Gardener, a Jamaican immigrant, had died as police were attempting to arrest her for deportation. It was in that year, during May, that he was awarded an Honorary Doctorate by Pace University, New York, in recognition of his work in striving for justice and equal rights.

Despite his clear left-wing credentials in the political sphere Bernie was rather conservative in other areas of his life. He was an ardent admirer of the Queen, a Euro-sceptic and advocate of old-fashioned schooling. The man who would one day take over his Tottenham Constituency seat,

Barrister David Lammy, said of Grant:-

"The first time I met Bernie, I came to see him with my parents to ask him for help to get me into a good school."

Lammy went on to become the first black British person to study at Harvard University in the United States. According to Lammy:-

"Many will understand when I say that you could not really describe yourself as a friend of Bernie's until he had occasion to bark at you...on one of the last times I saw him, he did just that - while lamenting the stance that I took on the vexed issue of Mike Tyson's entry into this country. Bernie argued passionately against his entry and considered Tyson as an unworthy role model for his young constituents. His concern for young people is well documented and remained a passion throughout his life."

Resettlement

Grant caused immense controversy by suggesting that a £100,000 option should be given to those wishing to return to Africa and the Caribbean, particularly the elderly who had given their working lives to Britain. On Tuesday 19th. December, 1995 Grant told the House of Commons that there was:-

"...nothing new about the British government providing financial assistance to people, including British citizens, who wish to resettle abroad."

He called for a "...realistic scheme to facilitate resettlement" for Britons with Caribbean heritage. Bernie made a thoughtful and informed argument that demonstrated the rational, economic and social sense of this proposition and the advantages for both Britain and the nations of the Caribbean. He said:-

"...it is not generally in the interests of any country to have a substantial number of people in its midst who honestly do not want to be in that country."

According to Grant, many of those who had approached him about the possibilities of such a scheme were:-

"...those who are most dependent on social benefits health and welfare services, and indeed are most likely to be subsidised in various ways for their housing costs. They are also likely to be tenants of local authority housing. It would not take too much imagination to calculate a 'social benefits equivalent' sum for a given number of people each year, which could be used as the basis for a budget for a resettlement scheme. Given the lower costs of living in the Caribbean, even after weekly 'benefit equivalent' payments, there would be substantial sums available for investment in housing, social care, and health insurance."

For Grant this would:-

"…certainly be a more effective means of helping the countries concerned than the current practice of sending down highly paid consultants to perform key jobs."

And would

"…be in the interests of Britain, not least because it would comprise a recognition of the huge damage which it has done to the Caribbean, both now and in the past. It is true to say that having created and exploited those countries through slavery and colonisation Britain is now abandoning them, now that its economic interests lie elsewhere. Having stolen so much, it would be more than fitting at this time in history for Britain to at least facilitate the return of those who wish to return. Some have said that even to mention this matter is to cause damage to race relations in this country, and to argue for a resettlement scheme is to give in to racism. I have even been accused of adopting the agenda of fascists and racists. Even the Secretary of State for Home Affairs told me recently that he feared that an enhanced resettlement scheme would make black people feel unwelcome here. I found that rich indeed coming from someone who has set back race relations by at least twenty years in the relatively short time that he has been in office.

I am not convinced by these arguments. This is about creating positive choices for black people, setting our own agenda for once, and about remembering where we came from. Some black people will want to stay in Britain, and the fight for racial equality will continue. I myself will continue to play my part in that struggle. It is true that some want to leave because they are sick and tired of the racism they face in this country. They are fed up with fighting racism, and I see no reason why they should be forced to do so. There are others however who quite honestly do not feel at home here, and others who despair of the predominant values and culture of this society, and fear for their children growing up in such a climate. Then there are others who quite simply wish to return to live with their families, and of course this feeling is the more common nowadays because of the absurdity of current immigration rules which keep families apart.

This house has no right to deny those people a choice about their future, and against the background of all that has been done to black people historically, this house owes it to them to allow them to exercise that choice. I speak on behalf of very large numbers in raising this matter tonight."

That year the Jamaican government estimated that some 2,000 people returned from Britain.

Activist

As his black parliamentary colleagues rose to the heights of New Labour's centrist government, Keith Vaz to the Foreign Office, Paul Boateng to the Home Office, and Diane Abbott to top-level state committees, Grant stayed true to his old-style trade union, populist democracy and the fight for black political influence within the Labour Party.

During the last years of the 1990s, despite undergoing a heart bypass operation and kidney failure in 1998, Grant remained a strong advocate of black and ethnic minority rights. However, many sensed that his views were mellowing as his actions moderated, but in the closing year of his life, Grant addressed the House of Commons saying that a just conclusion to the Stephen Lawrence case was "the last chance for British society to tackle racism." On the publication of a damning report into the inquiry about the murder, Bernie publicly advised that Sir Paul Condon, the Metropolitan Police Commissioner, should take early retirement. But it was Grant's wise counsel and investigations into racism and xenophobia (he was Chair of the Socialist Campaign Group of Labour MPs) that helped influence government actions following the death of the black teenager.

Grant took a lead in highlighting the rise of racism in Europe, not least in his capacity as the chair of the Standing Conference Against Racism in Europe (SCORE) and in 1997 he was appointed as member of the Select Committee on International Development. Bernie was the only MP amongst those appointed to the Home Secretary's Race Relations Forum in 1998.

In October of that year Bernie called for British withdrawal from Northern Ireland and Irish reunification, claiming that this was the only way towards peace in the province. He rejected the recent Labour Party policy document on Ireland because it gave loyalists a veto over the future of the whole island. Around the same time he was involved with a campaign for a statue to the Unknown Slave to be erected on a plinth in Trafalgar

Square, central London.

In January 2000 Grant confronted the then Culture Secretary, Chris Smith, with figures he had obtained from the Lottery operator Camelot, showing that his constituents had gambled £63 million on the National Lottery since it was launched five years previously, compared with the national constituency average of £38 million, whilst Lottery grants to Tottenham totalled just over £5 million. The figures supported the fears of churchmen and groups campaigning against poverty who warned that the Lottery would attract most support from people who could least afford it.

Grant called on Smith to investigate the lack of benefits to his constituents. In a letter to the Culture Secretary Bernie wrote:-

> "I am sure that you will appreciate that this huge discrepancy will be seen as a scandal. The net effect of the Lottery has been to take some £63 million out of one of the poorest local economies in the country and very little has been put back.
>
> The size of the discrepancy in my constituency raises some very serious questions as to the distributive implications of the National Lottery, the role that it is playing in society and the incentives it generates amongst the least well off."

He also made the point that minority groups had received a particularly poor return.

Bernie died at the Middlesex Hospital in London on Saturday 8th. April, 2000 at 7.30am, following a heart attack. He been suffering with a kidney complaint for some time and had been admitted to hospital overnight. But his family believed he had been recovering well. Bernie was 56 years old. Right up to his passing he remained a popular figure with his constituents, an outspoken nonconformist and controversial figure. His death marked almost four decades campaigning for racial justice and minority rights.

In 2006 Grant's biography celebrated one of the most charismatic Black British political leaders of modern times. It was written by his father.

Eric Grant

The story of Bernie's father is another inspiring chronicle. Eric Caesar Alexander Grant was born on 21st. December, 1913, in Bagotsville, Guyana. He too was the child of two teachers. At an early age he made the decision to follow in his parents footsteps. Motivated by the example of his mother and father and fortified with his own ability, at the age of eleven Eric won a partial scholarship to attend the Collegiate High School in Georgetown. He finished his School Leaving Examination in 1928 and with this qualification, at the age of fourteen, he began his teaching career at Rattray Memorial Congregational School.

However, his employment offered no salary, so whilst working in a pharmacy he took the preliminary exams and become a chemist. Although he worked several years in chemistry, thoughts of his first choice of vocation never left his mind and eventually he made the break and left to study for the Cambridge Examinations, intending to return to teaching. His first job after gaining his Junior and Senior Cambridge Certificates was a post at the St. Matthews High School. After just one year the Principal, impressed with his hard work and the quality of his teaching, asked him to become the Headmaster of St Matthews' branch school, Martin's AME Zion School.

Eric's reputation as an innovative educator continued to grow and in 1937 he was offered the Headship of La Harmonie Congregational School, situated in the Upper Demerara Region. The school and Eric excelled. He raised standards to a level at which pupils were able to pass the Primary School Leaving Certificate as well as the Eleven Plus and scholarship examinations. The young Headmaster also broadened the curriculum to encompass basket-weaving. Such was the quality of the school's production in this subject that pupils were able to generate finance to buy themselves books and stationery. Eric's vision was noted. After qualifying for his Third and Second Class Teachers' Certificates in 1944 he was asked to take up the position of Head of Ituni Undenominational School in the Bauxite area of Guyana. His rigorous leadership skills enabled him to make the maximum use of the resources available to him and inspire his staff to achieve unparalleled results and win national recognition.

In 1957 Eric came to Britain and the University of Reading to study for a Diploma in Rural Education. During the two year programme he was required to undertake teaching practice. He enjoyed his first exposure to teaching in the UK and the challenge of being the only black teacher in an all white school in Berkshire.

Following the completion of his studies, Eric returned to Guyana. After successfully tackling two more Headships, he went back to Reading University, this time to study for the Postgraduate Professional Teachers' Certificate, which he completed in 1965.

Back in Guyana, Eric became a Lecturer at the Environmental Teachers' Training College and in 1967 he took on the role of the Superintendent of the In-Service Teachers' Training College. He remained in that post until his retirement in 1973.

But it seems retirement was not for Eric and after a few months he returned to work for three years as the Principal of Linden Evening Institute, until 1976, when he was appointed as the Curriculum

Development Officer for Social Studies, Ministry of Education.

Eric 're-retired' in 1982 and returned to Britain to join his wife Lily, who was also an exceptional teacher, both in Guyana and in London. The Grant's five children had settled in the UK. Leyland, their eldest child was an engineering manager with British Telecom, Bernie (his second child) was deep into his political career, whilst Rosamund, Eric's oldest daughter was the author of a number of cookery books and a practicing psychotherapist and the two younger daughters, Waveney and Efua, worked in education and local government.

But Eric had not lost his passion for teaching and he became involved with the Lemuel Findlay Supplementary School in Tottenham. This work led to his being called back into active service when the then Chief Education Officer for Haringey suggested that he would make a fine supply teacher. Despite being almost 70 years of age, over eight years Eric taught in more than 60 primary schools in Haringey. He finally put an end to his classroom work in the 1980s, but carried on his commitment to education as a trustee of Lemuel Findlay.

In subsequent decades Eric took great pleasure in travelling all over the world, including North America, West Africa, Europe and the Caribbean. He wrote prolifically, in verse and prose, and amassed a huge selection of essays about his life and reflecting on his experiences.

Following the passing of his son Bernie, Eric started writing a book, *Dawn to Dusk*, about his son's life. The book was completed shortly before Eric passed away on Thursday, 3rd August, 2006, at the North Middlesex Hospital.

Eric left a lasting mark on the education system in Guyana as Head of six state primary schools and Principal of a state secondary school. He also set-up two private secondary schools. And by way of his teaching and general involvement in education he had impacted on hundreds of people's lives in London. According to Eric:-

"Teaching is the only profession that touches the skills of every profession, person, race and culture, yet Nobel prizes are rarely given to teachers per se, but to those who have had good teachers…"

This shows Eric's clear view of the role of the teacher, but also of how undervalued educationalists are in our society. But his fondness of the motto 'Learn, teach and serve your community' demonstrates an intimate understanding of the teaching role that many of us in that profession, be it in primary school or like myself higher education, would do well to ponder; we are essentially servants and not commanders of those we teach.

Eric Grant distinguished himself as an educationalist and a teacher and in later years, as a writer and poet. He was survived by his first wife Joan, his second wife Yvonne, his third wife Sharron, four of his siblings, his three sons from his first second marriage, Steven, Alex and Jimmy and his grandchildren..

Bernie Grant's Legacy

Bernie's white English wife, Sharon, was also his personal assistant and was very much his partner in work as well as in life. She was on the shortlist to succeed him as Labour candidate for the Tottenham Constituency, but was beaten by the then-27-year-old David Lammy, who won the by-election.

In his Maiden Speech to the House of Commons (Wednesday, 19th. July, 2000) David Lammy said of his predecessor: "the man who was one of the key reasons that I got into politics in the first place.

Lammy went on:-

> "I most sincerely thank the people of Tottenham for their confidence in my ability to represent them and hope that, in years to come, they will find me a worthy successor to this great man...Bernie's legacy will live on. He sits here with us now in the memory of all who knew him. I know that you will forgive me Bernie if I do not wear a dashiki today in your honour. In a very real sense, you are part of the reason I am here and for that I thank you and will never forget you."

Bernie Grant was one of the most charismatic black political leaders of modern times. His critics have implied that he never came up with a solitary tangible idea to make Britain more productive and throughout his career failed to put forward a single workable proposal as to how the massive problems of unemployment and housing that were the backdrop to his first years in Parliament, might have been alleviated via anything other than ponderous and far reaching benefit handouts of one type or another. From this perspective he might be said to have demanded much but have been totally unhelpful in terms of identifying how these demands might be facilitated. This analysis makes him more of a haranguer than a politician.

It has also been inferred that Grant's portrayal of black people together with his supposed continual 'playing of the card', caricatured communities and even whole nations as perennial victims and/or the potential recipients of the 'milk of guilt' or the 'bounty of blame'. The effect of this might have, to a certain extent, been cathartic, but overall may be understood as passing off an over-simplistic analysis of history and a 'route one' interpretation of the psychology of human interaction as fact. The result of this would have been to make a 'medicine show' of political debate that could only produce placebo rather than policy and leave Grant accused of making himself a reputation by peddling resentment and investment in pity and thus riding high on the most base of social attitudes.

However, for close to four decades, Grant had campaigned for racial justice and minority rights. Though in life he was an outspoken nonconformist, in death, Bernie Grant was praised from the heights of the Establishment, from Cabinet ministers and Scotland Yard to political associates and black community leaders.

From his funeral lectern, draped in the flag of Guyana, the tributes were manifold. Doreen Lawrence (the mother of Stephen) spoke of her respect and affection for Bernie. Jack Straw, then the Home Secretary, eulogized him as campaigner for the inquiry into the Lawrence case and said:-

> "Bernie's achievement was huge in making our society more tolerant and decent".

Chief Superintendent of Police Steven James remarked:-

> "Some people think it reasonable to support the view that Bernie Grant and the police were on different sides. Nothing could be further from the truth.

Lee Jasper, a long-standing Grant supporter, and Chair of the National Black Alliance and the campaign group Operation Black Vote, said:-

> "Bernie will be remembered as a hugely popular man of the people that every black man and woman should aspire to emulate."

Bernie's fellow Labour MP Frank Dobson, to whom Grant gave his support as the Labour Mayoral candidate for London in October 1999 (in preference to Ken Livingstone) was "saddened" by his friend's passing and said:-

> "I didn't always agree with him but he made a huge contribution to political life in London...I think his life represented the triumph of hope over cynicism because he decided to get involved and prove he could be selected and elected to Parliament...He was an example to everybody because he always said what he thought."

According to the Home Office Minister at the time of Bernie's death, Paul

Boateng, Grant was:-

> "A tireless fighter in the struggle for racial justice, his was an authentic and fearless voice in the black cause... who spoke with great authority and passion on issues... He will leave a gaping chasm in the political firmament."

According to the Conservative Party chairman Michael Ancram:-

> "Bernie Grant brought a special style to politics and was a respected member of the House of Commons. He will be missed. We send our thoughts and condolences to his family."

Narendra Makanji, of the London Borough of Haringey Council, said:-

> "He united workers in industries and the public services through the Black Trade Unionist Solidarity Movement; pulled together the Labour party black section in pursuing seats in councils and in parliament; and improved the bargaining position of agriculture workers in the Caribbean."

The Prime Minister, Tony Blair, whose work to reform ("modernise") the Labour Party was often opposed by Bernie (Grant had also attacked the efforts of Blair's predecessor Neil Kinnock in this task) said of Grant:-

> "He was someone for whom I had immense respect and affection...He was a dedicated and diligent constituency MP who worked tirelessly for the less well-off, whose commitment to social justice was unwavering and who also made a powerful contribution to development issues...He advised me regularly on issues relating to development and on our relations with Caribbean countries...He was someone who always made efforts to understand and respect other people's point of view. Bernie was also an inspiration to black people throughout the country. One day I hope it will be commonplace to have black and Asian MPs at Westminster. When that happens, it will in no small measure be a tribute to Bernie Grant and the inspirational lead he gave."

Sharon Grant said:-

> "Bernie touched the lives of so many people in a lifetime's work as both a national and local politician, and there will be great sadness today...We have lost a great fighter and a champion of justice for oppressed people everywhere...He had a huge heart and I guess that he just wore it out."

The Tottenham MP's send-off in April 2000 was probably the largest funeral for a black person that Britain has ever seen. His cortege threaded its way past key sites in his life. It stopped at Haringey Civic Centre, where he had once been Leader of the Council and his Tottenham offices. The procession paused in front of hundreds of onlookers for a minute's silence at the once riot-torn Broadwater Farm Estate, where he had Chaired the community centre. The cortege then moved on at a slow pace to Alexandra Palace where the funeral service took place. It was attended by more than 5,000 people; thousands more had lined the streets of Haringey as Bernie made his last journey.

Six pallbearers bore the silver-metal casket. Lance Sergeant Jason Sumner, of the 1st. Battalion Scots Guards, played the *Lament Flowers of the Forest*. Among the hundreds in the congregation were Clive Lloyd, the former West Indies cricket captain, and Jazzy B, founder member of the band Soul II Soul. At the service it was said that Bernie Grant had changed the course of British history. Whatever anyone might think of that statement it is undeniable that the world knew who Bernie Grant was and what he stood for.

Commemoration

In December 2006 the Ethnic Multicultural Media Academy (EMMA) honoured Bernie with a Special Award at the ceremony at the Grosvenor House Hotel. This might be understood as a testament to the way he had highlighted black issues and brought them to national prominence.

In 2004 an exhibition at Bruce Castle Museum commemorated the life of Bernie Grant. Set in the heart of the community that Bernie represented as an MP, Sharon Grant, his widow, had produced the exhibition so that future generations would not forget the work Bernie did for black communities. At the launch on 31st. March, Sharon said:-

> "This exhibition came about because after Bernie's death I was left with a huge volume of material...It was clearly of some historical significance. We wanted to make sure it was available for people in the future. I think he would want to be remembered as someone who understood his past...Someone who was influenced by that past and wanted to right the wrongs of that past."

Professor Chris Mullard, chairman of the Bernie Grant Trust and a personal friend of Bernie said:-

> "This celebrates his contribution in a real way, the way that he would want

it to be celebrated. Not like a statue, but actually a living set of programmes particularly for young people. We realised there was so much material and this was part of an educational process, a consciousness raising process."

The Bernie Grant Archive is made up of documents, news items and photographs taken during Bernie's political life. The material covers a range of activities he undertook, locally, nationally and internationally: his early work as a trade-unionist, as a Haringey councillor and finally as a Member of Parliament. Included are personal documents, news items, photographs, letters, flyers, Bernie's personal collection of political badges as well as hate mail sent by those opposed to the outspoken position taken by Grant on unjust policing.

Although seen by many as a contentious extremist, sailing closer to the shores of anarchy than socialism, others saw Bernie as principled and motivated by a strong sense of social and racial justice. For all this, Bernie Grant was an activist and a figure that evoked and provoked mixed emotions all his life. On the floor of the House of Commons he was outspoken in the cause of eliminating racism both in Britain and the world. He campaigned against racist policing methods, and deaths in custody, on institutionalised racism in health, housing and education, refugee rights and for greater resources for inner city areas. Internationally he fought for the elimination of overseas debt for poor nations, and for the recognition of the past injustices of colonisation and enslavement. He will also be remembered by many thousands for the individual attention he gave to their personal difficulties.

Bernie Grant, whose political life ended where it was lived, in Harcourt Road, Muswell Hill, channelled the concerns of his community to the highest levels of Government, and was regarded as the authentic voice of Britain's ethnic minorities. By the time of his death, the verbose activist of the 1970s and 1980s was seen as a statesman of great integrity. He heightened awareness of the inter-connectivity of struggles in Tottenham, London, Britain, Europe, Africa, the Caribbean and the USA. He cultivated the understanding that humanity is a single entity that needs to continue its struggle for justice, equality and emancipation.

The epitaph he desired was simply: "Bernie Grant - African Rebel". He certainly was an influence in terms of connecting black communities in Britain to Black nations and communities of the world. He was posthumously awarded an honorary doctorate degree by Middlesex University for services to education and cultural development for young people.

One of Grant's last battles was to establish a major arts and cultural facility in his Tottenham constituency, the International Centre for the Performing Arts (*The Bernie Grant Centre*). On 5th. November, 2004 the *Bernie Grant Centre*, the late MP's vision of a major black-led centre of excellence for the arts in Tottenham, received approval for a £14 million funding package including £6 million from the Millennium Commission and £3.5 million from Mayor Ken Livingstone's London Development Agency. The money would transform the former Tottenham swimming baths into a major performance and education centre fostering and displaying local and national artistic talent.

Combining performance, training and business support, the centre will reflect the cultural diversity of Tottenham, create jobs for local people and bring new opportunities for residents in one of Britain's most deprived areas to develop artistic and cultural talent.

Ironically, given Bernie's attack on the National Lottery, the tenth birthday of that 'institution' (that funds the Millennium Commission) was only days away and the *Bernie Grant Centre* will be hailed as an example of how the Lottery can transform communities. Sharon Grant, a driving force behind the project commented: "At last we are able to realise Bernie's dream of harnessing the creative talent of our diverse community."

CHAPTER 3
Michael Akintaro

The fearless seaman who stood up to gangsters and racists in London's
wartime West End

Michael Akintaro was amongst the last of a pioneering generation of
African seamen who helped lay the ground for the establishment of
London's post-war black community. Michael was one of an appreciable
number of Nigerians who settled in Britain in the 1930s, he was a
prominent fighter in the little known racial conflict that developed with the
arrival of the segregated American army during the Second World War.
His refusal to capitulate under racist attack made him a legend throughout
the West End and the whole of London.

Born on 2nd. June, 1914 into a Yoruba farming family at Odeomu,
near Ibadan, Michael grew up in the bustling city of Lagos. He was an
intelligent young man who, after gaining entry to grammar school, might
have attended University had it not been for the death of his mother in
1932. As it was his adventurous spirit took him to sea when he was just
eighteen.

His travel became his education. One of his most difficult lessons took
place in the Texas port of Galveston, where, for the first time he
encountered the brutality of segregation. This experience was to stay with
the young man for the rest of his life, shaping and strengthening his attitudes
and beliefs.

Michael made temporary homes in Newfoundland, Belgium and
Holland before making Liverpool his base. In 1937 he moved to London's
East End where many of his fellow Africans scrapped an impoverished
living among the Jewish community, but he soon broke away from the area's
poverty and headed for London's West End where he worked as a nightclub
caretaker and boiler man, supplementing his earnings with occasional work
as a film extra. At the famous Jig's Club, where he rubbed shoulders with
Jewish gamblers, he met visiting American entertainers including his hero,
pianist Fats Waller. Gaining insight into the lives of such people and
reflecting on his own experience, Michael began to understand that
creativity comes from questioning the type of informal and formal rules that
prevent people, whether because of colour, class or lack of experience, from
fully expressing themselves. He started to see that those who purposely set
in place unhelpful and limiting regulation on human action, through policy

or bureaucracy, or the more obvious forms of physical bullying, nearly always do so because of their own uncertainties, self-loathing, anxiety or resentment. However, for him this did not mean that these limitations, such as the barbarity of segregation, should not be questioned or seen as in any way correct or necessarily permanent.

The Fighter

It was through such conviction that Akintaro, who, although a small man, built a fearsome reputation for argument. He was never afraid to give vent to his individuality and struggle for what he, maybe sometimes alone, saw to be just. For him, the intimidation that is so often the tool of gangs of weaklings, even though they might hide behind labels such as 'government' or 'committee', should be challenged for what it is, though the practice of individual judgement and concentrated personal action. His bravery was famously employed when his fellow black entrepreneurs were threatened and attacked by London mobsters, predecessors of the Richardsons and the Krays. Later he was also to challenge perhaps the far more insidious institutional bullying that created segregation and maintained colonialism.

Michael was a family man, renowned for his devotion to his wife, Stella Bronstein, the daughter of a Whitechapel tailor from Odessa, Russia, whose family claimed kinship to Revolutionary leader Leon Trotsky. Along with their two children Michael and Stella became part of Camden Town's developing West African community.

With the outbreak of the Second World War Michael rejoined the merchant fleet. He was bound for Philadelphia when his ship broke in two after attack by aircraft. Rescued from a lifeboat wearing nothing but a vest, he spent two weeks in Aberdeen Hospital before returning to sea. Further injury ended his seagoing career and he finished his war service in a munitions factory.

By 1943 the West End streets were thronged with American troops. They provided entrepreneurial locals with a new source of income and Akintaro's Soho credentials stood him in good stead when he befriended black servicemen out on the town. At the time these black GIs could not gain entry to many places of entertainment. This inspired Michael to set up a modest operation in a small airless cellar off Denmark Street. With a radiogram for dancing and the unsuspecting American P/X stores as his source of liquor, he discovered black servicemen cared little for décor if they were free to dance with their chosen partner. Such social freedom angered some white Americans, who responded violently to the sight of inter-racial couples socialising. At this time one was not free to be with whom one wanted to be with. The regulations of clubs and other institutions, rules made by the unworldly and the ignorant, didn't allow this. Paternalism, the weapon of the social élite, was the order of the day. One's 'betters' decided what was right and what was 'good' for people, when they should do things and with whom. This constituted a system of control of time, space and interaction, wherein whom one was able to talk or be with was not decided by potential companions, but by groups of people who knew little of, and were remote from, the everyday lives of ordinary individuals. Michael, after his experience in Texas, was not going to accept that others knew what was 'good' for him and those he chose to work with. As such he fought hard to keep choices open for his clients.

All this meant that Akintaro experienced incredible overt and covert bigotry. He was subjected to both informal and official attack but he always retaliated in kind, whatever the odds. Insulted and pushed off the pavement on one occasion, his response led to his imprisonment, but this only enhanced his reputation within the growing black movement in Britain and the Empire.

Revolution

Following the Second World War, Guyanese revolutionary George Padmore called on Akintaro as a foot soldier in the fight against colonial rule.

George Padmore war born in Arouca, Trinidad in 1902. His real name was Malcolm Nurse and from a commitment to communism and decolonisation he later became a leading Pan-Africanist with anti-communist sympathies and one of the most influential African figures of the twentieth century. In 1924 he went to Tennessee and Fisk University to study medicine. He moved to New York and Howard University, and subsequently to Harvard Law School and it was during this period that he became active in the US Communist Party and changed his name to George Padmore.

Padmore established himself as an important black student leader, and became involved in the international communist movement, 'Comintern'. At the end of 1929 he travelled to the USSR where he took control of the Negro Bureau of the Communist International of Labour Unions and became Secretary of the International Trade Union Committee of Negro Workers. He also took the role as editor for the journal *Negro Worker*.

Padmore resigned from all these posts in 1934 and moved to London where he worked with C.L.R. James as well as a number of other West Indian and African intellectuals. Responding to the invasion of Ethiopia by Italy Padmore and James founded the *International African Services Bureau*. In his role as leader of the IASB George was amongst those who organised the 1945 Manchester Conference which was attended by W.E.B. DuBois,

Kwame Nkrumah, Jaja Wachuku and Jomo Kenyatta. The conference began to set the agenda for decolonisation in the post-war period.

When Ghana gained independence in 1957 George moved there and worked as an advisor to Kwame Nkrumah (who had become Prime Minister of the new state). Padmore eventually returned to London for medical treatment. He died there in September of 1959.

Akintaro helped distribute radical literature and met other anti-colonialists, including Padmore's financier, the redoubtable Nancy Cunard, and future Ghanaian president Kwame Nkrumah. Such people saw the value of allowing responsibility to be taken by those who felt ready to grasp and make use of it. This is the working through of trust, which itself can be thought of as a gift from the generous to those who seek to develop and extend themselves. Michael was always keen to show this type of belief in others. He understood that it is in the risk of allowing others to take responsibility that people grow, both those who seize responsibility and those who are secure and confident enough to let it go. For him, when responsibility is withheld that it is in fact the exertion of control. Michael saw that the wish to maintain and keep control is the tactic of the spiritually impoverished who feel that they have so much to lose and so little to gain from reaching out to others. This is a vicious circle that becomes tighter and tighter until in the end those at the centre are isolated in their own 'ways' and 'thoughts', stymied by Grid Iron rules of tradition and the tyranny of often outdated and pointlessly limiting regulations written in stone. The inevitable bitter end of the rigid and rabid rule follower is to find his or her self, as Hitler did, in a bunker dug deep in their own anal retention with a pistol of madness trained on their own head.

Friendship not Professionalism - The Way of the Yoruba

In 1953 Michael abandoned the nightlife. He joined the ministry of works as a hot water fitter, a job that took him from the Air Ministry to Buckingham Palace. On his retirement he was awarded the Imperial Service Medal.

Akintaro always maintained the Yoruba cultural practice of visiting friends and he made many in his long and productive life. In Yoruba culture friendship is a key factor in human activity. This intimate connectivity, that embodies the urge to give and be with others in an active and interactive way. From a Yoruban point of view, that is how we extend and develop ourselves. It is in the continuous growing cycles of friendship that human beings might become all that they can be. This friendship encompasses compassion, flexibility, generosity, toleration, forms of love and acceptance.

Why didn't Michael formalise his role? Why did he not enter a career as a teacher, community or social worker? Surely this would have enhanced his ability to help his community? Maybe he saw that the qualities of friendship found in the Yoruba tradition cannot be replicated in the artificial associations of the professional/client relationship as exemplified in social work or formal education, which are often formulated with notions of 'boundary', 'distance' and accusations of collusion in the background. Professional interaction is often encumbered by strictly secular, but essentially sacred codes of conduct that are watched over and enforced by the priestly class of the professional élite, those who hold sway over the sacrament of qualification or promotion. The resulting doctrine or ideology of professional discipline and control can seriously curtail, if not totally obliterate spontaneous expression and creativity through the threat of professional or career sanctions. The need to be 'careful' or 'clean' can work to distance the professional from the true value or experience of life that is found in the close mutuality of friendship with others. As such, those soaked in the professional culture can find themselves hygienically removed from the risk-taking process (professional distance) of the giving and receiving of trust and the self-expression that is the flower of the same. It would be convenient to think this might only affect 'the professional role', but how often does the professional detect his or herself 'acting professionally', or using 'professional skill' and 'professional language' with partners, parents and children? Perhaps this is why Michael kept well clear of taking on the shackles of professionalism.

Michael claimed to prefer the company of traditional 'age group' associates, but was generous to younger ones too. Blessed with impressive recall and an unusual capacity for historical analysis, he brought the past alive for his listeners, enlightening them to the struggle and sacrifices of his generation, sharing the insights gained from tribulation, even when memories were painful. He was not afraid to give advice, even tell others what he thought was right and wrong. Equally he listened to the opinions of others. The honesty gave rise to energetic debate and argument. These were total pumping workouts of rationality, often salted with the type of dynamic and positive aggression that sparks people into action. This is far removed from the covert and polite assignations of 'professional dialogue' wherein the coded language of policy and procedure can be fashioned into highly camouflaged 'man-traps'.

Michael Akintaro died on 15th. September, 2000. He was survived by a son and a daughter, three grandchildren and one great-grand daughter. He was an extraordinary ordinary man, wrought in the commitment to act and the will to activate. Michael lived his convictions in action. Through this activism he showed us that to be an educator is not the province of the qualified or the professional but is the product of certain attitudes, experience and beliefs. But beyond this, by his life he exemplified that awareness, enlightenment, wisdom and insight are born of generosity, trust, the willingness to be active in taking risks by encouragement and the facilitation of self-determination and expression. This in turn creates in us the winding, dangerous, unpredictable but exciting and beautiful paths to personal and social freedom.

In contemporary professional (formal and informal) education there is much determined preaching about 'teaching methods' and adapting to the 'way people learn'. Too often this throws out the simple acts of talking and listening and replaces them with an over-commitment to cold and predictable power-point presentations, cartoon like tricks of the sterile interactive whiteboard and other equally inane toys seemingly designed as much to distract minds as engage them. Spontaneity and the incumbent risks (the excitement and adventure) of learning and teaching are substituted by preconceived, banal, pre-packed and over-processed lesson plans (the junk food of education).

The educator, thus divorced from their own organic and dynamic expression as embodied in their capability to listen and talk (to have regard for and respond to others) justify their actions by claiming, as if directed by an internal handbook, how they are 'adapting the learning environment' or 'responding to learning needs.' This of course is meaningless jargon. It doesn't take too much to work out that what are often portrayed as 'contemporary methods' at best shut out as much learning as they facilitate (because many people learn best by listening and talking). At worse these mechanistic 'techniques' represent patronising assumptions about the supposed deficit of learners; 'they will not be able to handle 'conventional' forms of teaching'. In short those who come to learn (adults, teenagers and children) are treated like infants in an old fashioned primary school, wherein people are seen not as developing human beings but as half formed creatures that are essentially lacking.

This might be recognised as a hangover from the colonial past and the influence of class prejudice and discrimination. Akintaro would have us question this situation, and tell us to make the world our classroom and to bring the classrooms into the world though the simple, but at the same time wondrous exchange of expression, wherein all learn from each other. This is the legacy of Yoruba and wider African educational forms, embodied in Great Zimbabwe and the vision of 'Ujamaa' as adapted by Julius Kambarage Nyerere. As Michal might have said, there is much to gain, and little to lose.

CHAPTER 4
Nawal al-El Saadawi

Dissidence and Creativity - a path to creativity and the challenging of
inequality for social and political change occur

Born into a well educated family in 1931 in the small village of Kafr Tahal, Egypt, Nawal al-El Saadawi has been called 'the Simone de Beauvoir of the Arab world.' She is a writer and psychiatrist but she has described herself as a feminist and a militant. She has had a major influence on the lives of women, and perhaps in particular women of colour, all over the world. She has witnessed humiliating and unfair treatment, both in her profession as a doctor and as a writer. This has led her to speak out in support of political and sexual rights for women and constantly reiterate women's ability to take power in the form of resistance. As a result she has been imprisoned (this is detailed in her book *My Travels Around the World*) and arrested on a number of occasions - as such she is a person that is set in the process of history, making it and challenging its legacy. As much as any writer can Nawal has changed the world. She has done this through the liberation of mind that has been achieved by of millions of people (women and men) particularly in those parts of the world called 'the third', the 'non-industrialised' or 'the south' (all expressions that she dismisses as divisive, for Nawal, there is just one world) using her ideas to find means of self expression.

Refusing to accept the limitations imposed on women, especially those from rural backgrounds, by both religious and colonial oppression, Nawal qualified as a doctor in 1955. From this foundation she went on to become Egypt's Director of Public Health. Her writing career of close to 40 years has focused on the plight of women. In 1972, her first work of non-fiction, *Women and Sex*, provoked antagonism from the upper echelon of the political and theological hierarchy in Egypt and the wider Arab and Muslim world. Her response to the Egyptian Human Rights Organisation's estimate that at least 90 percent of young women in Egyptian villages had been victims of female genital 'circumcision' was to name such practices as part of the punishment for being born a woman. This conviction led directly to her dismissal from her position as director of Education in Egypt's Ministry of Health, and as Chief Editor of *Health* magazine. She was also prevented from practicing as a medical practitioner and as a consequence lost her position as Assistant General Secretary in the Medical Association of Egypt.

However between 1973 and 1976 Saadawi worked in research at the Ain Shams University in the Faculty of Medicine, looking at women and neurosis. In 1979 she became the United Nations Advisor for the Women's Programme in Africa (ECA) and the Middle East (ECWA).

In 1980, following a protracted struggle for the intellectual and social freedom of Egyptian women, a fight that had cost Nawal any chance of employment in her nation's political or bureaucratic structure, she was imprisoned under by the regime of Anwar Sadat. However, this did nothing to deter her. Following her release after the assignation of Sadat she founded the *Arab Women's Solidarity Association* and devoted her time to writing, becoming an international journalist and speaker on issues effecting women. Now she is the author of many books, both fiction and non-fiction and has received a number of literary awards. Her efforts, even in the face of the banning of her books and the rise of a variety of fundamentalisms all over the world, have encompassed a huge area. Nawal has looked at the role of women in African literature and the sexual politics of development initiatives. She has questioned the whole idea of Third World development, the notion of an 'Arab world', tourism in a 'post-colonial' age and the practice of writing itself. She has examined the nature of cultural identity and the subversive potential of creativity. Throughout she has been a leader in the fight against female genital mutilation and as forthrightly addressed problems facing the internationalisation of the women's movement. Her challenge to the religious and social conventions surrounding the politics of sex, particularly under some relatively recent interpretations of Islam, is constant in her work as is a critique of class and patriarchal systems of control. Her personal quest for equality has provided a novel and bold perspective on the power of women in resistance against poverty, racism and fundamentalism. Much of Nawal's writing has been published in Lebanon because the majority of her work has been banned in Egypt. However, refusing the reverse imprisonment of banishment she has recently returned to Egypt following a five-year exile.

Dissidence and Creativity

Nawal argues that dissidence is a clear path to creativity. For her, conformity too often involves the stifling of the creative powers that she feels are an integral and defining part of human nature. Relating to the Arabic interpretation of the word Nawal understands 'dissidence' as a struggle to create, to bring something original or new into the world. According to Nawal, one cannot be dissident without being creative. She asks: "Can I have the passion and knowledge required to change the powerful oppressive system of family and government without being creative?" (1997; 158)

Self-government

Nawal does not believe we are really free. She has said that she "discovered that democracy is an illusion" in the West, and even more an illusion in the non-industrialised world. But she does want people to be free, and to be "independent and to govern themselves". She has little time for governments, for her there is not much to choose between them, whether in the West, the East, the North, or the South. For Nawal there is something wrong with the idea of governing others. She writes, "I govern myself I don't need somebody to govern me, either in the state or at home".

In Nawal's perfect society people would be encouraged to govern themselves. This makes the positive assumption that people are capable, and are able to govern themselves, but for Nawal they are prevented from doing that all the time. This idea looks to the potential that people have rather than what they lack; it is the antithesis of the deficit model that fuels the professional role. Therefore it is anti-professional. The role of the professional is to meet the needs of others, addressing the perceived 'deficit' of others. To this extent it can be seen that for Nawal professional activity would be seen as essentially colonising in character.

Nawal believes that society is abandoning traditional forms of government, very slowly. She argues that non-governmental groups and societies are growing. She points out that in non-industrialised regions these groups are semi-governmental, the governments of these areas having attempted to dominate the non-governmental and the civil groups, but they are, in her words, "coming up". For her, "There is a process that's going on to unveil the minds of people" as governments "work in very subtle ways to control the brains of people, and to brainwash through the media". However, Nawal asks, "how can a government maintain power?" According to her, "People in the government are few. How can the few dominate the majority?" Here she is pointing out that there is potential for us to express ourselves and critique the nature of the state or society. However, she believes that this cannot be done through the agencies of the state or be mediated by state sponsored employees whose interests lie in the propagation or support of state ideals and values. The few dominating the majority is made possible by the majority being ready to be guided or educated by the minority. For Nawal, this situation is reminiscent of the colonial situation.

For example, one often comes across the idea in certain professional arenas that we should help others 'celebrate difference'. In the colonial situation the colonial government needs to make sure that people do not unite against them. As such, it is imperative to make sure that groups are played off one against the other in competition for what resources are available for 'the natives'. In order to do this, difference has to be constantly reiterated and demarcation lines of difference need to be made clear (as in multiculturalism).

However, as is evident from one of the central principles of the National Blood Transfusion Service, the kind of semi-governmental organisation of the type Nawal writes about, our aim should be to provide services on the basis of common human needs: "there must be no allocation of resources which could create a sense of separateness between people". It is the explicit or implicit institutionalisation of separateness, whether categorised in terms of income, class, race, colour or religion, rather than the recognition of the similarities between people and their needs which causes much of the world's suffering.

Colonialism and Slavery

The problem of the many controlling the few is, for Nawal, historically connected with slavery. For her slavery meant that a few people, maybe one 'lord', governed hundreds or thousands of people. This history has left a kind of psychic heritage that is re-energised in education and the media. Domination is not essentially economic, or military, for her it is a subtle form of mental domination. As such, the central question for Nawal is: how people can get rid of this invasion to their brains by the media and by education in universities? The answer, according to Nawal, is that we need, in the first instance, to become conscious of this situation; we have to know politics in order to challenge politics.

This process is evident in Nawal's own life story. She moved from village life to university then into a profession as a doctor. The very process, although damaging, has helped her to see the world as she does; it has enabled her to express her ideas, in more than language. Nawal recognises this ambiguity but states that, "I had to study medicine to get rid of it." For her, we start by knowing. She had to go to school and to university. When she graduated as a medical doctor and as a physician, it was at that point that she started to challenge the medical profession and to see that the profession (like all professions) is commercial. Professions exploit people, but, she says, she could not have known that if she hadn't studied medicine.

Do not mistake this point of view for the rather trite idea that one is best placed within a profession in order to change it. The clear message here is that professions change those who move into them. When you know about a profession, for Nawal, it is at this point you can change it, but it cannot be changed from within. As her biography illustrates, the 'dissenting voice' speaking out within a profession, is soon rejected by that profession. She herself is an example of this.

According to Nawal, ordinary people do not encroach on others; its people who have power who encroach on the others. The powerful encroach on others through their social agents, the army, the family, the police, the professions, medical, social and legal. Nawal has experienced such encroachments in a very physical way. She was circumcised as a child. As a physician she has consistently condemned this practice as well as the practice of male circumcision and, what she calls, 'psychological circumcision'. She argues that there is a lot of silence in connection with the physical abuse of circumcision, but Nawal argues that the covert psychological interventions are just as damaging as more overt physical atrocities. She contests that the physical is visible, and sometimes the visible is less dangerous than the invisible oppression. The psychological assaults of the educational and welfare professional, according to Nawal, are forms of invisible oppression or psychological circumcision.

Nawal argues that it is in the process of living together that we mature. As adults we are not children but even as children we are maturing all the time. A level of government action, that is mediated by its professional agents, that is intrusive, prevents this maturation. In effect this retards the maturation process in that the professions separate people as individual 'clients'; they are plucked from their context and subjected to the gaze of the professional and the intrusion of professional practice. People do not, by nature, need teachers, social workers, judges, lawyers, or even doctors. In fact, it is these psychological circumcisers that prevent people dealing with each other and so maturing.

Religion

Nawal has said that in her utopia there would be no established religion and no books. She is very much against the idea of a 'fixed text'. She sees Holy books as political books. The Old Testament, the New Testament or the Qu'ran, are, for her, political books. They speak about war, invasion of other people's countries, ethnic cleansing, of inheritance, of money, this, as a focus, for her, has little to do with justice, morality, or spirituality.

However, Nawal argues that all texts that become 'holy', be they by Freire, Freud or Marx, are limiting. The words espoused and sanctified in contemporary texts, words like 'unconscious', 'socialism', or 'post-modernism', 'education', 'dialogue', 'autonomy' or 'reflection', should be most rigorously critiqued and held up to scrutiny in order that their usefulness in everyday life my be 'problematised'. According to Nawal, holy books or holy words limit our action and so our creative potential. She wants ideas like justice, freedom and love - that have meaning and associated action in everyday life for the mass of people and not just a chosen professional or religious elite - to play a much greater part in our thinking and action. She believes that we worship the text, whether divine or human, and this enslaves us when we seek to 'do' the words. In effect we are just following instructions, as in a rite.

Words

In her writing Nawal asks us to look again at words, concepts and expressions like 'democracy', 'family planning', 'globalisation', 'post-modernism', 'education' and 'human rights' and the invention of the idea of a 'self'. For her these notions have been used to conceal contemporary forms of colonisation. She says:-

> "I think the conception of justice and freedom and love became complex and ambiguous and so complicated because we live in a very hypocritical society that tries to twist language and the language has double meaning. Peace means war, democracy means oppression. Language should be clear, so we understand each other. No monopoly, no playing, no games, no political games, no linguistic games, because I am really fed up with the linguistic games of the so-called 'post-modern era', which itself is part of the linguist game, the very name is part of the linguistic games …We find ourselves lost in an avalanche of words which appear very dissident, and which multiply and reproduce themselves endlessly…. We drown in these words; we are suffocated by them. It is the zero-sum game of words in which you lose your power to understand."

This process of developing 'professional words' creates a reliance on academics and professionals to interpret the world. These are the elites with a direct stake in often oppressive systems. Understanding is mediated through them, a group of people with little experience of poverty or hard laborious work - they do not know what it means to work hard on machines. This process masks the character of reality that can only be realised through the experience of people in the process of loving and living.

As such, Nawal exhorts us to be critical of ideas such as 'the self' generated as it has been within the type of commercial/educational complex she has referred to. For her, the notion of 'self' separates people into an often artificial individuality, replacing the broad range of 'real' human relationships based on interdependence and mutuality with notions of 'personal independence' and 'autonomy.' Within this dialogue (it is merely a dialogue for it is not critical, as in dialectic) dependence, the very humane action of one human being relying on another, whilst the other allows themselves to be relied upon (being 'supportive') becomes a sort of dirty word.

Once you start to understand Nawal's project, many taken for granted concepts or seemingly benign polices can be seen to be no more than the wrapping on an effort to maintain power structures. These structures are often less formal, more covert than they were maybe a hundred years ago, but they are clear descendants of systems based on slavery and blatant colonialism.

One example might be the 'drop the dept' campaign of a few years ago. The idea here was that the mass of 'ordinary' people in the industrialised world would pressurise the 'evil bankers' to cancel debt of the non-industrialised nations. This campaign was supported by US President Bill Clinton, British Prime Minister Tony Blair, the Church of England and Chelsea supporter and stand-up comedian David Baddiel.

Just suppose that this campaign had been completely successful and the major banks and financial organisations, to which most of the money was owed, passed-on the loss to shareholders. This would have resulted in shareholders withdrawing their capital, placing it elsewhere and the eventual demise of these organisations. It would, in short, have been financial suicide. The losses would have realistically been passed-on, via interest rates and so on to borrowers. This would have made it harder for employers in the developed world to invest to create employment or maintain existing jobs, particularly those involving unskilled labour. Housing would have become less accessible as any type of borrowing would have been more expensive. Food, clothing, anything manufactured, would also have become relatively more costly. So, in the short term, those who would have paid the most would have been the poorest in industrialised societies.

However, this would not have been the end of the story. The same financial institutions would not have been looking to lend any more money to what would have been the 'bad debtor' nations, no more than they would to individuals who have a record of not paying debts. Even if they did, the interest rates would have been even more crippling than they are at present. This being the case, non-industrialised nations, if they were to continue to build their infrastructures, would have been obliged to borrow directly from the governments who had most vehemently supported the 'drop the debt' campaign. This would have given these governments direct control over the national policies of non-industrialised states. As might be becoming clear, the result of this would be economic and political colonialism, a covert, less formal incarnation of former empires. This danger is by no means passed as the issue of debt continues to be a political chess piece.

As such, for Nawal, we need to place a great deal more reliance on our own experience in interaction with the experience of others. This being the case, books should be secondary. She has said: "we need to use our senses, images, feelings, music, - we learn from music and dancing. We have also to use our bodies." Here she is not thinking of organised sporting or musical events or commercial 'gigs' of one type or another; she loathes these. She has called such situations a form of madness, heightened in competition. This, for her, is a surrogate form of war, symbolised in all forms of competition, from the exam result to the football field, from the tests for five-year-olds, to the quest to win investors by minimising safety costs, and carries social and historical symbolism. Nawal argues:-

> "It is an artificial need; this artificial need was created by the class patriarchal system, the slave system. To convince us that war is inevitable. That it's hormonal, it's natural. No, I think war is unnatural and people can live without war, without this competition. So, all these needs are really created artificially by the system."

For Nawal, the style of playing is more important than say the number of goals scored. Teamwork and an atmosphere of friendship should be fostered. This requires our notion of success to change, but also the individual/group relationship. This can only happen in a society that sees the achievement of justice and equality as the basic criteria of success.

Nawal the person – Summation
This chapter can only give you a taste of Nawal al-El Saadawi's thinking, but it might give a glimpse of her as a person of soul and someone deeply committed to humanity. She has been denigrated many times, but she is not a person to create enemy figures. She may stand out against particular views or policies but she does not see herself being against individual human beings. She has said:-

> "People can change, people make mistakes, people are sometimes evil, and they do evil things because they are pushed to that. I believe in the benign nature of human beings. I don't believe that people are inheriting this malignant, un-divine nature. I think we are born in a very benign good nature, a human nature, but we loose our humanity because of political systems."

According to Nawal, we are brought up to think that dreams are not part of our reality, we despise our dreams. But she asks us to "remember our dreams" they will give light to our life. She recalls:-

"When I was in prison I was living on my dreams. It gave me a lot of power. Prison taught me that freedom is very important, but it taught me also that I'm ready to lose my freedom ... for a different society. Because, I am not ready to live in a very unjust, oppressive society, and just be free like that. I felt the linkage between our freedom as individuals and the freedom of others. Though I was in prison, I was ready to continue in prison; in a way it gave me a lot of insight that what I am doing is right, and I am not ready to sign something to the president so he will free me. No, I will never do that. I will continue to criticise... even if it keeps me in prison. Before I went to prison I had the illusion that prison is like death. But when you know prison, you lose your fear."

I will finish this chapter by echoing the dedication Nawal makes at the start of her Reader in that it might give any reader some idea of the nature of the path to liberating thinking and freedom:-

"To the women and men who choose to pay the price and be free rather than continue to pay the price of slavery."

The above text was developed from material from interviews with and the writing of Nawal al-El Saadawi.

CHAPTER 5

Leroy Eldridge Cleaver
A Soul on Fire

Known as 'El Rage' within the Black Panther movement, there can have been few more unlikely literary lions than Eldridge Cleaver. Born poor on 31st. August, 1935, the bulk of his education would be had by reading and writing by the red night lights of some of the most fearsome locations within the American penal system; San Quentin, Folsom and Soledad prisons.

Eldridge got his first job after his family moved to Phoenix, Arizona. He was a shoe shine boy. Later the Cleaver's moved to Los Angeles, part of the great migration of blacks to California. The family were obliged to live in a succession of rooming houses, low grade accommodation, crowded with poor families, plagued with rats and cock-roaches.

From the start, Eldridge was an outsider. Called a 'hick' because of the way he talked, dressed and wore his hair, the young Cleaver learned to fight at an early age, and soon took to the streets. As a boy he was in constant trouble with the law, hanging out first with fellow black kids, and then, when he decided they weren't tough enough, with Chicanos.

For all this, in his book, *Soul on Ice* he produced one of the most compelling accounts of the black experience in America ever to be written. It was a massive achievement, overcoming tremendous obstacles. Looking back he recalled: "I wanted to send waves of consternation through the white race."

To a great extent he succeeded. The book inspired young radicals and horrified mainstream society. It was published in 1968, but was written whilst Cleaver was in prison, the place, up to that point, where he had spent most of his adult life.

Eldridge's parents' separated when he was just twelve years old. This caused him to plunge into a deep depressive state. He was convicted of bicycle theft at the age of fifteen, and sent to reform school in Whittier, California. In 1950 this was quite a horrifying place, and the older boys soon inducted Eldridge into trading in marijuana.

When he got back in to the wide world Eldridge entered Belmont High School, where his size and strength earned him a place in the gridiron football team, but by 1953 he found himself back in the reformatory, this time for dealing in weed. He and his friends were making hundreds of

dollars a week in this trade, very big money indeed in mid-Twentieth Century urban America. His arrest for this crime prevented him from graduating from Belmont. Eldridge finished high school at Preston School of Industry, a juvenile detention facility, association with the same would kill almost any chance of a decent job in the future. In 1954 Eldridge was transferred to Soledad Prison.

That same year, the United States Supreme Court ruled segregated education illegal in the landmark case of *Brown v. Board of Education of Topeka.* The following year, the arrest of Rosa Parks for refusing to give up her bus seat to a white man in Montgomery, Alabama, sparked off the Montgomery bus boycott and the direct-action civil rights movement. Watching the events unfold on the prison's television, Cleaver and his fellow inmates saw the hypocrisy of America. They were incarcerated for breaking the law; yet those whites who were not obeying the laws against segregation remained free.

In his bitterness, Cleaver developed the theory that his crimes were right because they were a revolt against the evils of white America. He vowed to step outside the white man's law; he promised himself that the only laws he would obey from then on would be his own. Just a few days after he got out of Soledad he was again arrested for possession of cannabis. He was sentence to serve two and a half years in California State Prison, back at Soledad.

Following his release in 1956, Cleaver put his theory into practice, deliberately committing crimes against the 'enemy' white world, an eleven-month rampage of crime in which he returned to selling marijuana, and became a weekend rapist. At first his victims were black women; later, white - often prostitutes working from motels. Rape was an insurrectionary act, he recalled candidly in *Soul on Ice.* He confessed to battering black women in preparation for the rape of white women. He later recalled that:-

> "It delighted me that I was defying and trampling upon the white man's law, upon his system of values, and that I was defiling his women. This point, I believe was most satisfying to me because I was very resentful over the historical fact that the white man has used the black woman. I felt I was getting revenge."

Such acts were symptomatic of Cleaver's awful confusion, his violent, but straightforward way of dealing with complex social and political issues that were still a mystery to him.

Caught and convicted of assault with intent to kill, the twenty-two-year-old Cleaver was sentenced to two to fourteen years. He was placed first in

San Quentin and then in Folsom, the hell-hole prison of the California State system, where inmates were lucky to survive a long term sentence.

In prison, in deep despair, and with no one but himself for company, Eldridge began to regret his crimes. He had lost the assurance that any crime against white society was right as well as all respect for himself. In desperation he began to write down his thoughts and record his feelings. He wrote in open and almost frantic fashion and flung wide a new vista in terms of his perception of himself and the world. He concluded that in committing crimes for their own sake, he had been running away from his problems instead of trying to solve them. He wrote later:-

"After I returned to prison, I took a long look at myself and for the first time in my life admitted that I was wrong, that I had gone astray - astray not so much from the white man's law as from being human, civilised. My pride as a man dissolved and my whole fragile structure seemed to collapse, completely shattered. That is why I started to write. To save myself."

In the most hurtful and unlikely environment, Cleaver began to educate himself. He devoured the works of Thomas Paine, Voltaire, Karl Marx and W.E.B. Du Bois, and began to develop a personal philosophy of what it meant to be black in a white America. Blessed with keen intellectual powers, this was the beginning of his transformation from a convict to a political activist. Inspired by George Jackson, the prisoner/author of *Soledad Brother*, Eldridge started to write with conviction and intelligence. It was the prison essays and letters that he wrote at this time that were to form the basis of *Soul on Ice*. He began to use the pen to get out of the Pen.

It was at this point that Cleaver joined the Nation of Islam. When a split occurred between Malcolm X and Elijah Muhammad, leader of the Nation of Islam, Cleaver sided with Malcolm. After the split, Malcolm made a pilgrimage to Mecca, the holy city of world Islam. On his return he announced that he now believed it was possible for blacks and whites to live together in friendship. But Malcolm was assassinated before he was able to do more than begin his Organisation of African-American Unity. Like so many others, Eldridge Cleaver was devastated by the news of the murder of Malcolm before he could set about putting his new beliefs into action.

In 1965, after eight years in prison, Eldridge wrote to Beverly Axelrod, a white San Franciscan lawyer, known for her work in civil liberties cases. He asked her to plead his case for parole. That letter began a romantic association between the Attorney and the convict based on a lyrical and tender correspondence (Eldridge and Beverly established an enduring relationship founded on affection and mutual respect). Axelrod was interested in him and his writings, and she showed some of his manuscripts to Edward Keating, a founder of the *Ramparts* magazine, then amongst the most radical journals in America. Keating was impressed. He sent Cleaver's work to some white writers on the East Coast for appraisal. Keating insisted that Cleaver's writing proved that he was a reformed person, arguing further that his talent ensured him a livelihood once outside prison. Keating and his writer friends successfully pressed the California prison authorities to release Eldridge.

Freed on parole in November 1966, Cleaver had a book contract and a job with *Ramparts*. He wanted to make a clean break with his old life, so he moved to San Francisco, where he and other young black artists founded the Black House (a satire on the White House) to serve as an African-American cultural centre. But Cleaver believed that the problems of his people could not be solved through culture. In *Soul on Ice* he wrote that he, like Malcolm X, was convinced that:-

> "The Negro's basic situation cannot really change without structural changes in America's political and economic system."

As such, Eldridge was soon enmeshed in a whirlwind of radical events and personalities. It was whilst writing an assignment for *Ramparts* that he met Huey Newton and Bobby Seale, founders of the Black Panther Party. Their swagger and audacity captivated Cleaver and they were impressed by his ability to survive Folsom. He joined the Panthers in February 1967. Because of his writing skill Cleaver was named Minister of Information. He had an imposing physical presence, and was an articulate speaker. He had a keen ear for the quotable quote and this made him an even more effective communicator. As such, Cleaver would prove to be of great value in the early development of the Party.

The Panther Party have a reputation for aggression, but they were involved with relatively few violent incidents. In the main their tactics were essentially non-violent. In the early stages of their development the Panthers were a black self-defence movement based in the slums of Oakland, California, trying to stem the police harassment of blacks in the ghetto. As such they had an advocacy ethos that extended to campaigning for better housing, health and education for black people. But they were to become an energetic, innovatory social movement, establishing youth projects, breakfast clubs, shelters for the homeless, child care facilities for the poor and the first mass testing for sickle cell anaemia, which was taking a huge toll on black people in the USA at that time. The Panthers built an award winning school wherein people were graded according to ability rather than age. They created, within black communities, provision and facilities free from what they saw as the colonial intervention of the state sponsored professionals. This being the case, the Panthers were a social upsurge comparable to the Paris Commune in their humanistic and political objectives.

It was around Easter, 1967, in connection with an article that he was writing for *Ramparts*, looking at Stokely Carmichael (Kwame Ture) that Cleaver travelled with Carmichael to a conference organised at Fisk University in Nashville, Tennessee. One of the organisers of that conference was Kathleen Neal, the daughter of an American Foreign Service Officer. She was working for the Student Nonviolent Co-ordinating Committee (SNCC). She and Cleaver fell in love and were married in December 1967. Kathleen Cleaver joined the Black Panther Party and became communications secretary (she has now become a prolific writer on civil rights issues).

On 15th. April, 1967, Cleaver spoke at an anti-Vietnam War rally attended by 65,000 people. He articulated the Black Panther Party's support of the National Liberation Front in Vietnam, who, for him, were fighting against domination by the United States. Cleaver likened Black people in the United States to a colony ruled by the white mother country. He reiterated the Panther call for blacks to arm themselves in self-defence. The rally and Cleaver's speech were well publicised. Not long afterward, Cleaver's parole officer informed him that in the future he would have to submit all speeches for approval. Only after his attorneys prepared to appeal the matter in court, on the ground that Cleaver's right to free speech was being violated, did the parole authorities back down.

With the assistance of his attorney, Beverly Axelrod, Cleaver helped the Party to launch its newspaper, *The Black Panther*. The first issue was produced on 25th. April, 1967. Its opening headline addressed the killing of a young Black man by police. While overseeing the publication of the paper, Eldridge continued a myriad of other activities. By virtue of his unique story and his articles in *Ramparts* (his books *Soul on Ice* and *Post-Prison Writings and Speeches* were not yet published) he had a national platform, and he used his position to publicise the Black Panther Party.

The Panthers began to arouse a seething hostility among the police, which eventually led to shoot-outs. One such confrontation took place following Panther attempts to quell rioting after the assassination of Martin Luther King. During this incident a young black man, Bobby Hutton, lost his life. According to Cleaver the killing happened whilst Hutton was being taken into custody rather than, as the police would have it, during the fire-fight. Bobby Hutton was shot twelve times and became the first of many

Panther martyrs. Cleaver described the incident later:-

> "Then they snatched Little Bobby away from me and shoved him forward,
> telling him to run for the car. It was a sickening sight. Little Bobby,
> coughing and choking on the night air that was burning his lungs as my own
> were burning from the tear gas, stumbled forward as best he could, and after
> he travelled about ten yards the pigs cut lose on him with their guns."

Cleaver was wounded in the same skirmish, his parole was rescinded and he
was sent back to jail, but he was freed after two months on a writ of habeas
corpus by a California superior-court judge who ruled that he was a political
prisoner.

Eldridge saw the shoot-out with the police as his first experience of
freedom, in that he had been free for the hour and a half that the gun battle
had lasted, from what he called the repressive forces because they, in his
words: "...couldn't put their hand on me because we were shooting it out
with them..."

Cleaver ran for President in 1968, as a candidate for the Peace and
Freedom Party, an anti-war movement involving both blacks and whites.
He poled 30,000 votes, a massive total at a time when many of his potential
supporters would not have had the literacy skills needed to gain eligibility to
vote. At the same time Eldridge began to lecture on racism at the University
of California at Berkeley, and other Universities throughout the United
States to the intense annoyance of the then Governor of California, Ronald
Reagan, who at the time remarked that:-

> "If Eldridge Cleaver is allowed to teach our children, they may come home
> one night and slit our throats."

Given his paranoia it is perhaps not surprising that Reagan attempted to
silence Cleaver. However in the process the Governor provoked mass
demonstrations by black and white students.

In November, 1968, a higher Apellate court ruled that Cleaver should
return to jail. In response he went underground and escaped via Canada to
Cuba, later leaving there for a glossy white villa overlooking Algiers. Here
he became something of an expatriate American celebrity. From North
African exile he launched an international wing of the Panthers.

Eventually, Cleaver fell out with the Algerian authorities and, with his
wife and two children, moved on, dividing the next three years between
living in Paris and an apartment he had bought on the Cote d'Azur. He also
travelled widely during this time, meeting many world leaders, including

Kim Il-sung, the then Prime Minister of North Korea. However, political disenchantment was gradually taking a hold on Eldridge and he began to suffer serious bouts of depression.

It was during a stay at his French coastal retreat, on the balcony overlooking the Mediterranean, that he had a vision. Gazing at the sky he saw his profile in the moon. Then, across the face of the moon he saw some of the people who had inspired him in his struggles: Fidel Castro, Mao Tse-tung, Karl Marx. Each one appeared for a moment then dropped out of sight, like fallen heroes. He recalled in *Soul on Ice* that:-

> "Finally, at the end of the procession, in dazzling, shimmering light, the image of Jesus Christ appeared. This was the last straw."

Cleaver converted to Christianity and returned, voluntarily, to the United States in 1975. He had seen the light but there were dark days ahead. His travel had educated him, he once remarked:-

> "I ran into the Egyptian police and the Algerian police and the North Korean police and Idi Amin's police in Uganda. I began to miss the Oakland police. The last time I saw them suckers I was shooting at them."

Cleaver pleaded guilty to the charges stemming from the shoot-out, but most of the more serious charges against him were dropped. He spent eight months in jail, was given five years probation and 5,000 hours of community service.

Adopting a conservative point of view, Cleaver ran unsuccessfully in a Republican primary for the United States Senate. He tried his hand at fashion designing and ran a recycling operation in California. His marriage ended in divorce in 1987, after he succumbed to the allure of crack cocaine and petty crime.

But for all this, according to Richard Rose, at that point professor of religion and philosophy at the University of La Verne, a small liberal arts college near Los Angeles, where Eldridge was working as a racial diversity consultant at the time of his death: "He was a gentle spirit. His presence of nonconformity was still there, and he was his own person."

The Legacy

Eldridge Cleaver was an enigma trapped within a paradox. As a writer he possessed a powerful voice and a rare gift; he had a few years of influential political activism, but the sum total of his life was somewhere between a soul on ice and a soul on fire. He was a troubled spirit few people ever really got to know. But this should not allow us, the spectators, to underestimate his achievements. This man came from nowhere and nothing, less than nothing, as a convict and a rapist, to educate himself (perhaps the only alternative to indoctrination) and shake the very foundations of American society. But what did he give us? What did Eldridge Cleaver leave to this world? I think he left us, black and white, with at least two legacies.

1.The legacy of political philosophy

Power is nothing without control. Cleaver once said that: "Respect commands itself and it can neither be given nor withheld when it is due."

This sums up his political stance. It is a position that spurns the colonial and patronising idea that people can be empowered by others. It is an argument that sees power arising out of the individual and the collective, that seeks to create or take power, rather than await the powerful to distribute their power, which, is the fantasy of 'empowerment' promoted by those with an investment in maintaining the social status quo. The Panthers, for a time, exemplified his ideas in practice. If one relies on someone else to provide power, it is they, the provider of power, who will decide where, how much and what order of power is distributed. This is why the giving of power is a contradiction in terms; power, is, almost by definition, something that is taken rather than given. From the point of view of the Panthers and Eldridge, if you think someone is giving you power (empowering you) it is likely that you are mistaken and that in actuality you are being disempowered (you are from the start if you think you are being empowered).

From Eldridge's (and the Panthers) perspective education (for example) is mediated though the structures of a corrupt and oppressive society, as such it can be little more than a form of indoctrination, designed to strengthen that society. Why would the power élite that control any system do otherwise; where would there motivation for this come from?

Cleaver saw the civil rights movement as an exemplifying how the prevailing power systems maintain control covertly, whilst seemingly appearing to 'give power' (empower). He once said that the civil rights movement had given blacks access to hot dog stands, but had never addressed economic freedom, economic justice or democracy. Britain's equal opportunities legislation can be seen in the same light. What looks like liberatory policies are in fact, for Cleaver, forms of amelioration and tokenism.

Cleaver thought that the murder of Martin Luther King demonstrated the fear surrounding the potential for black economic democracy. He pointed out that as soon as King started turning towards the economic (nonracial) arena in Nashville, supporting the garbage man's strike, he was murdered. In 1997 Eldridge remarked that:-

"...if one called a meeting about segregation only Louis Farrakhan and David Dukes would come; call a meeting about money and everybody would come - that's where the rubber hits the road."

For Cleaver, the expanding black middle class in America were a useful indicator of how the economic system is cornered by the traditional power élite. He claimed that:-

"The Black middle class have followed an assimilationist ethic. They have become white and they've adopted all the worse features of America in terms of not caring about other people...the black bourgeoisie is as corrupt and immoral as the white bourgeoisie..."

For Cleaver, this process was reiterated by the recruitment of black protest leaders to the power élite. This, according to Cleaver has meant that, what he called the Black protest machinery has been transformed into the political machinery of the state. This, for Cleaver, has:-

"...stripped the black community of any kind of organisational machinery and consequently it left us floundering and treading water in a miserable state. That is why the number one task that we have in the Black community is a coup d'etat against our present leadership to strip them from that machinery that controls the community so that new ideas and new people can percolate up and then we can have a new agenda...we're under the dictatorship of the black bourgeoisie...and they're not any more concerned with the poorer black people than the rich whites are concerned with poor white people."

For Cleaver it is not impossible to deal with the problems of blacks in isolation; the effort to do this just comes down to a form of categorisation that only benefits the power élite in society. He said that, "we've got to get rid of special problems." This is a classically Marxist approach, but for Eldridge he drew his conclusions from experience. According to him, what we need to do is a much broader project than one based on misguided ideas of creating equality through State mechanisms that are inherently racist as they are built on the need to propagate institutional inequality/exploitation in terms of resources and wealth. He said:"we have to eliminate the economic basis of the underclass by providing jobs, not handouts."

The Panthers always had a strong economic emphasis in their programme. Cleaver had it that:

> "We had a direct challenge to the whole exploitation of the capitalist economy…we understood the relationship to our freedom and our access to economic remuneration and not just a little job because that is whimsical."
> The man on top can change that any time he wants to. That's why I was always so down on being totally dependent on the welfare system because when the winds blow differently in Washington, they can cut you off…this is a dangerous dependency.
> I talked about stuff that went beyond welfare. I rejected welfare because we need to be involved not just with the federal budget but with the private sector because the federal government gets its money from the private sector, so we have to be involved in owning and have an influence over the productive capacity of this country or else we are going to be perpetually dependent upon the largess of those who rule."

As such, Cleaver was arguing that the welfare system was designed to continue the status quo, maintaining the position of the poor in a net of apolitical, apathetic dependency. For Cleaver, why else would the welfare system exist in an aggressively oppressive capitalist state like the USA? Here, he echoes Franz Fanon's analysis of the 'colonial mentality', in Black Skins, White Masks.

2. Care about each other as the political and economic foundation of society

Cleaver saw the ideas of Louis Farrakhan and the Nation of Islam as essentially racist, for Eldridge: "The Afro-American people are not a racist people. We are an anti-racist people." He would have agreed with General Colin Powell's contention that black People, after coming so far, "cannot afford to take a detour through the swamps of hatred."

Society's problems are, at base, for Eldridge, founded on the contention 'that we do not care about each other'. That ethic was maybe always there. Tobe Johnson, a professor at Morehouse College Atlanta, just after Cleaver's death said of Eldridge that: "He could be thought of as a hero…At the time, it was inspirational for us here in the South to see a group like that out in Oakland providing breakfasts, providing shelter for the needy."

Eldridge understood, as did the Panthers as a movement, that the basis of political liberation does not lie in acts of legislation, or in the hands of the power élite, nor in education sponsored by the same. Our potential for freedom has its seeds in the small acts of kindness we can do for each other. This, in the end, may be the essence of Cleaver's political legacy.

The legacy of Redemption

Much of Eldridge Cleaver's life can be understood as a process of redemption. In the very last days of the Twentieth Century this became something of an American theme, as exemplified in Tony Kaye's 1998 film *American History X*. This depicts the conversion of a young white man to a fascist murder and his eventual redemption. Such a process is something we all seek to a greater or lesser extent; it is the want to find our better selves, to restore faith in ourselves and those who made us who we are.

Cleaver made a 180 degree turn in his life. He set himself a course to seek redemption for his past crimes: through his speeches, campaigning, writing and political action. He was a fugitive from justice, having forfeited bail in connection with serious felony charges. As a result of a dramatic spiritual experience he said that he suddenly realised that he had run as far as he wanted to run and was willing to turn himself in and face the music - whatever that might involve - and it was possible that it could have meant an 82 year prison sentence.

His 'vision' or 'understanding' led him directly to a final act of redemption, the last part of a process started by his reading and writing. He set out to seek his own redemption by making what restitution he could. In the end, that is what we would all perhaps hope for. To make good, or at least make restitution for, our mistakes.

Redemption can be understood as an essential ingredient in terms of human well-being. It is the capacity or the means we have to forgive ourselves and others. Without this, without restitution, without acceptance and tolerance, we would find ourselves miserable and contemplating suicide.

Eldridge showed us, by his life, that if we allow redemption, coupled with restitution, forgiveness, tolerance and acceptance to work for all humanity we might be more able to survive in this fractured world. This is the basis of humanitarianism and foundation of all the world's great religions. But do we see much evidence of this when we look around our society? Do we ever let the criminal off the hook? Even after they have served their time we know them as 'ex-offenders'. We often harass them wherever they live.

Against the advice of Christ our forgiveness does not seem to stretch to 70 times 7. We appear to believe in retribution rather than redemption. Maybe Eldridge Cleaver's struggle for redemption can remind us of the potential we stifle by our demands for punishment of those who offend our sensibilities, our own ethical or moral positions; the standards that we sometimes seem to desire to impose on or colonise others with, as if they are, taken for granted, better or superior to those held by others (those we blame and punish). It was this type of imposition that Eldridge and the Panthers struggled against. For them, all that could arise from punishment was resentment, so the fight was to end the institutional punishment of blacks so that a true liberation of humanity might come about.

Obituary

Eldridge Cleaver once remarked that: "too much agreement kills the chat." As such, I do not think he expected or hoped for all those who listened to him to agree with him. It may be there is still some mileage in his contention that: "All the gods are dead except the god of war". That is, we can only begin to move towards the truth by contention: indeed, when we all agree that we have found the truth, maybe we are not too far from the German National Socialists of the 1930's and 1940's (and what we have actually found is one big lie).

Eldridge used what he had. He could have been stymied by bewailing that he had not got what he wanted, but instead he moved with the resources to hand. There he was, in a cold, dark, lonely cell, a person from the most deprived of backgrounds, struggling to express himself in a profoundly unforgiving situation, lacking even a decent light. In comparison you or I have it all, except the attitude, or the will, or the strength.

Eldridge once said: "You cannot unring the bell", but maybe one can explain how and why it has tolled (or even, as Mohammad Ali said when this phrase was quoted to him, "Well, ring another bell"). Shortly before his death Cleaver reflected:-

> "Everybody changes, not just me. I was pulled over in my car with my secretary for a traffic thing, and one of the officers walked up to the car and saw me sitting inside. He took off his hat and said, 'Hey Eldridge, remember me?' He used to be a Panther. It was hard to believe."

In his last book is a dedication. It reads:"Jesus Christ, our Lord and Saviour, Who can do for everyone what He did for me." Just a month before his death he declared: "I've gone beyond civil rights and human rights to creation rights."

Change is the way of all things and as far as change is redemption, it makes, from what we were, what we are and might become. The life of Leroy Eldridge Cleaver mesmerised and alarmed a society not then accustomed to inflammatory rhetoric of the type he dealt in; a truth, not easy to listen to. He was a passionate rebel, something of a visionary. Writer and former Panther David Hilliard said of him:-

> "I thought Eldridge was the reincarnation of Malcolm X. I'd never heard such power, such eloquence."

Roland Freeman, the highly regarded photodocumentarian whose work has been exhibited world wide (also an ex-Panther) pointed out that:-

> "Eldridge played a very critical role in the struggle of the 1960s and the 1970's. He was a symbol."

Leroy finished his life as political philosopher, but first he was the ordinary, frail human being to be found in us all. Perhaps his daughter, Joju Younghi Cleaver, summed him up best when at his memorial service she spoke of her father as:-

> "A caring man who loved his people, meaning everyone under creation."

She said her father had:-

> "left very strong fires that burn brightly in my brother and as bright as ever in my heart."

The former spokesman of the US Black Panther movement and author of *Soul on Ice*, Leroy Eldridge Cleaver died on 1st. May, 1998, at 6.20 am, aged 62. The cause of his death was withheld at the family's request, but later it was revealed that he died of a heart attack. He left a son and a daughter and is survived by his ex-wife.

Eldridge was born in Warbbaseka, Arkansas on 31st. August, 1935, the son of Leroy (a pianist, who during World War II got a job as a dining car waiter for a railway line) and Thelma (a janitress). From a background of the most abject poverty, that it is hard for us to imagine, he was to become one of the most eloquent American voices of the late 1960s. I hope that you, in reading about him have felt his redemptive heat and in that you will find the grace to forgive yourself and others.

CHAPTER 6

Kwame Ture (Stokely Carmichael)
Political activist, civil rights leader, philosopher and poet.

The basics of the short life of Stokely Carmichael, who became Kwame Ture in 1969, betray little of his uniqueness. He was born in Port-of-Spain, Trinidad on 29th. June, 1941. He married twice. Each of these unions produced a son. He died in Conakry, Guinea, on 15th. November, 1998, but when the black power movement scared much of white America out of its wits, and triggered a historic pulse of pride through a generation of black Americans, no star burned in its firmament fiercer and less compromising than that of Stokely Carmichael. Thirty years on, the names that populated that brief but dramatic dawn still have a heroic ring: Huey Newton, Bobby Seale, Leroi Jones, Eldridge Cleaver and, of course, Stokely himself. Of them all, he stayed truest to his original principles. Not for him recantation and conversion to the pragmatics of American Politics taken on by Cleaver. Not for him the compromise of Seale, who accepted an alliance with white radicals to further the struggle, but ended up writing books about barbecuing. For the man who would be Kwame Ture, the very notion of compromise was a sell-out. In 1969 he decamped to Guinea, where he spent the rest of his life advocating a unified socialist Pan-African state; the last hope, he said, for blacks to break the white race's stranglehold on global power.

Stokely Carmichael was a rebel almost from the moment he set foot on American soil. As a child in Trinidad he was looked after by aunts and his grandmother. At the age of eleven he went to join his parents who had emigrated to find work in America. By the time he became a teenager Stokely was a Harlem boy. Long afterwards he raged against the British education he received in one of Her Majesty's colonies. He claimed that Tranquillity Boys School "drugged" him into accepting white supremacy; he recalled eagerly waving the Union Jack during a Royal visit and remembered that: "At school we were made to memorise Kipling's, 'White Man's Burden', and told we didn't exist till a white man called Sir Walter Raleigh discovered us." In 1967 he recalled: "We went to the movies and yelled for Tarzan to beat the hell out of Africa." If the Tsars of Hollywood and the captains of colonial education had known the nature of the seeds they were planting in the exceptional little boy who was Stokely Carmichael

they would have lost one or two nights sleep in their comfortable beds.

At least Trinidad was ostensibly black-run. Not so Harlem and theAt least Trinidad was ostensibly black-run. Not so Harlem and the United States of the 1950s, where white police protected white wealth, white politicians passed white laws and the blacks just had to put up with it. In New York, right from his first days there, Stokely encountered a more virulent form of racial discrimination than he'd known in his colonial days and on his own admission he became something of an urban tearaway. He observed how his father, a carpenter who supplemented his income by driving a taxi, worked himself to death: "and he died just the way he started: poor and black".

The young Stokely experimented with marijuana. When the family moved to the Bronx, despite being a very intelligent young man, he cultivated a reputation for fighting, drinking and being a pretty good thief as the only black member of a gang known as the Morris Park Dukes. Even so, at the highly regarded Bronx High School of Science, he immersed himself in political theory and philosophy. His affluent white classmates became his associates and as he said: "I dated white girls. I was the good little nigger and everybody was being nice to me." Later in life he hated recalling this time that he saw as a period of personal and psychological capitulation on his part.

Carmichael's political awareness was sparked by television reports of the sit-ins organised in the late 1950s by Martin Luther King and the Southern Christian Leadership Conference (SCLC) at segregationist restaurants in the Deep South. Stokely regarded them as publicity stunts until he saw pictures of the violence that the police inflicted on demonstrators. This changed his analysis of the situation dramatically.

By the time he left high school, Carmichael was emerging as a left-wing radical. He was a student of Marx and Darwin, and his knowledge energized his continued horror and anger at the official brutality of the Southern States and the beatings meted out to black college students for ignoring the unwritten code of racial segregation. In the early 1960s he joined the Congress for Racial Equality and took his place on the picket lines protesting against white supremacy.

In 1961 Stokely was organising integration on buses as a member of the Freedom Ride movement, taking coach trips through the Southern States to challenge their segregationist travel laws. He soon found himself on the wrong end of the truncheons. He recalled: "After a few beatings, I realised it was either them or me. I preferred me." The future black militant was born.

Turning down scholarships at several white universities, Carmichael chose to attend the predominantly black Howard University in Washington DC. After graduating in 1964 with a degree in philosophy, he threw himself full-time into the civil rights struggle. As an organiser for the Student Non-violent Coordinating Committee, Carmichael spent most of the next three years in the South, organising hundreds of volunteers, working to set up schools, teaching black people how to write and creating black medical clinics. In Lowndes County, Mississippi (the poorest state in the Union at that time) a rural area with a two-thirds black population and a virtually all-white electorate, Stokely worked to encouraged blacks to register for the vote. He raised the number of black voters from 70 to 2,600; a 53 percent black electorate. He went on to create the all-black Lowndes County Freedom Organisation, to meet a local ordinance, aimed at illiterate voters. It took as its symbol a leaping, snarling black panther. He observed:-

"A man needs a black panther on his side when he and his family must endure loss of job, eviction, starvation and sometimes death for political activity."

This intense and radical activity required a rare boldness and bravery. Murder was a constant threat and for his pains Carmichael was arrested some three dozen times (after being picked-up for the 32nd time he lost count). He endured constant official intimidation and was savagely beaten on several occasions by prison wardens, particularly during a seven-week term in a Mississippi prison. But the young man had style, looks (he was tall and sparely built), and was a spellbinding orator. One admirer described him as, 'a Nubian god'. Another remarked how he "gave the impression he could walk through Dixie in broad daylight, using the Confederate flag for a handkerchief."

By the mid-1960s Carmichael was an iconic militant in the process of development. In March 1965, at a conference in Waveland, Carmichael spoke of the need for the SNCC to return to its roots in the black community. That was a seminal moment and the sense of his argument was clear to both white and black members, who through Stokely's intelligent analysis were persuaded that they had separate political tasks.

In 1966 and 1967 Carmichael travelled widely, lecturing in Spain, Czechoslovakia, North Vietnam, Africa and Cuba. At Chalk Farm, in London, he spoke on the 'Dialectics of Liberation' and the 'Demystification of Violence'. After his eleven day visit the Labour Home Secretary, Roy Jenkins (the man who was to help found the short lived British Social Democratic Party and champion electoral reform by way of proportional representation) announced that Carmichael would not be allowed to re-enter the UK.

Stokely's defining moment came on 16th. June, 1966, just three weeks before his 25th birthday and a month after being elected chair of the SNCC. He had just been released after yet another arrest, and was addressing a crowd in Greenwood, Mississippi, as part of a Freedom March following the shooting and wounding of James Meredith, the first black American to be admitted to the University of Mississippi, while conducting a solitary march. As the police moved towards Stokely he yelled to the crowd:-

"We've been saying 'Freedom' for six years. What we are going to start saying now is; 'Black Power!'"

The audience took up the cry. The phrase galvanised, polarised and ultimately split black America. It effectively distanced him from Martin Luther King's emphasis on peaceful political struggle. Years later he elaborated on the split:-

"One simple definition separated us...He saw non-violence as a principle, which means it had to be used at all times, under all conditions. I saw it as a tactic. If it was working I would use it; if it isn't working, I'm picking up guns because I want my freedom by any means necessary."

Carmichael explained what he meant by Black Power as: "Negroes taking over local government in communities where they are in the majority." As such Black Power referred to political and economic self empowerment. He wrote:-

"We want control of the communities we live in and we want to stop the exploitation of non-white people around the world."

But the phrase not only horrified whites. Martin Luther King, striving to achieve black equality through non-violence, called the Black Power slogan "an unfortunate choice of words". Nevertheless it appealed to militant young blacks who had been robbed of leadership by the assassination of Malcolm X eighteen months earlier. Under Carmichael the Black Power movement set itself against moderation and co-operation with white authorities, and turned its back on King's ideas of patient progress towards integration. Black Power soon became the war cry on the lips of young blacks all over America.

During the 1960s Carmichael broke new ground in black politics by insisting that blacks in America had to achieve liberation by their own efforts, even if this meant the use of violence. In an article in the *New York Review of Books* he claimed that black Americans were a propertyless people in a country where property was valued above all else, and in a society which did not function by morality and love but by power and money. In his masterpiece *Black Power* (1967 - written with Charles Hamilton) Carmichael called for unity among black people and urged them to recognise their heritage, and build a sense of community to: "define their own goals." He backed up his written word in his speeches, encouraging his listeners to smash "everything white civilisation had created".

In *Black Power* Carmichael defined racism as not merely exclusiveness, but: "exclusion for the purpose of subjugating or maintaining subjugation." He believed that blacks must own property and develop the economic power to disrupt. He pointed out that American blacks had not succeeded in bettering their lot by trusting the panaceas of white liberals. He became one of the first to insist that blacks should stand proudly by their own traditions and culture.

Carmichael was able to make a rigorous academic analysis of the plight of the America's black people. He quoted Machiavelli, Sartre, Camus, Mao and Che Guevara on the importance of hating the white supremacist. He made these truculent points with grace and charm during 1967 and 1968, a period when America was afire with race riots. He was a mesmeric speaker, combining the outrage of the outcast with eloquent articulateness. He once claimed that: "To ask Negroes to get in the Democratic Party is like asking Jews to join the Nazi Party."

In 1968 he proclaimed: "When white America killed Dr. King it declared war on us. Our retaliation won't be in the court room, but in the streets of America." He warned: "Black people know they have to get guns. I don't think there is any alternative to retribution. It will be war to the death. I speak as just one Negro, ready to die. My life means nothing."

In this mood Carmichael dismissed liberals as bumble heads, do-gooders and nosy-parkers and redefined integration as: "You do what I tell you to do and then you can sit at the table with us." At this point Stokely became the incarnation of violent black separatism and nationalism. He had become impatient with what he saw as the less than modest gains of non-violence. He had also got fed-up with the seeming indifference of the white-controlled legislature to brutal acts committed against non-violent black protesters by police. In 1967, he finally broke with the SNCC after telling a meeting in Havana that the SNCC were preparing urban guerrilla forces to fight to the death. He was officially sacked as the National Chair in 1968. However, in that year he was appointed honorary Prime Minister by the

Black Panther Party.

Although the BPP was founded by Newton and Seale, it was Stokely that brought the symbol of the black panther into race relations. He had become an ardent critic of the war in Vietnam. "Why should a Negro", he demanded to know, "go 8,000 miles to shoot a man that ain't never called you 'nigger'?" He advised the black Americans sent to Vietnam to join the Vietcong in the struggle against the white colonisers. This was part of a personal war on the whole of the white-dominated industrialized world. "The trouble with the West" he complained in 1968, "is that it feels it has the right to give everybody their independence. I'm amazed when I pick up the paper and read that England has decided to give me my independence. All they can do is stop oppressing me, get off my back."

In America, Stokely's "burn, baby burn" dictum of anarchic yet directed violence was a dramatic, active alternative to the politics of passivism that, from his perspective, had got black people nowhere in nearly a hundred years. But even the Panthers proved too moderate for Carmichael. As they proposed to make ad hoc working arrangements with radical whites groups, Stokely left. He had been involved for less than a year, but such alliances he said "led to complete subversion of blacks by whites." Still more alarming to Carmichael, they risked removing the grounds of protest. "America does not belong to the blacks", he thundered as he turned his back on the Panthers. In response, Eldridge Cleaver, the Panthers' Minister for Information, wrote an open letter to Carmichael chiding him for his "paranoid fear" of whites. For Carmichael however the only way to fight racism was with an emphasis on race.

In 1969, with the famous South African singer Miriam Makeba, whom he married in 1968, Carmichael left the United States and made for Africa, urging all America's blacks to do likewise. He set up home in Guinea and later changed his name to Kwame Ture after Kwame Nkrumah, the first leader of an independent Ghana, and Sekou Toure, the president of Guinea and the sole leader in former French Africa who had spurned the patronage of the French President, Charles de Gaulle, when his country won independence.

Kwame was always much more conscious of Africa than many of his Black Power peers. In 1968 he said: "We are an African people with an African ideology."

In Guinea Kwame studied French, continued to advocate revolution, and took up the cause of Pan-Africanism under the banner of Nkrumah's All-African People's Revolutionary Party (AAPRP). He claimed that: "It is only the power of a unified socialist Africa that can intervene on behalf of the Africans scattered all over the world to ensure their proper respect."

Following a divorce he married Malyatou Barry, a Guinean doctor. This relationship also ended in divorce. As time went on Ture came to personify the black militant movement but he was also, all too often, its solitary voice. Increasingly, in his African retreat, he was ignored by the Western media. But he continued to make regular recruitment campaigns for the AAPRP in American and other universities. He began to devote his efforts to fighting the corners of outcast counties like Libya and Cuba, trying to do his best to challenge the propaganda of a media dominated by American neo-colonial interests. He has been repeatedly misrepresented by the same. For example, in 1969 he was reported to have he told the Indians of Guyana that they could never be part of the Black Power movement. This was not an attack on the Indians but on the means by which they took and held power: through reliance on American capitalism. At the same time he was accused of telling women that there was no place for them in the revolutionary movement except on their backs. This again, in context, was not a statement disparaging the overall potential contribution of women. He was making the point that while women relied on masculine aid for their liberation they would only get to be where masculine, capitalists wanted them.

However, he was never cowed by the risks of misinterpretation. In 1970 Ture was banned from entering his native Trinidad for fear he would encourage revolt, by energising the Black Power movement there (which was later suppressed). Back in Lowndes County in 1974 he reminded his audience that the white man had sinned against his black neighbour "and there will be no remission of sin without the shedding of blood". In London in 1983 as a guest of the Hackney Black People's Association, Kwame called for the destruction of capitalism. The Brixton riots of 1981, he felt, had failed due to insufficient organisation (anyone who was there would agree with this). He advised that the purchase of hand grenades might be a good idea. Insane? Well, some people took him seriously. When he attempted to return to Britain in 1984 he was once more forbidden entry.

In the same year Sekou Toure died. He had let Kwame (and many, many others) down badly, turning out to be a torturer and a murder of political opponents. Under the new regime Ture was even briefly imprisoned at one point.

In the 1990s Kwame continued to wax eloquent against Israel, capitalism, America and Zionism (which he saw as a type of colonialism) on American campuses, mostly to all-black audiences. He stayed true to his socialism and his Marxist roots, as America bred a new black middle class and a black political élite (conscripted to the political interests of America's white ruling class) to undermine and corrupt the revolutionary potential of black America. But Kwame's sheer unswerving zealotry earned its own respect. One thousand people, including leaders of the black establishment he so despised, attended a testimonial dinner for him in Washington in April 1998. Most of those attending knew that Kwame was dying of cancer (he claimed he had been infected with the disease by the FBI. Not such a fantastic notion; they have done worse and more bizarre things). This was the last chance to pay tribute to the man. Not because they agreed with him, but because they wanted to thank him for being on the barricades when the barricades were truly dangerous.

To the end, Ture kept his rhetorical swagger and his style. Often he wore the green fatigues of a soldier in the Guinean army. In 1992 he wrote in his postscript to Black Power:-

"Since we shed blood sporadically and in a disorganised manner for reform, let us permanently organise ourselves and make revolution."

Kwame Ture died on a Sunday, aged 57. He had been undergoing treatment for prostate cancer in New York for many months, but decided to return to Africa when his condition became irreversible. Jesse Jackson visited Kwame three times at his home in Guinea during a trip to Africa and reported that Ture had said that he "wanted for his last days to be in Guinea and in West Africa" and wanted "to be among the people of Africa". Jackson went on:-

"He was committed to ending racial apartheid in our country. He helped to bring those walls down."

Kwame Ture was a most effective organiser, capable of breaking through class and racial barriers by the force of his personality, by his fabulous good looks and by his political sophistication. He was flamboyant and outspoken. He had been determined to give his life to transforming America and Africa. His attitude to violence was indeed revolutionary. He saw capitalism as a violent social form and as such it could only produce violence. For Kwame, if we are faced with overt violence we either respond in kind or die. But he had another side that saw that covert and subtle violence needs to be answered too and he understood that we do not necessarily need guns to do violence to the system; he knew we can undermine it with humanity and the care for and the love of each other. This is why he was so adamant that people should come together and respond in a unified manner. Facts like his serving on Bertrand Russell's international war crimes tribunal have been forgotten. What is recalled are words quoted out of context in order to damn him as mad-man, for example the often quoted statement that Hitler was the white man he most admired as "a genius". Our outrage blinds us to what Ture was getting at, that Hitler convinced basically good people that evil was moral; Hitler overtly demonstrated the nature of racial supremacy - the ideology that Ture hated with all his being.

Kwame Ture will perhaps some day be recognised as one of the great human beings of the late Twentieth Century. His followers and fellow travellers have all failed to live up to the type aspirations he held. He realised that all change comes down to small personal actions, the collective of which is revolution. He demonstrated this even in the way he answered the phone: "Ready for the revolution."

CHAPTER 7

Ludwig and Malcolm

How two people who never met and could not have met offer an organic
understanding from subtle, concentrated and committed interaction: the
Philosophy of Mutuality.

Ludwig Wittgenstein is regarded by many as one of the most influential
philosophers of the Twentieth century. His two great works *Tractatus Logico-
Philosophicus*, published in 1921 and Philosophical Investigations, published
posthumously in 1953, have inspired a vast secondary literature and have
done much to shape subsequent developments in philosophy, especially
within the analytic tradition.

One might fill a library with the books written about Malcolm X. Such
is the extent of the exploration of his relatively short life it would seem there
is little of interest or novelty left to say about him. He is an icon of African-
American culture and a seminal figure within the wider social discourse and
modern history. However, here I want not so focus on his stature as an
orator or activist, which is massive. I want to demonstrate the nature of his
philosophy, the culmination of this being his last days following his
enlightening trip to Mecca.

Malcolm, like Wittgenstein had a charismatic personality. Both have
exerted a powerful fascination upon artists, playwrights, poets, novelists,
musicians, and even moviemakers. As such their fame has spread far
beyond the confines of, in Wittgenstein's case, academic life and in
Malcolm's, the province of civil rights in America.

In spite of the widespread acknowledgement of his genius, there is a
sense in which Wittgenstein's thought has made very little impression on the
intellectual life of the last fifty years. As he himself realised, his style of
thinking is directly at odds with that which dominates our present era. His
work is opposed, as he once put it: "to the spirit that informs the vast stream
of European and American civilisation in which all of us stand."

Despite all of Hollywood's interest, much the same story might be
applied to Malcolm. He created a way of thinking about civil rights and the
position of black people in America (and across the world) that went against
the norm, but when this was to an appreciable extent embraced by the
cannon, he moved on and developed his thought to again take himself to
the very frontier of thinking and potential action. This was, of course, the

point at which he was most dangerous in terms of disrupting the status quo. Also like Wittgenstein his figure abides, but his ideas have, to some extent, become hidden by his profile.

Over half a century after Wittgenstein's death, one can see more clearly than ever, this feeling, that he was swimming against the current, was entirely justified. If one wanted a convenient label to describe the tide he laboured to make headway through, one might describe it as 'scientism': the view that every intelligible question has either a scientific solution or no solution at all. This spills over into the mental health and related welfare/educational disciplines of the industrialised world, in that they claim an understanding of individuals, groups and communities. These 'insights' (which are, in reality, no more than mere hypotheses) are generated through observation, recording and analysis.

It is against this view that Wittgenstein resolutely set his face, and it is in this respect that unfortunately, his work has almost no discernible impact on the intellectual life of our age. People want to be able to think that they can, by scientific method, predict and so control the world. A whole industry of 'planning' has been based on this assumption that has spurned sub-species like 'time-management' and 'quality assurance'.

Science is premised on various forms of categorisation. The idea of scientifically differentiating types of people is the cradle of race theory (and by association racism). It is clear that Malcolm was challenging this when he was at the very pinnacle of his perceptive powers:

> "We don't judge a man because of the color of his skin. We don't judge you because you're white; we don't judge you because you're black; we don't judge you because you're brown. We judge you because of what you do and what you practice."
> Malcolm X, in Malcolm X: *The Last Speeches*

Scientism takes many forms. In the humanities (which provide many of the means by which education and welfare are delivered and mediated) as they are now pursued in our universities, examine philosophy, literature, music, art and the behaviour of people as if these facets of human behaviour were sciences like biology or chemistry. Researchers and students are compelled to spell out their 'methodology', and make the effort to 'contribute to the literature' in their chosen field. The assumption, made seemingly unproblematically, that almost anything can be explained via the scientific method, has led to vast quantities of bad academic and professional writing, which is characterised by bogus theorising, shallow and often spurious specialisation and the development of a plethora of pseudo-

technical vocabulary designed to disguise traditional academic disciplines and common sense everyday activity, as specialised forms of technical enquiry. Wittgenstein would have looked upon these developments and wept. Malcolm may also have seen them for the means of obscuration they are.

There are many, many questions to which we do not have scientific answers, not because they are deep impenetrable mysteries, but simply because they are not scientific questions. These include almost all questions that really matter to us. Questions about love, life, art, history, culture, the nature of equality, music and people. All these questions relate to the attempt to understand ourselves better. The scientific tool may indeed involve the asking of a question, but such questions are not generally going to give us a useful answer about non-scientific activity. The problem with science is that it presents itself as being self-evident. Evidence is the fulcrum of scientific truth and its purpose is to leave no room for critique. However, this is potentially restrictive of human interaction and growth. Malcolm understood this. The progress of non-scientific reasoning is not about problem solving, it is about generating a constant reassessment of the nature of reality, achieving particular truths that are constantly in question:-

> "I think all of us should be critics of each other. Whenever you can't stand criticism you can never grow. I don't think that it serves any purpose for the leaders of our people to waste their time fighting each other needlessly. I think that we accomplish more when we sit down in private and iron out whatever differences that may exist and try and then do something constructive for the benefit of our people. But on the other hand, I don't think that we should be above criticism. I don't think that anyone should be above criticism."
>
> Malcolm X, in Malcolm X: *The Last Speeches*

There is a widespread notion in intellectual life today that sees the great scandal of our time as being our lack a scientific theory of consciousness, or, as it is sometimes put, of "the self". Look at the time spent in universities and in the professional context trying to understand, or expose to inspection and examination 'the self'. The implied assumption is that in the absence of such a theory we do not really understand what consciousness or the self is. And so, at the moment there is a great interdisciplinary effort, involving physicists, computer scientists, cognitive psychologists, philosophers, and welfare/educational professionals, to remedy this lack and to come up with tenable scientific answers to the questions: what is consciousness: what is the self: who am I?

One of the leading competitors in this crowded field is a theory advanced by Sir Roger Penrose, a professor of mathematics at the University of Oxford in England, who pursues an active interest in 'recreational maths' which he shared with his father. He argues that human thought is created at the level of the mind through quantum collapse processes in microtubules, protein structures found in the skeleton of a neuron. This means that for Penrose a stream of consciousness is an orchestrated sequence of quantum (very small) events, taking place in the brain. According to him, a moment of consciousness is produced by a sub-protein in the brain called a tubulin. This normally exists in the superposed (transposed) states, characteristic of sub-atomic particles but which Penrose argues, has the remarkable ability to collapse its super-positions all by itself – thus producing a conscious moment. The theory is, on Penrose's own admission, "speculative" and it strikes many as being bizarrely improbable. But what hits the layperson straight in the face as most strange is the prevalent assumption that even if it is not correct this is the kind of theory we want in order to understand consciousness better.

Suppose we discovered that Penrose's theory was correct, would we, in making that discovery, understand ourselves any better? Would our mental angst or psychological suffering be any less? This is another way of asking, 'Is a scientific theory the only kind of understanding?' Do any of the scientific techniques or theories that a youth or social worker or psychiatrist may know about make them any more able to comprehend or help with the everyday experience of a person, than say a baker or a bartender? Well, one might ask, 'Is there any other kind of theory than a scientific one?' It is Wittgenstein's answer to that question which is his perhaps his greatest and most neglected achievement.

As Malcolm's intellectual development took a critical turn later in his life, Wittgenstein's philosophical thought underwent significant and even fundamental changes between his early and his later work, but his opposition to scientism was constant. In his later work he saw the difference between science and philosophy. At that point he believed that this was not the difference between two sets of truths, one expressible in language and the other not, one which can be stated and the other only shown. Rather he understood that they were two very distinct forms of understanding; the theoretical and the non-theoretical. Scientific understanding is given through the construction and testing of hypotheses and theories. Philosophical understanding on the other hand is resolutely non-theoretical. What we are after in philosophy, according to Wittgenstein, is the understanding that consists in seeing connections; how one thing relates to or connects with another. This is the essence of Malcolm's insight during and after his experience of pilgrimage. He saw the connections between people rather than their separateness and understood that progress of any kind could only be achieved through human beings interacting with each other.

In appealing to this kind of understanding Wittgenstein was not, as he was in the *Tratatus* invoking a mysterious and esoteric type of ineffable truth. If we want examples of non-theoretical understanding, they lie readily to hand in ordinary life. It is the kind of understanding that we typically have in mind when we say that we understand a poem, a piece of music, a person or even a sentence. Think for example of the case of a small child learning her native language. When she begins to understand what is said to her, is it because she has formulated a theory? We can say this if we like, and many philosophers, linguists and psychologists have said just that. But it is, to say the very least, a misleading way to describe what is going on.

The criterion we use as standard to evidence that a child understands what is said to her is that she behaves appropriately. She shows that she understands the phrase 'put this piece of paper in the bin', for example, by obeying the instruction. In order to show that she has understood, she does not, it ought to go without saying, have to convince us of the truth of any particular theory. Thus we can, and very often do, use the notion of understanding outside the context of theory construction.

Another example and one very close to Wittgenstein's heart, is the understanding of music. How does one demonstrate that one has comprehended of a piece of music? Well, perhaps by playing it expressively or by using the right sort of metaphors to describe it; 'This phrase is like a question', 'this one is like a conclusion' etc., etc. And how does one explain what expressive playing is? What is needed for this, according to Wittgenstein, is a culture. For him, If someone is brought up in a particular culture, and then reacts to music in such and such a way, you can teach her the use of the phrase, 'expressive playing'. Thus what is required for this type of understanding is a form of life; a set of communally shared habits and practices, together with the ability to hear and see the connections made by the practitioners of this form of life. For example, I recently played a piece of Turkish Gypsy music to a group of second year undergraduate youth work students. I started to try to explain something about what was being played with saying: "This music…" but, before I could go on a mature student, an experienced worker, heckled "is shit!"

What can be taken from this is that this person did not have a culture, communally shared habits and practices, that may have allowed her to hear and see the connections made by the practitioners (Turkish Gypsies) of this form of life. To have this she would need to be generous/secure enough to be ready to listen to and enter into a shared experience of exploration either with Turkish Gypsies musicians or others with some connection with this music (like me!); this was not to be. Hence any sincere comment she might have made about this music could be no more discriminating on the basis of ignorance (prejudice). This is not a reason to be angry with this person, but it is an understanding (not a scientific theory) of her response.

The expression "is shit!" is a personal response to a communal condition (although I cannot construe anything telling or useful about this woman's community from her individual behaviour) that in the context of higher education one might hope would be temporarily suppressed or mediated. In the milieu of youth work, wherein there are constant connections with cultural representatives not necessarily concomitant with one's own, it would of course 'unprofessional' and in some instances highly dangerous to react in such a way, albeit explicable. But this is expecting a person to act in a consistent, scientific manner; weighing up the pros and cons and then acting according to the resultant theory. But instead humans are inclined by all sorts of other considerations to basically reveal more about their instincts and anxieties in everyday life than they are to adhere in their behaviour to scientifically generated responses.

Certainly this person can be made more aware of the possible reactions to her prejudice, be taught not to express her feelings in such a way. This is a sort of scientific lesson; 'experience suggests that this will have that reaction, so if you don't want that, don't do this'. And of course, even though this encourages a type of deception, maybe even lying, it works. But it will not make her appreciate Turkish Gypsy music. She might still see it as 'shit', she just won't voice that opinion and so not reveal her prejudice/ignorance.

What is true of music is also true of most ordinary language. Wittgenstein argues, in *Philosophical Investigations*, that understanding a sentence is much more akin to understanding a theme in music than one may think. The understanding of a sentence also requires participation in the form of life, the language game to which it belongs. The reason computers have no real understanding of the sentences they process is not that they lack sufficient neuronal complexity, but that they are not, and cannot be participants in the culture to which those sentences belong. For Wittgenstein a sentence does not acquire its meaning through the correlation, one-to-one, of its words with objects in the world. It acquires its meaning through the use that is made of it in the communal life of human beings. This is how intelligence develops and understanding grows (en it?).

In his book *Shadows of the Mind*, Roger Penrose suggests that deep problems in artificial intelligence, physics, and the philosophy of mind are closely connected. He presents a detailed argument, using another theory, 'Gödel's theorem', to conclude that human thought cannot be simulated by any computation. This leads him to the conclusion that physics is 'noncomputable', and he presents suggestions about how 'non-computability' may enter into a theory of quantum gravity and that this happens in the realm of mind, as we have seen, through quantum collapse processes in microtubules. This is a very different explanation from that offered by Wittgenstein. Very simplistically, Penrose proposes a mechanical explanation of operation whereas Wittgenstein offers an organic clarification of a developmental process. Malcolm exemplifies this in much of his thinking, for example he argued:-

> "I'm the man you think you are. And if it doesn't take legislation to make you a man and get your rights recognized, don't even talk that legislative talk to me. No, if we're both human beings, we'll both do the same thing. And if you want to know what I'll do, figure out what you'll do. I'll do the same thing – only more of it."
> Malcolm X, in *Malcolm X Speaks: Selected Speeches and Statements*

Here Malcolm is making the point that behaviour is essentially an interactive process. No matter what rules or regulations are put in place, no matter what may constitute the scientific norm, people will conform or rebel according to the organic and social situation they are presented with, so the so called rules, or norm, will be in a constant state of flux and as such a level of novelty and unpredictability will always reign, hence Malcolm will do more of it. That is his decision, putting his unique stamp on the world.

Malcolm's position might seem straightforward and in a way it is. In the same sense Wittgenstein's position may sound trivially true and certainly he regarded this to be the case. He once described his work as a *"synopsis of triviality"*. However, its importance derives from the fact that when we are thinking philosophically, we are apt to forget these trivialities and thus end up in the seemingly absurd confusion offered by Penrose, who, in effect imagines that we will understand ourselves better if we study the quantum behaviour of the sub-atomic particles inside our brains. It is a similar illusion that we might grasp precisely what is going on in a group or a community by analysing the behaviour of the individuals that make up that entity. This is a belief analogous to the conviction that a study of acoustics will help one understand the music of Beethoven.

Why do we need reminding of triviality? Well, we seem to be bewitched into thinking that if we lack a scientific theory of something we lack any understanding of it at all. But maybe we can 'just understand'. Wittgenstein writes in the *Blue Book* (the *Blue* and *Brown Books* are notebooks from Wittgenstein's later period, originally dictated to his students in Cambridge in the 1930s, and circulated, not without precaution and secrecy). This is probably the most straightforward introduction to Wittgenstein's work:-

> "Philosophers constantly see the method of science before their eyes...and are irresistibly tempted to ask and answer questions in the way science does. This tendency leads the philosopher into complete darkness."

In this condition we seem in danger of knowing about everything and understanding nothing. We can know all the procedures involved and duties emanating from equal opportunities legislation. We can be well versed in the rhetoric of diversity, but this does not mean we comprehend or grasp the nature of discrimination or the experience of discrimination and prejudice. This can only be understood by way of the sharing of experience in a spirit of mutuality. This was the underlying message in much of Malcolm's oration and teaching.

One of the most important differences between the method of science and the non-theoretical understanding that is exemplified in music, art, philosophy and ordinary life, is that science aims at a level of generality that necessarily eludes these other forms of understanding. This is why the understanding of people can never be a science and why to try to use forms of scientism to grasp what is happening between people is to practice obscuration.

To understand a person is to be able to tell for example whether s/he means what they say or not; whether their expressions of feeling are genuine of feigned. How does one acquire this sort of understanding? This is the question that Wittgenstein raises right at the end of Philosophical Investigations. Is there, he asks, such a thing as expert judgement about the genuineness of the expressions of feeling? His answer to this is that he believes there is. Even here there are those whose judgement is better and those whose judgement is worse. More correct prognoses will generally issue from the judgements of those with better knowledge of humankind. Can one learn this knowledge? Wittgenstein argues that some can. Not, however by taking a course in it, even if it does come with a fine piece of paper signed by an institutional dignitary. It can only be learnt through experience and the effort to understand others. Can someone else be another person's teacher in this? 'Certainly', says Wittgenstein. From time to time you can give someone the right tip or a useful nudge, this is the nature of learning and teaching (answering questions with 'non-instructive' questions such as 'what do you think?' is not genuinely teaching and can lead more often than not to frustration on the part of the person who asked the original question, rather than learning).

The evidence upon which such expert judgements about people are based is, according to Wittgenstein imponderable, resistant to the general formulation characteristic of science, or even to the weighing up characteristic of legal evidence. Imponderable evidence Wittgenstein writes includes subtleties of glance, of gesture, of tone. I may recognise a genuine loving look, distinguish it from a pretended one, but I may be quite incapable of describing the difference. However, if I were a very talented painter I might conceivably represent the genuine and simulated glance in pictures, but would this stand up in court?

The fact that we're dealing here with imponderables should not mislead us into believing that all claims to understand people are spurious or built upon shaky foundations. Once, when Wittgenstein was discussing his favourite novel, Fyodor Mikhailovich Dostoevsky's *The Brothers Karamazov*, with his friend and fellow Cambridge philosopher Maurice Drury. Drury mentioned that he found the character of Father Zossima extremely impressive. Of Zossima, Dostoevsky writes:-

> "It was said that by permitting everyone for so many years to come to bare their hearts and beg his advice and healing words, he had absorbed so many secrets, sorrows and avows into his soul that in the end he had acquired so fine a perception that he could tell at the first glance from the face of a stranger what he had come for. What he wanted and what type of torment wracked his conscience."

"Yes" replied Wittgenstein, "there really have been people like that who could see directly into the souls of other people, and advise them." Avoiding asking simply what they thought (a'la the modern day charlatans that we laughingly call 'counsellors' – even though they scrupulously avoid the giving of counsel)

An inner process stands in need of outward criteria, according to one of the most often quoted aphorisms (short pithy truths) of philosophical investigation. It is less often realised what an emphasis Wittgenstein placed on the need for sensitive perception of those outward criteria in all their imponderability. Where does one find such acute sensitivity? Not typically in the works of psychologists but in those of the great artists, musicians, novelists and the likes of Malcolm:

> "I for one will join in with anyone, I don't care what color you are, as long

as you want to change this miserable condition that exists on this earth."
By Any Means Necessary: Speeches, Interviews, and a Letter, by Malcolm X

These couple of lines quite clearly demonstrate the necessary 'inward process', the willingness to 'join with anyone', that might be reflected in the 'outward criteria', the 'change' in 'this miserable condition that exists on this earth'.

Wittgenstein writes, in Culture and Value: "People nowadays think that scientists exist to instruct them. Poets, musicians etc., to give them pleasure. The idea that these have something to teach them does not occur to them."

At a time such as we are living though, wherein the humanities, and by implication the welfare and education industries, are institutionally obliged to pretend to be sciences, we need more than ever the lessons about understanding that Wittgenstein, the arts and Malcolm have to teach us.

X
Everything we don't understand
      is explained
      in Art
      The Sun
      Beats inside us
      The Spirit courses in and out

A circling transbluesency
      pumping Detroit Red inside, deep thru us
      like a Sea
                        & who calls us bitter
                        has bitten us
                        & from that wound
                                    pours Malcolm

                              Amiri Baraka
                                    "Little
                                    by
                                    Little"

CHAPTER 8

Hanan Ashrawi

A Philosophy of Truth - The ethic of Amanha.

Dr. Hanan Ashrawi has for decades been a compelling and influential voice in the contemporary theatre of Middle Eastern politics and a central figure in the struggle for a Palestinian homeland. She has been a tireless campaigner for human rights and has distinguished herself in both the academic and political arenas. Her academic expertise has played a vital role in the development and recognition of Palestinian culture, while her longstanding political activism on behalf of the Palestinian people has contributed greatly to the development of an independent and self-governing Palestine.

Ashrawi received her Bachelor and Master's degrees in literature in the Department of English at the American University of Beirut. After earning her PhD. in Medieval and Comparative Literature from the University of Virginia, Charlottesville, Dr. Ashrawi returned to her homeland in 1973. She established the Department of English at Birzeit University on the West Bank, just as the University was transforming itself from a two-year college to a four-year institution of higher learning. She served as Chair of the English department from 1973 to 1978, and again from 1981 to 1984. From 1986 to 1990 she served the University as Dean of the Faculty of Arts.

Ashrawi's political activism in Palestine began almost as early as her academic career at Birzeit. In 1974, while the University was being intermittently closed by the Israeli military, she founded the Birzeit University Legal Aid Committee/Human Rights Action Project. Her political activity developed dramatically in 1988 during the Intifada uprising. It was at this point that she joined the Intifada Political Committee, at the same time serving on its Diplomatic Committee. Hanan was involved in this work until 1993. From 1991 to 1993 she was the Official Spokesperson of the Palestinian Delegation to the Middle East Peace Process and a member of the Leadership/Guidance Committee and Executive Committee of the Delegation.

In 1993, with the signing of the peace accords by Arafat and Rabin, Palestinian self-rule was established and Ashrawi headed the Preparatory Committee of the Palestinian Independent Commission for Citizens' Rights in Jerusalem. She was the Founder and Commissioner General of that committee until 1995. From 1996 to 1998 she served as Minister of Higher Education and Research. In August of 1998 she founded the Palestinian Initiative for the Promotion of Global Dialogue and Democracy, and has served as secretary general. From 1996 Hanan served as an elected member of the Palestinian Legislative Council, Jerusalem District.

Ashrawi was a member of the Independent International Commission on Kosovo and of numerous international advisory boards including the Council on Foreign Relations, the World Bank Middle East and North Africa Region (MENA), and the United Nations Research Institute for Social Development (UNRISD). She remained a faculty member at Birzeit University until 1995.

Hanan has published numerous poems, short stories, papers and articles on Palestinian culture, literature, and politics and edited the *Anthology of Palestinian Literature*. She is author of *The Modern Palestinian Short Story: An Introduction to Practical Criticism; Contemporary Palestinian Literature under Occupation; Contemporary Palestinian Poetry and Fiction; and Literary Translation: Theory and Practice*. In addition to these publications set in the field of literature, Ashrawi's most recent writings include *From Intifada to Independence, Birthing the Nation* and her autobiography, *This Side of Peace: A Personal Account*. What follows is drawn from this body of work and some of Hanan's many publicised interviews and discussions.

On Being a Writer

When Hanan Ashrawi started writing she used the environment most familiar to her, recording memories of family picnics, games and jokes. She has said that she has a special reverence for words. Both of her parents had a love for language. Her father wrote and her mother was also a very avid reader, and she discussed things with her family. But from before her third birthday Hanan saw magic in books and was intrigued by their mystery. She has recalled being fascinated with how her sisters were able to open books solve the ambiguities of words and language and began to see how spoken and written language can open worlds. That wonder has always stayed with her.

Ashrawi's father took her seriously as a writer from when she was a small girl. He advised her to keep a notebook with her at all times, and offered warm suggestions about how she might improve her work. He told her to record whatever struck her, thoughts, ideas, reflections on her reading. This encouragement, in her childhood's formative years, to record and review her experience, was a corner stone in development of her awareness of self and others. Her consideration or what was going on for her and others gave her a broad view of her context and the meaning of activity, her own actions and the behaviour of others, that fed a growing sensitivity and capacity for empathy.

Hanan's father counselled that she should write her responses down as they occurred to her. He discussed what she had written with her. She has recollected how he encouraged her to read, taking time out of his extremely busy work as a doctor (one who responded, day and night, to every call), to talk to his youngest daughter, still not ten years old, about style, language, substance, and humanity. But this wasn't a passive relationship with language, it was an active interchange. She felt she had to capture it and use her own perceptions, her own words, to communicate.

Those who take the time to read Ashrawi's *This Side of Peace* will discover that she became a talented writer, not just in a scholarly sense. Her prose are measured, having an attractive clarity and a beauty of flow. For her the crucial point about being a writer is not about being published or even read, or whether the writer has a special relationship with language (something Ashrawi has had since her childhood) or the way the writer uses language. She started writing a short story once about a panhandler or a beggar. Her father felt it was extremely sensitive, and told her, "You see things, you see beyond the surface, and you challenge the prevailing wisdom." This is a gift she has managed to hold on to, but admits to having taken it for granted. However, Hanan has not been able to devote herself to the type of writing she loves most - reality intrudes and she has accepted that one cannot always have the luxury of doing what one wants to do all the time. But she has confessed that she would much rather be an academic and a writer.

Here we see a consequence of thinking about the world. The more we do it, the more questions we come up with. This in itself can be dangerous, like Ashrawi, we can be led into situations where injustice and crime dominate. However, there is maybe one thing that is more dangerous than asking questions and that's the decision not to ask them. Practice has made writing and reflection come easily to Hanan:-

> "I wrote this book (This Side of Peace) in four or five months, writing every night after midnight, two or three hours in between doing lots of other things. But it was not cathartic, it was a source of achievement and I felt that I had to be honest to that period, I had to record it, I had to state it. Otherwise it would be distorted or usurped."

As we read these words we can start to understand that Hanan's commitment to writing is also a working through of a responsibility to project an authentic, 'non-distorted' perspective, what might be called 'a truth'. There is little point to reflective writing unless it plays out some duty to veracity, as it is a form of exploration and discovery, a special relationship with language and the use of language, more than the pursuit of a written aesthetic. Words, in themselves, have no power. The power words can express is the force that humans give to them. Words can articulate or explain relationships between people but it is in these relationships where potential resides and Ashrawi allows us to tap into this power.

The main part of *This Side of Peace* is about Hanan's involvement in the middle-eastern peace process, but this contribution was motivated by her Palestinian identity, the consideration that has shaped her writing. Her words are directed by an effort to find a voice for the Palestinian people. According to Ashrawi, even before the creation of the state of Israel, Palestinians had been removed from international consciousness even though Palestine is a nation that has a remarkable cultural heritage that includes a musical and literary tradition. She sees that the total disruption of Palestinian life has made them absent, silent and invisible, except as labels and stereotypes.

How often does this happen in everyday life? People are sometimes, first and foremost, described as a 'type', male, female, black, white, Gay or straight. To this extent the individual classified disappears as a unique person. We see them as a category, a 'young person' or one who has been 'excluded'. This may cause us to miss the things about them (the person categorised) that are much more important, their loves, desires, wishes, hopes, fears, talents and genius. Someone designated as having special needs or as one who is excluded, may well be limited by these labels in a manner that outweighs any benefits that might be derived from such classification. Ashrawi has spoken of her feeling that:-

"I had to give an authentic voice to a Palestinian reality that was constantly being distorted, subjected to other people's agendas and language."

It is worth thinking about the fact that we, as individuals, carry a range of agendas, including those of the agencies and organisations we work for and those who fund the same and/or who pay our wages. The professional also uses a language that others, outside the professional sphere, may not have access to. They 'engage' with 'clients' using this language and described their behaviour to 'peers' or 'colleagues' in the same coded, or as Ashrawi would have it, 'distorted' way. Class and ethnic élites have similar barriers around their interaction. Hanan looks to address this:

"From the beginning I felt we had to use our own language, we had to present ourselves by ourselves. We had to stop what I described as the confiscation of our voice and our will. We had to be there. We had to get an audience as a means of getting credibility and establishing our presence, not in a defensive or apologetic way but in a very human way. To challenge people on their own terms and turf, so to speak."

Hanan is not looking for people to represent her or others. She seeks no 'advocate' but simply claims the right to a voice and a language. How often do people have their voice taken away by the good intentions of professionals, who, in effect have similar aims, in terms of outcome, as the control ambitions of ruling groups in the colonial context? The well meaning end up speaking for the apparently voiceless; they become their voice; the alien translators (and so colonisers) of other people's experience. Ashrawi proposes a more humane and developmental approach, seeking to work alongside people in their project to find a voice. The authentic voice may well be drowned out by the din of the classification. For instance, in 2003 Ashrawi was awarded the Sydney Peace Prize. This created controversy amongst conservative Australians, who disapproved of Hanan's selection, accusing her of being a terrorism apologist. The professional espousing their views, for example that, 'young black men are like this' or that women require differential 'treatment', is simply a professional view, developed in a specific milieu, dominated by the language arising out of professional qualification and the requirements of social, state and agency agendas. It is not necessarily how things are or should be.

For Hanan, words and language are very important in the process of telling a story, which is a vehicle for affirmation of identity. She argues that Arabs have an affinity with language, but she insists one can never really separate the language from the identity. For her, how one uses language is shaped by personal perception and the language that one deploys shapes how we perceive things. According to Hanan, national identity finds its best expression in an honest use of a personal narrative and this must be used by Palestinians because they have been abstracted and depersonalized, they have been turned into numbers or victims, or labelled in an extremely racist, stereotypical way. She insists that the most effective way to challenge ignorance is by telling the truth, through our humanity, using our own words.

How can we move towards seeing people as individuals, with their own unique stories, rather than perceiving them through the way society and/or professional practice classifies and so depersonalises them? What seems clear from Ashrawi's position is that we will not get to know someone or gain their trust by seeing them thorough the spectacles of categorisation or from behind the fence of professionalism, the barriers of its language, values and what/who it represents.

On Activism

Ashrawi was inducted into politics by her fundamental identity, belonging to
a people who were stateless. As such, political life became almost inevitable
when she returned to her hometown on the West Bank. She took up
teaching and became a Dean of Faculty, but found herself protecting her
students. She feels she started her political life the moment she was born.
According to Hanan Palestinians come into this world with a responsibility
and a challenge. She sees being a Palestinian as something that's very
controversial, something you can't take for granted as it evokes serious,
extreme responses.

Hanan's political activism first came to the fore when she was a student
in Beirut working with refugees and then with the revolution. But she
experienced a turning point in 1967, when Israel occupied the West Bank
and Gaza. Her father had long predicted this would happen, but she had
felt that was part of his legacy, his past, not hers. However, from that point
she considered herself an activist, be it in Beirut or the United States. When
Hanan returned home, after a very difficult journey, she started a legal aid
committee to defend students and human rights projects. But at the same
time she was involved in the student movement. She recalls that the
students and faculty then were one, there was no distinction and they would
demonstrate together. She was arrested with her students several times.

Ashrawi recalled how she took the painful responsibility of cradling the
head of a dying student. She saw herself doing this in both her role as an
academic but also as a human being; she was not able to separate these two
aspects of herself in such a dramatic and distressing moment. She has felt
she has had to look after students and has carried them wounded in her car,
gone through checkpoints and tear gas and bullets to take them to hospitals.
For her, she has merged the academic, the political, the personal, the
human, the struggle, and has refused to fragment herself as a human being
or divide her roles. She insists on being all these things together: not just a
dean, or a teacher, or a mother, maybe even a priest.

This attitude flies in the face of many of the taken for granted
categorisations we come across every day in the media and in the
educational environment. Collectively we are convinced to feel that we can
separate or fragment ourselves into mutually exclusive persona; the
professional and the person, in work, out of work. This view, as Hanan
points out, essentially undermines our human nature; we are integrated
beings not our social or employment classification. By splitting ourselves up
in this way we literally lose our personal integrity. For Ashrawi, the most

authentic response we can give, the most edifying way of being with someone, is as the individual we are and all that that is, denying nothing of our own personhood. In this way we offer integrity and commitment. We are not approaching 'the other' in the form of the 'client', a pupil, or a student, but a person, like ourselves, vulnerable, but strong, fearful yet courageous. In comparison the clinical, sterile attitude of 'the professional intervention', the purely 'educational encounter' is prosaic, perfunctory and inherently unproductive. I do not stop being part of the institution at 5pm and do 'my own thing' until 9am the next morning; I am always, in and out of the institution, doing my own thing. Anything else is either a silly lie or a contorted creation of fragmented experience. The person who has subjected themselves to such serial dichotomies cannot give totally of themselves at any given moment because they are in effect never totally themselves; they have been categorised to bits.

Hanan has described herself as an envoy not a diplomat, being and perceiving herself to be of the people and not 'official'. For her, this has allowed her to exercise her option for directness and honesty. However, over the last decade her role has developed and now she sees herself as a voice, a spokesperson, but also somebody who would embody, who would express her people's fullness of experience, history, character, pain, aspirations, everything simultaneously without all the distortions of diplomatic talk and political doublespeak, but directly and honestly.

For many of us, this would mean moving away from the doublespeak of professional jargon or particular class or ethnic language codes. We would need to start to see people again as chatting, gossiping, discussing, talking, rather than 'entering into dialogue'and 'intervening'. We would once more see people thinking, considering, dreaming and imagining and see the basic absurdity of phrases like 'thinking in and on action' and 'reflecting on practice'. I am unlikely to express my pain and aspirations with someone who is unwilling or unable to share and value my fullness and experience in an authentic sense. As such the professional might do well to reclaim the personhood that professional language and action can distort. For Ashrawi, to do the people we work with justice, one needs to be part of them, to share their pain, their sorrow, their struggle, and their aspirations. She has never felt that she came from outside the people, but rather, feels she is one of the people and that she needed to convey this in an honest and candid manner.

In *This Side of Peace* Hanan makes the point that her family have helped her a lot in her struggles. She emphasises the need for *amanha*, this is a broad expression of trust. Her family, her mother and father and siblings, her husband and daughters, have been a major source of strength and love for her. She has seen the unquestioning, unconditional, unlimited, quality of this support and knows it as a source of strength for her. Her commitment to the human dimension of the Palestinians through their history but also the future is another foundation in her life, understanding the pain that Palestinians have suffered through no fault of their own. All this is creative of *Amanha*, a trust. For Ashrawi, when one is given something in trust that is an *amanha*. But it also goes beyond that to mean that you will hold that trust with integrity and honesty that you will carry out what you've been entrusted with.

This brings together what we have been looking at so far:-

Integrity - not being split in terms of identity or attitude.
Honesty - looking to develop our human responses and not be
overridden by professional, class or ethnic concerns.
Trust - that arises out of trusting and honesty, it is this that allows us
to be entrusted.

Ashrawi claims that she has always felt she has been entrusted to present *This Side of Peace* as a personal account and not a 'memoir,' because she didn't want it to be a memoir. It's a personal account, because she believes that the collective is always seen through the individual narrative. And, for her, there were so many individual narratives, much more moving, much more tragic maybe, or even dramatic than hers. But she was determined to get to the reality of the Palestinian experience, and as such felt obliged to use the 'gateway' of the personal narrative. This required complete honesty as it was taking the responsibility of carrying the *amanha* of the people through being honest with herself in her own articulation of the story.

This effort for frankness in the personal account rather than looking for the truth in interpretations of group or categorical action, which may be little more than projections of those who earn a living out of such activity, is a quest for honesty and the finding of a voice. It has caused Hanan to confront power systems and if we take on such a project we can expect no less. In order to sustain such a stance she argues that one has to continue with dedication, maybe obsessive zeal, in a sense one creates an alternative and more authentic power. For her, the power of honesty, of principles and values are much more powerful than political power, personal power and self interest. Because she had no personal agenda and because she felt she was empowered by the trust she had, she wasn't going to be intimidated or deflected. She felt she could speak up, speak out and face all sorts of traditional power, whether it is in the hands of an Israeli soldier with a gun, an assassin with a machine gun, or even courts, military courts under the occupation, or with her own people and systems of power that deal with authority and people who view themselves as being above the law. Because it was not a personal agenda, it was a national agenda that found an articulation through a personal experience and was vindicated by the collective human experience that gave Hanan strength, drive and confidence. And she felt she wasn't alone or vulnerable.

You can see this chapter as attempting to emulate Ashrawi's position. It is an attempt to speak out and harness authentic power; that power that lies in you and others to change the world, not change in a corrupt system, but generate a change of system, wherein we might develop in a non-distorted fashion.

In *This Side of Peace* Hanan emphasised that women have played a distinctive role in the Palestinian movement. According to her the Palestinian women's movement is an old movement, having started in the 1920s. But the gender-sensitive agenda started in the 1970s, because it was at that time that Palestinian women decided to organize and start working on issues of bringing women's perceptions to politics, to social organization, to resistance. This happened because women were part of the resistance and, later on, part of the Intifada under occupation. Ashrawi sees Palestinian women as being tremendously strong and has conjectured that might be the case in all patriarchal and male-dominated societies, because the women have to struggle in such situations. The battle for excellence, for credentials, has to be fought every day. Women are obliged to validate themselves constantly, to stand up to tremendous discriminatory practices, whether inherited traditions, imposed norms or male perceptions of power and control.

It is instructive that Ashrawi sees women as strong, not as weak and vulnerable. She doesn't want to see women protected but she wants them to take part in things, she does not feel that segregating them into 'gender specific' groups, to undergo a type of apartheid (separate development) is useful, because she sees their strength developing through full and active participation. Ashrawi argues that it is women's struggle that has made them strong. When she was Minister of Higher Education women students did much better than men. The top ten students, or the top fifty or the top hundred would always be women. For Hanan this was because they had the harder struggle, because they had a harder life, but also because women have a sense of solidarity and do not work alone. Ashrawi argues that women work within collective networks and try to bring to the agenda sensitivity by way of approach and language. But they also bring daring, because women have been at the forefront of resistance and as such have taken risks and have stood up to traditional norms or expressions of power.

Ashrawi wrote a poem called *Women and Things* which describes the power of women in different ways, and a series of short stories called *Women on the Hilltop*. For her these show how she feels, that women, no matter where they come from, not only bring with them a sort of elemental or biological or natural force for life, but also a strength and a willingness to take risks and to confront and to stand up with pride, because they don't look at themselves through their own self-interest but through the interest of the people as a whole, the cause, the issues, rather than personalities.

Ashrawi's whole philosophy is about risk taking. In this she shares the message of Corneille's *The Cid* (1636): *To win without risk is to triumph without glory*. Our human glory might be found in our honesty and authenticity. Without it, what are we?

On Questioning

Hanan as come to see the place where language, contemplation and love of family are merged with international negotiations with the representatives of intransigent power, as essentially a learning situation, which of course means being involved in a process of constant questioning. But for her, confidence comes from self-respect. To demand respect of others you have to respect yourself and you have to be confident to stand up also to injustice and not to accept it, not to be intimidated.

You see, it is hard for me to say what I feel, to take risks, to be honest unless I have self-respect, faith in myself. But until I develop this confidence how will I gain the respect of others? Not through my fear, that energises my need to be dishonest and inauthentic. Insecurity may be understood as the source of deception; a lack of faith in myself might cause me to hide my feelings and not say what I think, because I don't really believe what I have to say is 'good enough'. I begin to fear questioning the rules because others must know better than me. Ashrawi says she has always enjoyed letting her students know that they can question and provoke. Even when she was a minister she always told them: "Provoke reality, don't acquiesce to it. Challenge it. Speak up." She wanted people to develop the courage to speak out, not to be complacent, not to accept the givens, not to accept also, as her father said, the limits. "To be daring," he said, "be daring in the pursuit of right, of what is right, justice." As such, Ashrawi sees that a sense of daring, of questioning, of not being deflected, comes also from a recognition that your humanity is what you have in common with others.

Hanan believes that there is a common language that emerges, regardless of whether it's Arabic, English, French, German or Japanese. There is a common human language that recognizes no boundaries. At the same time, the human will and the human spirit are the determining factors in everything one does. She accepts that there will always be small-minded, narrow-minded, power-driven, power-hungry people who will try to set limits, who will try to place constraints on people. But, for Ashrawi, the human spirit refuses such constraints. The willingness to take risks and to vindicate our humanity is essential to her.

Hanan sees this risk taking as being carried out through words, but words coupled with action. She has a love of words, seeing them as an embodiment of how we think, how we feel, what we believe. However, if they are not said or written even the most brilliant idea, unarticulated, will never exist in the world. Words show how our life flows, the way we perceive ourselves and others and tell of the way we deal with others, and the way we take up challenges; words show our lives as a fusion.

For Ashrawi no person is compartmentalized or separate. Each one of us is made up of many different aspects, and we should not curtail one of our roles or any aspect of our identity. She believes this is living an integrated life which produces an integrated human being and an integrated reality.

Ashrawi is married to Emile Ashrawi. Together they have two daughters, Amal (born in 1977) and Zeina (born in 1981). The political philosopher, academic and intellectual Edward Said has said of Ashrawi: "She is the creator and speaker of the new language of the Palestinians." As such, she might have the hope 'we', all of 'us', might be involved in the creation of a new language. Not the turgid, banal, distorted, doublespeak of professional jargon, but a rich expression based on honesty and *amanha*. A language that can create a risky but exciting and life enhancing path in the footsteps the African concept of Ujaama; mutual respect and understanding.

CHAPTER 9

Ericka Huggins
Panther Path Maker

Ericka Huggins might be seen as a unique example of a community activist, although her contribution to the cause of humanitarianism and civil rights is part of a long tradition of female campaigners. There are a range of personal qualities and individual facets that make Huggins interesting to those of us involved in community action of one type or another; she is a committed educationalist and a continuing intellectual presence within the sphere of civil rights and diversity issues. However, it is not her devotion to pedagogy that has sustained her involvement and dedication. Her passion and energy have many souses, but the power of her credo probably emanates from in her ability to sculpt action out of a deep motivational seam of care and love.

Ericka was just 15 when she first became aware of her fervour for justice. Her soul was stirred as she joined Martin Luther King's Freedom March in the spring of 1963, which took place in Washington, the city that was her home. The Freedom March was initiated to pressurize Congress to adopt long promised Civil Rights legislation. But the March, which brought together major civil rights, labour, and religious groups, was also the consolidation of the huge growth in protest activities. It was the culmination of a wave of demonstrations across the USA that, as a concentrated protest, were more extensive than any before or after that point in American history. This massive upsurge of sentiment and political zeal was an eruption from the very heart of communities, black and white, across the USA. It was unmediated by professional intervention, indeed it is likely this tsunami of dissent would have been significantly stifled by attempts on the part of professionals to orchestrate its course There was something about it that was entirely 'of the people' that arose from a very basic need to demand an end to forms of oppression. To this extent, it was an attempt to cast off the yoke of the label of 'the oppressed'.

Almost a thousand actions were mounted in over a hundred southern cities, resulting in over twenty thousand arrests. In that spring of 1963, Erika knew the event would have an impact on the African-American community that would last for generations. It was already having an enormous impact on her life. She understood then that she wanted to serve her people.

Huggins was in high school in Washington when she heard about the march and remembered it as "the most amazing thing I had ever heard." She knew who Martin Luther King was and she wanted to go, but Erika's parents forbade her to take part. She reminded her mother that she had always spoken of the need to step forward for their people and to make a difference. But she replied that she didn't mean for her daughter to do it. But Erika went anyway. While on the march, the thing that moved the teenager most was when the famous singer Lena Horne stood up at the microphone and sang the word 'Freedom'. It rang out over the heads of the marchers and sent a chill down Erika's spine.

On 19th. June, President Kennedy sent Congress the promised civil rights bill, which offered federal protection to African Americans seeking to vote, to shop, to eat out, and to be educated on equal terms. For Ericka the action and its consequences exemplified that change could be brought about by the activity of the people; it demonstrated that ordinary folks had the potential to change their condition and destiny. It became clear to many of those involved in the demonstrations of 1963 that no individual or group had to accept their treatment as fate or an unalterable condition of existence. The lesson was that power could be accessed without the dead-hand of State intervention, which only distracted communities from taking power by the pretence that power might be given. It was then obvious that in a milieu wherein inequality was a given, demonstration was a superior means of gaining justice than forms of inevitably one sided negotiation.

The Freedom March ignited a passionate appetite in Ericka for social action and she went on to become a member of the Black Panther Party. The Panthers were perceived as violent, but what Huggins saw herself participating in was an effort bringing to expose the violence of the American State from slavery onwards and that the response would have to be one of defence.

Erika became a committed campaigner on campus and she was involved in a string of protest meetings, demonstrations and student actions. It was when she went to Lincoln University that she realized that black student organizations were the way in which she could get involved in promoting the African-American cause. But Huggins also understood that "it wasn't enough to be sitting on the college campus". Action needed to be taken! She felt that the world at that time needed people to "step forward". Police brutality against the African-American community was rife, partly because there were groups and individuals from that community saying 'no', "loudly, on every level".

Having read about young people of the Black Panther Party who were patrolling the police and encouraging people to say no to police brutality, Erika wanted to be part it. It seemed for her that from the day of the March on Washington and the time that she drove to California to find the Black Panthers, there was no gap at all. She called it "a momentous continuum in my own life."

Huggins explained the disparity of the metering out of justice, comparing a white and a Black man who received a parking ticket. From her experiences a Black man might have been beaten for the ticket, while a white man would just have been given the ticket and told to have a nice day. For her, the Panthers she became part of saw themselves as people who wanted to dismantle oppression on various levels - one of which was police brutality and another was a system of government that did not support human beings in living the quality of life that they deserved by right of their birth.

Ericka lost the father of her child in January 1969. Her husband, Panther activist John Huggins, was killed, according to Ericka, because instead of selling dope to Black people, he was involved in educating young people from Black communities in the south. For Ericka the US government and media collaborated to portray her husband's death as a black on black crime, and later the FBI was found to have been deeply implicated in the murder of John Huggins. Ericka recalled a conversation she had the day after her husband was killed:-

> "A woman said to me, 'This is too hard for me. Do you know what I'm going to do? I'm going to straighten my hair, and I'm going to become an airline stewardess.' A whole lot of people did that to survive."

However, Huggins decided on a different, probably the very opposite course. From the tragedy of John's death Ericka developed a practical analysis of power, understanding the need to build coalitions with other oppressed groups and soon after her husband's death she became a writer for and editor of the *Black Panther Intercommunal News Service*. Later, in 1969, she was made leader of the Black Panther Party in New Haven, making her the most influential voice of the movement in California.

Her consciousness of the need for collaboration grew and she began to make the point that the Panthers needed to begin to reach out to a wider constituency than relatively small groups of radical Blacks. This was understood by some as a kind of 'selling out', but Huggins was one of the first radical leaders within the black community to understand that a single militant group can, at best remain just that; an exemplar of extremism, rebellion that is obliged to constantly teeter on the edge of extinction. She saw that a truly radical movement must radicalize the majority if it is to bring about change. This meant placing a great deal of faith in the human urge for justice.

But, her fortitude, intelligence and probably her will to strengthen and 'de-isolate' the Panthers via collaborative efforts, made her a dangerous enemy for the racist establishment in America. This, together with her relationship to John, plus her gender, led to the authorities seeing her as a huge symbolic and practical threat. In May 1969, Ericka was charged with kidnapping and conspiracy to commit a crime. All this was premised on of little more than an acquaintanceship with a group who had become involved in internecine violence. Panther National Leader Bobby Seale was also implicated. Yale Law School graduate Charles R. Garry was the defence lawyer for Seale.

Garry, a Marxist, employed unique form of radicalism; he used dialectical tactics to oppose the judicial system. His simple but all-encompassing theory was that there should be no prisons because most crimes are acts of survival based on a criminal system that protects property and class interests. The only effect of prison was to seal the victim's fate. He also felt that some people were treated unfairly or even tortured by the moralism of a blind and archaic legal system. This has become an underpinning foundation of much of the writing of former Panther women.

Catherine Roraback was the defence lawyer for Ericka Huggins. She had been known as New Haven's community lawyer. She upheld the tradition of the law as an instrument for protecting individual rights, for facilitating social change, and generally for maintaining the ground rules of an open, democratic society.

The trial and Ericka's case is significant in the history of American law in that it revolved around the efforts to discredit the prominent leadership of the BPP. The trial was an attempt to destroy the Panthers via the courts and was in effect a show trial. The pursuit of the case against the actual murderers became practically dormant. The court proceedings lasted two years. Throughout this time Ericka was held, mostly in solitary confinement and kept apart from her daughter. However, the case was eventually dismissed. But Ericka's sacrifice was not in vein. The trial and its outcome played a significant part in pressurizing the US government to create affirmative action programmes and other federally-funded schemes for the inclusion of Blacks, which in turn resulted in better schools and better jobs for black people.

From 1973 to 1981 Ericka was Director of the Oakland Community School; a community run and supported child development centre and elementary school in East Oakland. But the seed-bed of this institution was the Panther run breakfast school. Ericka, who had been involved from the start, recalled how the police repeatedly stormed into breakfast programs while children were being fed, guns ready. The police were often 'riot-equipped' tactical units who destroyed the food and the room while claiming to look for non-existent 'contraband' or 'fugitives.' This tactic scared many, and to some extent was a successful strategy in limiting the community support for the program.

In the mid-1990s, Mai Huggins, the daughter of Ericka and John Huggins, as a 26 year old said: "By the time my mother was my age she had had a baby, lost her husband, been in prison for two years, worked in free breakfast programs and helped start a school." In one sentence she had portrayed her mother's incredible resilience and the root of her contribution to the liberation of black people in the United States. But at the same time Ericka had shown that women could take an active and powerful role in the politics of liberation, even as a single parent, under incredible pressure from the full force of a massively powerful and corrupt police force backed by its legal confederates. Ericka's book of poetry, *Insights and Poems*, co-authored by Huey Newton, published in 1974, reflects on some of this.

Ericka has noted that the Panthers have often been branded by the white media as "glorified gangsters." Recently, Hugh Pearson's book, *The Shadow of the Panther: Huey Newton and the Price of Black Power in America*, has resuscitated this perspective. "I tell the truth," says Pearson. "It's not my responsibility to edit and hide the truth." But Blanche Richardson, manager of Oakland's Marcus Book Store, has taken issue with Pearson's account of the the BP allegation. "My biggest complaint with the book," she said, "is its vicious inaccuracy." It's the eternal Panther question: revolutionaries or criminals? In a time when sections of our own society are being demonized by the media in conjunction with the State, this makes for interesting reflection. But the presence on the stage of thought of women like Ericka Huggins helps us remember the consequences of and the responses to such pernicious activity.

Another branch of the retrospective assault on the integrity of the BPP is the allegation that it was packed with men who were all about "the rights of our people" while holding chauvinistic views of women. Ericka Huggins says about accusations of sexism: "There were some men who could (not) have cared less about what women thought about anything, and there were some men who were on the right page."

History, in Huggins' words, has been "decontaminated," leaving out much of the accomplishments of the Panthers. While some are intrigued by the Panthers, the image of 'angry Black people' prevails, especially with the white middle-class. The 1996 motion picture Forrest Gump (a massive box office triumph for director Robert Zemeckis and actor Tom Hanks in the lead role) perhaps summed up this perception, depicting the organization in a stark militant light. The movie followed the trends of media sources of the past, focusing on forceful and angry individuals, while ignoring or making light of the police brutality and oppression that caused such a stance.

While the Black Panthers are rarely featured in mainstream newspapers, in the past twenty-five years, the media has continued to focus on violence as opposed to the social programmes the Party implemented. Several prominent figures in the Party have written memoirs and autobiographies including Elaine Brown's *Taste of Power* and David Hilliard's *This Side of Glory*. Yet these sources will only help people learn about the Panthers if they are proactive and interested in this part of what has become black history and as such part of the history of western capitalism.

Ericka Huggins currently lectures on the African-American influence on the Human Rights Movement, the Black Panther Party Community Programmes and the impact of women leaders in the Black Panther Party. She has taught meditation and mindfulness in California public elementary and secondary schools for over 20 years and is currently part of a global project to offer spiritual awareness to children, teenagers and young adults. She lives in Oakland, California and is working on her autobiography. She looks back on her time with the Panthers as productive, but is aware that their legacy is to continue action rather than settle for the way things are:-

"There were a number of things that we did, including declaring the need for a whole different government. There were lots of mistakes and incredible flaws in what we did, but there were also many successful things, including community support and education programs as well as helping to change the way in which African-American people think and speak about themselves. Sadly, however, there is still so much to be done."

This action cannot be generated by the State and its professional agents. It is not something that will ever be seen as 'reasonable' because whilst people are treated unreasonably reason is the prisoner of those who are doing the treating. Salaried employees of the unjust State are not in a position to undermine the State. Some think they can change the State, but it seems more likely that the State, in Orwellian tradition, is more able to change them. It seems then that those of us in the realm of professional care and education, with our ambitions to be 'arbiters of justice', 'educators', or 'advocates for young people', have problems and flaws, that although quite unlike those of the Panthers, are, at least, as profound. Does professional activity have room for the soft and deep resources of care and love? Is trust, in any meaningful way possible without these constituents of our humanity?

The social world continues to change and evolve; history is made, and the spirit of the Black Panther's lives on. Ericka Huggins has expressed the hope that people will remember the organisation she gave thirteen years of her life to as one that was dedicated to the end of human suffering: "guided by human love for people." The Panthers "love [d the] people in our community." In the words of Fred Hampton: "I'm gon' die for the People! [. . .] 'Cause I live for the People! [. . .] 'Cause I love the People!"

CHAPTER 10
Peter Mokaba

Youth worker and political educator. Roar, young lions, roar. No education
before liberation

As the youth service in Britain began to be populated by the generation that
had been youth themselves in 1960s the service made a subtle yet definite
transformation.   It became a professional location, concerned with
'changing the world' more than, as had been the case before and just after
World War II.   Work (paid and voluntary, part-time and full-time) with
young people began to be seen much more as a vocation that sought, in one
way or another, to mould youth into 'decent' members of society. By the
mid to late 1970s members of this 'sixties cadre' were beginning to take up
roles in training institutions and some propagated the idea that youth
workers should be concerned with the 'political education' of those they
worked with, others called it 'political' or 'social' literacy. The rather pallid
ancestor of this cause is the effort to educate people in 'citizenship' although
we in Britain live in a monarchy wherein we are all subjects of our Britannic
Majesty; the State is not a republic and as such the aim to promote
citizenship is something of a misnomer.

       This being the case it seems worth while looking at what political
education might be, beyond the mostly tokenistic, generation of youth
councils or parliaments (which reflect and complement Eurocentric,
professional/middle-class traditions and values and are necessarily made up
of the more conformist/conventional users of youth provisions) that many
of those involved in the youth service (as providers and consumers) might be
familiar with, and ask ourselves if political education is something that
informal educators (these are the people who used to be youth and
community workers but have aggrandised themselves with a title that no one
really understands, apart from a few narcolepsy inducing pedants, who seem
to be constantly revising the definition anyway), should be integrating into
practice as part of a process wherein young people might become more
aware of and more active in the world. Peter Mokaba is an example of
someone who did just this and did in fact, along with the young people he
touched, helped to change the world.

       When Nelson Mandela was inaugurated as president of South Africa on
10th. May, 1994, he appointed Peter Mokaba as Deputy Minister for

Environmental Affairs and Tourism. The flamboyant and exuberant Mokaba had been one of the most militant of the senior members of the African National Congress (ANC) and as a Member of Parliament in the new Government that had been voted to power that famous spring, was not about to change tack. He was to have a frenzied, event packed, although short career before he passed away at the age of just 43, on 9th. June, 2002.

What follows will trace the early biography of Peter Mokaba, but it will also examine his life and work as an example of a political educator in practice. In this process I look at Mokaba's values and purposes and compare and contrast it with the practice of what we might understand as the political content of youth work (informal education) in the contemporary British context.

I briefly met Peter in 1982, whilst coaching athletics in the township of East London. He was always a great football fan, and whilst I knew little about the team he gave his allegiance to, Orlando Pirates, he was familiar with my claret and blue love, the Hammers, who live and lose in another East London. Although four years younger than myself, by the time we met, Peter was a veteran subversive, having crossed swords with the white establishment in South Africa on many occasions. His philosophy, at that time, was strident and uncompromising, but nevertheless, his intelligence shone through and although our encounter was limited, his desire and passion did much to energise and politicise my own practice as a youth worker. It would be wrong to say we kept in touch, but we did exchange letters and latterly the odd e-mail. However, this motivated me to follow his life and work. He became a discussion point with associates in southern Africa who sent me newspaper cuttings and information (sometimes gossip) relating to this often zephyr like person. Later I would, now and then, scan the Internet for news about him, and there always seemed to be some. What follows draws on these relationships and that material.

The Lion Cub
Peter Mokaba was born on 7th. January, 1959 to Albert Mogodi and Priscilla Mapitsi Mokaba. The couple were migrant workers, finding what employment they could in and around Johannesburg. As such, from and early age, Peter was exposed to the inequities, injustices and violence of the apartheid system; a kind of ossified class régime based on race and the contortion of a particular Christian doctrine.

Peter's family was forcibly removed to Mankweng Township near Pietersburg, which is now called Polokwane, but was then the northern capital of rightwing Afrikanerdom and as such an area of staunch racial segregation, in the Northern Province, Northern Transvaal. This beautiful part of the world, where the sun envelops the African skies and lush landscape in a moody incandescent blush of gold as it rises and sets, was always to be the area from which Peter would draw his strongest support as an activist and politician.

Mokaba always saw his experience of poverty, violence and social exclusion during his young life as the source of his determination to excel at everything he did. Yet he did not just have a blind ambition for personal success; he believed that any of his accomplishments needed to be part of a general movement within the oppressed people in South Africa if it was to be meaningful or even real. For him personal development was intimately connected to the wider social context and the overall development of his community and compatriots. This being the case, Peter was determined not simply to fight his way out of poverty and build a successful career, but he was also resolute to struggle against the forces that created and maintained poverty and help build a more egalitarian nation. In Mankweng he lived as a squatter in shacks and moved from one yard to the next. As he mixed and played with the children of the rich he would often be reminded of the poverty he and his family represented. But he would always promise those around him that when he was old enough he would end his family's poverty. Peter told his father that when he became an adult he would not allow himself to be humiliated by another man, like his father had - particularly a white man. Peter's father argued that all Africans faced this humiliation.

Here was Mokaba's motivation to become conscious of the political situation; the need or want for something better. It is very hard to develop any deep political conviction or definite libratory direction without such an impetus. We need some vision and imagination to gain an orientation. So, the first steps in the development of political thinking might be the cultivation of the imagination. The exercise of our imaginative capacities is the necessary precursor to and the means of enhancing our powers of consideration and reflection, which engender a greater general awareness. However, our imagination might also be thought of as the midwife to our aspirations, dreams and hopes.

Peter knew that he could not begin to become part of a force that might alter the situation of blacks in South Africa unless he understood the processes and character of the regime that held non-whites under the oppression of poverty. In other words he understood that he needed knowledge on which to found his ambitions and aspirations. He grasped the fact that wanting change is not enough; we need to have knowledge of the control systems that maintain the oppressive status quo in order to begin to build alternative, more egalitarian and/or inclusive means of decision-making. The process of gaining this knowledge and putting it into practice could be seen as a path to wisdom that leads us out of political naivety and social ignorance.

Education for Freedom

Peter recalled his early efforts to ensure his capability to gain such knowledge, but this was to be an education in itself, leading to his first 'industrial action'. During holidays and after school hours he would pick up piece-work jobs to raise funds for his school fees. He worked at the 'Half Price Store' in Pietersburg, as a handyman in a building construction company and as a gardener for Reverend Van der Merwe of the Dutch Reformed Church near Turfloop. He laboured for a week for the latter employer. When at the end of the week he went to collect his wages the Reverend gave him two-and-a-half cents. Together with his co-gardener, Morrow Rasefate, Peter protested and demanded more. The 'man of God' unleashed his dogs on them. They managed to out run the creatures and get home to relative safety.

Here you might see that Peter's initial education was a process by which he gained knowledge and so understanding, but education is not understanding, neither is it awareness, enlightenment or wisdom. Education may well be a seedbed that can give rise to comprehension and wisdom, but if the means of education are controlled by a power or State that wishes to promote a particular perception of the world then the potential for education is subverted into a form of propaganda and/or indoctrination. Such is the case in Britain.

Unlike the young Mokaba, the youth of contemporary Britain are surrounded by professionals whose role is to 'educate' them. Professional training is, for the most part, financed (by way of loans and other funding) by the State. Professional educators are employed by the State or agencies directly or indirectly funded by the State and accountable via forms of State inspection. With the growth in number and influence of these 'educators', with their appearance on the very streets of our cities, towns and villages, so the kind of space to learn that Mokaba had has diminished. The 'learning space' might be understood to have become colonised by education professionals who represent and promote, in one way or another, the interests and aims of the State, for example producing a 'skilled' (flexible and cheap) workforce, attempt to alleviate pressure on welfare and health services (focus on teenage pregnancy, promoting 'fitness' programmes') and working alongside the police to control young people (Youth Offending Teams etc.).

As he grew, Peter, throughout the last quarter of the twentieth century, channelled his energy into the burgeoning youthful rebellion against the

South African apartheid State. He was inspired to early political action by
Ongkopotse Tiro and the black consciousness poets. More directly he was
motivated by Winnie Kgware, at the Hwiti High School in Mankweng.
This seat of leaning seemingly encouraged its students to be outspoken. Its
graduates included the likes of Olive Shisana, who was to become the
Director-General of the Department of Health in South Africa and who
fought her way through a number of controversies. The immunologist
William Makgoba, who later would take Wits University to the brink of civil
war over his candidacy for the vice-chancellorship was also a Hwiti scholar.
As part of this tradition Peter spent his high school years involved in the
political organisation of his fellow students. This of course meant getting
deeper and deeper into politics and confrontation with the State. At the age
of 17 Peter told the young people around him to "Roar, young lions, roar"
and under the battle cry of "No education before liberation" he immersed
himself in the emancipation politics of the era that culminated in the
student uprisings of 1976. He became a leader of the northern school
boycotts and one of the many student activists who expressed the militancy
of what would come to be known as the '76 generation, the 'Young Lions'
that roared, motivated by the call to the youth of Africa to engage in
struggle and to build a caring society, a just nation and a humane world.

Peter remembered 1976 and how Soweto erupted. Hwiti High School
was quick to play its part. As the president of the SRC Peter organised the
striking students to make for the villages and the mountains around the area,
seeing this was a better strategy by which to fight the police all out; face-to-
face conflict was doomed to end in a massacre. But his tactics were also to
promote and maintain unity. The young people learnt how to make petrol
bombs and in their first of operation attempted to set the school alight. This
failed but Mma Kgware, upon learning about this, seriously reprimanded
Peter. She said problems did not emanate from the school building but the
police and Bantu education. She was of course correct. The school had
played a crucial part in the basic political education of the young people
that had enabled them to react when threatened and not just accept
oppression. The strike at Hwiti and the running battles with the police
lasted until the end of the year. It says much for Mokaba and Hwiti that the
young people were never defeated by the full force of State control.

The general consciousness that education is impossible under oppressive
conditions might be questioned in terms of political education. Peter, at an
early age, realised that State education will only propagate the State within
which it exists; it will reflect the values and norms of that State. This is as
true of the British or American States as it was of the racist South African
State. The white dominated government would not, could not, tolerate

structures or institutions that questioned or threatened its existence. Therefore what were ostensibly educational institutions were, in the context of the Apartheid State, in reality places of indoctrination. Hence Mokaba's instinct to burn down the school buildings. However, that he saw the folly of this was testament to his acknowledgement that Hwiti had subverted the system. Kgware worked with him and through this discourse Peter became aware that those same buildings could be useful if they could be deployed against the State (like a tank captured from the enemy enemy a'la tactics approved of by Che Guevara's *Theory of Guerilla Warfare*). He began to understand that education need not be defined or confined by concrete structures but was the product of attitudes and the will of those that seek education by questioning the accepted theoretical paradigm and/or the dominant ideas of any given society or power structure. Hence, any unproblematic acceptance of theory or doctrine is anti-liberatory and that includes the theory/doctrine of informal education!

The mid 1970's were a seminal time in African history. The student uprisings of 1976 drew new battle-lines in the struggle against apartheid. Although the ANC Youth League produced some of the country's most radical leaders in the 1950s, the mass of the youth were not directly involved in national politics before what was, effectively, the revolt of the young. This was the start of a youth militancy that would be a central factor again and again in the South Africa's struggle for liberation. There was no question it was radicalism that was required as what was being proposed was a change of system. As such, the kind of bureaucratic structures that youth workers in Britain might encourage young people to take part in, 'youth parliaments' or 'user committees', would have been useless in that the very notion of centralised, representative democracy would have been in line with the existing dominant form of social control and as such could only compliment and reinforce the same. This is perhaps why the setting up of such structures seems to have become a preoccupation within the context of British youth work practice, often under the banner of 'citizenship'. Such organisation not only replicates Eurocentric and class forms of control, the very means by which youth are dominated by adult society, it implicates youth in the controlling adult regime. It could be said that the young are being recruited in the cause of their own oppression (colonisation).

Youth, as a group, might be understood as the most oppressed group in society. Perhaps, as in 1970s South Africa, because of this they have the least to lose from uprising against those that oppress and exploit them. Amongst other things the young cannot vote in local or national elections, they may not own property, they are disallowed from purchasing certain commodities and partaking in particular forms of 'adult' entertainment.

The young may not officially gamble, they cannot get married, there are strictures on their sex lives that do not apply to adults. They do not have equal employment rights relative to adults and they are not allowed to drive. They get what is called 'education' whether they want it or not (they are forced to go to school). They have never, as a group, requested even informal education, yet it is imposed upon them. This begs the question can compulsory education (State enforced/funded/controlled education) be education?

This being the case the youth parliament, users committee or any form of State motivated/directed collective activity, can be understood as being not much more than a means to indoctrinate the young into believing that this form of administrative activity provides them with a foothold in power and a tool deflecting them from what would be just rebellion given their relative lack of civil rights.

Predictably his youth work activism marked Mokaba out as a target for the authorities and he was obliged to go on the run for much of the 1970s. With many of his comrades he took to the mountains to evade arrest, but he was finally captured in November 1977 and charged with public violence. He was detained without trial in Pietersburg Prison, together with three other accused. There were 28 state witnesses against them, including the school principal. However, all those witnesses refused to give evidence, but Peter and his comrades were found guilty and given a suspended sentence and fined.

One morning at the beginning of 1977, as Peter was preparing to go to school, Mr. Mammabolo, the principal, came to his door. He delivered two letters: one from Hwiti High School and the other from the Lebowa Bantustan government. The former was to inform Peter that he had been barred from attending school. The second letter was a notice informing him that he had been banned from attending any school in the province.

Such exclusion is of course the predictable reward for speaking out and or refusing to take part in a corrupt and corrupting system without question, and illustrated that in State education there was no room for the critiquing of the prevailing political paradigm. This in turn demonstrated that State education to be, in reality, a form of political indoctrination with the promotion of the State's interests at heart.

Later on the same day Peter went to school. Vice-Principal Seabela came into Peter's class and instructed him to stretch out his hand for him to mete out punishment. Seabela lashed at Peter's hand until it bled. When he was finished Peter asked him for the rod and asked Seabela to give him his hand. Predictably the Vice-Principal refused, but Peter took the rod and lashed Seabela all over his body. Having given Seabela a taste of his own medicine Mokaba gave him back his rod. Peter then walked to the administration offices and demanded that he be refunded his school fees. An argument ensued followed by a tussle but they finally refunded him his fees. Peter had faced up to the bullies and had exposed them to be what all bullies are: cowards. But he had also shown that sometimes titles like 'teacher', 'tutor', 'informal educator', 'principal', 'supervisor' and 'manager' are merely verbal masks worn by official bullies. They might not use physical rods, but their psychological weapons are even more dangerous because they are mostly used in a covert (informal) way, aimed not at the hand, but at the mind. Tools of 'empowerment', processes of 'dialogue' and 'intervention' are used to extend the control of the State and persuade young people to, in one way or another, conform.

Determined to gain his basic educational qualifications Peter completed matriculation alone in 1978, taking on a variety of jobs to pay his way.

Learning Liberation

In 1979 Mokaba taught maths and science at Makgoka high school in Moria City and in 1980 he registered at the University of the North, but he was also continuing his political education. That same year Peter left South Africa for Swaziland, entering illegally through the fence at Piet Retief. Having been detained briefly by the Swazi police and surviving an attack by the apartheid regime on the house where he was staying, Mokaba journeyed to Maputo in Mozambique. Given the choice of furthering his studies or undergoing military training, Mokaba chose to go to Angola to train as a commander for Umkhonto we Sizwe, the ANC's military wing. He received his political and military training under the command of Comrade Mzwai Piliso and a group of Russian and Cuban instructors. Among other things they created a huge library for him to go through. When Peter complained that all he needed was a gun, Comrade Piliso convinced him that politics was primary in the ANC. Piliso taught that it was not the gun but the man behind the gun who wins the war. Such a man should not only be loyal but understand that loyalty needed to be the outcome of awareness and understanding and not be blind.

After training with the Angolans, Cubans and Soviet comrades Peter was deployed in a number of MK (Umkhonto we Sizwe) camps until he was selected to re-enter South Africa through Swaziland. Mokaba's orders were to operate as a pioneer, setting up bases for those who would follow and to train new recruits within South Africa to conduct economic sabotage and prepare for people's war and insurrection.

Perhaps you can see that Peter had reached a point in his life when he began to choose his educational route, not the road of 'normalisation' but a path that was impossible to take within the legitimate structures of the State. He could not operate from within the State system unless he was supporting that system. If, working for the State, you challenge the codes and discipline of that State it would, quite logically, reject you. How could it do otherwise and survive? Control systems and organisations tend to propagate themselves rather than employ people who will undermine their structure and influence. Experience tells us that individuals, far from subverting large organisations and systems of control, compromise and change in the face of the overpowering influence of the same.

The ANC, Peter's chosen educational institution, was the complete antithesis of the South African Apartheid State, which had arisen out of the need or desire to legitimate minority domination and reinforce forms of oppression.

Peter became a lone operative, establishing arms caches and preparing the ground for other guerrillas. At the University at Turfloop he took charge of an underground 'defence unit' on the campus. In 1982 Peter was arrested in Lebowakgomo after completing his mission and preparing to leave the country. He was tried for membership of the ANC, possessing weapons and having undergone military training in Angola and Mozambique. Peter was tortured and humiliated by the police in an effort to get him to tell them where arms might be hidden and betray his comrades. Mokaba refused to tell his captors anything and asked to be killed rather than allow himself to aid the régime that was persecuting him.

After months of brutal interrogation, Peter was finally charged. Later his Comrade Jerome Maake was involved in his trial and was also charged. The proceedings were a complete fraud. Mokaba was found guilty and sentenced to six years' imprisonment. Both men were taken to Robben Island.

In 1982 as in 1977 Mokaba was detained under the Terrorism Act. In the notorious Robben Island jail Peter found himself in the midst of yet another conduit of 'alternative' education; an active school, where formal and political education was prioritised. Like many others before and after him, prison became a rich mine of learning for liberation. It is ironic that the very heart of State control can be the one place where political education rather than forms of State indoctrination can hold sway. Tellingly prison, unlike the wider environment, is a place where many have nothing to lose by ingesting radical education and little to gain from embracing the kind of State indoctrination that produces agents of State control such as teachers, social and youth workers (informal educators).

After a year Mokaba's appeal against his sentence had worked through the South African legal system. The Appeal Court found that evidence against him had been manufactured. He and his co-accused were transported to Pollsmoor. At Pollsmoor they went through the formalities of being released. They were given suits and instructed to leave. Just as they stepped out of the door they were rearrested and recharged. Peter was not released again until 1st. March, 1985.

Peter's subsequent rearrest was based on the same charges that had put him on Robben Island. He was tried in Pietersburg and sentenced to three years, suspended for five years. Again, this illustrates that those who are seen as acting contrary to the State interests will not, cannot, be tolerated by the State. If the State tolerated people and ideas that undermined the State, the State, and those who benefit from it, would quickly perish. This is not a new insight; it is a fundamental tenet of the thinking of Karl Marx.

Youth Working for Emancipation

After he left Robben Island Mokaba chose to return to work among the youth of South Africa. His energy, practical experience and fiery vision quickly took him to the forefront of youth involvement in political action. He had emerged from incarceration as a committed fighter, a relentless organiser and an inspiring leader.

Throughout the first years of the 1980s Peter was an underground operative for Umkhonto we Sizwe. The consequence of this was that he spent over half the decade either in detention or on trial. He survived, by his count, up to 18 different murder attempts. Shots were fired at him and his home was firebombed. There were suggestions that these were attacks by political rivals within the ANC. But at least one would-be assassin later confessed that he had been ordered by the South African security police to kill Mokaba.

The Mankweng Youth Congress was formed in 1985 and Peter was elected to its leadership. He then served as education officer for the Northern Transvaal United Democratic Front (UDF) and was active with the Regional Youth Co-ordinating Committee, building youth congresses in the area. He also played a key role in ensuring vigorous opposition to the planned independence of KwaNdebele in 1986 (this was a Bantustan whereon the Apartheid government purchased nineteen white owned farms and installed a 'self-rule' government in 1981, so creating a semi-independent homeland for the Matabele people. Siyabuswa was designated as its capital, but in 1986 the capital was relocated to KwaMhlanga. KwaNdebele was re-integrated into South Africa on 26th. April, 1994. It now forms part of the Mpumalanga province).

The congresses were interesting social formations, akin to the soviets of newly revolutionary Russia, but set in the African village tradition, being based on loose formal structures, informal discourse, debate, argumentation and questioning. Theoretically this type of interaction is not the dialogue of informal education practice (that is set within State education/control structures and formations) in that it is, in essence, generated by political motivations and has as its logical end point social transformation rather than effecting personal change that facilitates the finding of a place within an existing oppressive, non-egalitarian society.

The congresses might be understood as authentic forms of localised political action that collectively generated a national dialectic, the product of a questioning and developing discourse, aimed at generating new ideas rather than maintaining defunct ideologies. The congresses became a powerful source of energy for national liberation. Discourse producing the dialectic might be understood as a contrast to dialogue that as an interactional form, tends to reproduce itself rather than anything novel, radical or blatantly critical of accepted norms. Youth Parliaments etc., might be understood as the contorted dialogical antithesis of the congresses that might look similar but are in fact refineries of impuissance that indoctrinate individuals into the acceptance of powerlessness by camouflaging impotence as influence and circular tokenistic dialogue as critique that must be acted on.

The South African Youth Congress Organisation
The united congresses gave rise to the South African Youth Congress Organisation (SAYCO) which was a consolidation of the numerous Congress-orientated youth organisations that had sprung up in various localities. Within the SAYCO there was consensus on such principles as a unitary rather than a federal structure and the promotion of a political and social structure free of racial bias.

In March 1987, although threatened with arrest, Mokaba led a group of students over the Zimbabwean border where they gained ANC approval to establish the South African Youth Congress. Almost the entire SAYCO Executive went all the way to Harare, crossing borders illegally to meet with the leadership of the ANC. At the end of 1987 Peter was again criss-crossing the borderlands of southern Africa. This time he was accompanied by a group of 'traditional leaders', seeking sanction for the establishment of the Congress of Traditional Leaders of South Africa. The CONTRALESA was initiated and founded.

As such, Mokaba created the ground for consensus amongst a range of differing rural interests and so again had been a driving force of social change. With something of the same thing in mind but in the urban context he was to found the Northern Transvaal People's Congress (NOTPECO), which was formed to organise migrant workers in metropolitan areas, particularly the hostels.

Soon after this Peter was elected the first president of the SAYCO at its secret national launch at a venue in the Western Cape, he declared that the formation of the SAYCO showed that the State of Emergency could not destroy political opposition. The launch was part of his efforts to continually rally opposition to the apartheid government throughout the states of emergency that characterised the South Africa of the 1980s. Everybody in the liberation movement was taken by surprise as the launch of SAYCO was announced in the middle of a particularly harsh state of emergency. Many thought that it would only be a matter of time before the fledgling organisation would be destroyed by arrests and repression and the SAYCO was subject to constant and fierce attack by the Apartheid State. It is sadly nearly always the case that progressive organisations are met by State attack. Perhaps the only good thing about this might be that one can recognise the institutions that meet State demands or reinforce its values, as they are demonstrably the most prosperous in terms of funding if not membership and intellectual resources. But the SAYCO did not succumb and it did not just survive, it thrived! Through the daring and defiant act of launching an overt organisation in a critical period in South African history, the SAYCO captured the imagination of and inspired militancy in thousands of young people.

On this impetus the SAYCO grew to be the powerhouse of the Mass Democratic Movement (MDM) in the last years before the ban on political organisations was lifted in February 1990. By the time the ANC returned from exile that year the Youth Congress numbered something more than 1.5 million members. Many more millions looked to Mokaba as their leader. This made him hugely influential, and his influence reached way beyond the rural homeland. Well into the 1990s he was one of the few ANC leaders to command the unreserved respect of township militants.

The SAYCO were not just a debating body; this was no 'youth parliament'. It had wide-ranging, 'maps on the table', sessions with senior members of the Politico Military Council (PMC) of the ANC, including the Commander of Umkhonto we Sizwe, Joe Modise. During these meetings Mokaba flouted many sacrosanct rules and in the process began to help define events in the struggle to end apartheid. Representatives of the SAYCO won responsibility for both the mass political front and the armed campaign. This invigorated the ANC strategy of sustained partial strikes which would gradually build into a national armed general strike (as adopted by the Kabwe Conference in 1985).

Umkhonto we Sizwe

Peter was arrested again in March 1988 and sent to Pietersburg to stand trial on charges of commanding MK (Umkhonto we Sizwe) structures in the Northern Transvaal. Co-accused with him was Malebane Tswai and Thabo Masemola, who refused to testify against him. Mokaba was detained for 14 months before the State dropped its terrorism case against him. While he was in jail, Peter's mother, Priscilla, brought an urgent application to restrain the police from assaulting him. It was claimed that he was kept manacled for days on end. Shortly before the application was due to be heard, his mother was arrested. She was to be detained for nine months, just one of the many times that Mokaba's family was targeted by the apartheid regime. After months of detention Mokaba was acquitted and Tswai and Masemola were sentenced to four years each. On his release Mokaba declared:-

> "We need every nerve, every fibre, every activity and aspect of morality of the youth to service the aims of the national democratic struggle. Our guiding words are: 'Rather die to a person than let the enemy pass.'"

For his own safety Mokaba lived for a time in Lusaka, but he returned to South Africa with a mandate from the leadership to try to persuade Winnie Mandela, then alienated from the United Democratic Front, to help her reintegrate with the ANC. He later summed up that task with the contention: "that was a battle."

The late 1980's were the zenith of Peter's activity as a youth worker and political educator. His career had not been based on a wish, desire or a duty to educate, but something more primal than this; a passion and/or a lust for emancipation arising out of the experience of oppression. For Mokaba, what might be called 'authentic education' is political otherwise what might be called education is at best training or instruction or at worst indoctrination or propaganda. This means that authentic education is hardly ever an end in itself. At the same time it can not be a means to implement change, as change is a given and a constant, it happens whatever we do or don't do. However education can be used within a strategy of development, for example as a weapon in the struggle for liberation. We often confuse development with 'growth' and 'expansion' and they are not the same, just as education is not wisdom and reflection is not consideration, awareness or imagination. Essentially reflection is focused on 'what has been', consideration is an intellectual exercise about the nature of things, awareness is about 'what is', and imagination is perhaps the most dangerous process of mind as it can fabricate 'what might be', based on 'what was' and 'what is'. It is this that enables us to envisage the world other than it is. Education, authentic (political) education can help us realise this 'alternative' reality. This is not just a changed world but a world that we have caused to become as we imagined it might be.

After the ANC became recognised in South Africa as a legitimate organisation in February 1990, Mokaba was appointed interim president of the ANC Youth League (ANCYL) after SAYCO decided to dissolve. He became the National Chairperson of the Provisional National Youth Committee and in July 1991 Peter was elected to the National Executive Committee of the ANC. He was voted president of the ANCYL in December of that year and continued to lead South Africa's youth until elected to Parliament in 1994.

In 1990, Mokaba was detained again. F. W de Klerk's government threatened to charge him for inciting the mass chanting, "Kill the Boer! Kill the farmer", the slogan that was to be associated with him for the rest of his life. However, he wasn't referring to any particular Boer or farmer, but the idea that there should be differentiated élites, but this battle cry was, perhaps understandably, never really understood. For all this, his response to the oppressor was typical. The King of the Young Lions roared telling de Klerk to, "Go to hell!"

Thirty years of political education.
By the start of the 1990s Mokaba had become a legendary social reformer. He had taken up arms to change the lives of his people for the better and succeeded. As a guerrilla fighter he, at times, seemed to be battling almost as a complete army by himself. He organised, educated, advised, led and inspired the young and the old, the literate and the illiterate, the rural and urban. He had a huge love for what he saw as the people's army and was a total believer in the power of the oppressed to throw off that insignia and liberate themselves. Like Steve Biko he argued that the moment one rejects the identity as one of the oppressed she or he is free. These rare qualities, together with incredible intelligence, caused him to swiftly mature as an all-round underground organiser and underpinned his unique qualities as an ANC revolutionary.

His election to government was a great confirmation of the effectiveness of his early days at Hwiti High School where he 'developed' as a confident young black man with purpose in his eyes and full of the excitement that is driven by the perceived possibility of positive transformation and the constant quest for knowledge. Although Peter's education had been repeatedly interrupted by State harassment and arrest, he had a life-long passion for learning and he never stopped studying, completing a Masters degree in Development Management at the University of the Witwatersrand. 'Developers' often tend to stimulate the development of others by and as a consequence of their own development and Peter inspired others to develop their political understanding and activity. His daring attitude, which bordered on recklessness at times, made him an enterprising operative. A taker of chances, everything about his assignments was big and of course his achievements matched his endeavour.

In life there are individuals whose personal characters leave an imprint on historic events. Peter Mokaba was one. But like us all he had choices, it's just that his were made in the most dangerous of environments. His desire for political and social change as opposed to the inward looking and relatively selfish ambition for personal change, which happens anyway when we commit ourselves to wider betterment, was forged out of painful experience, but this was the source of Peter's commitment to political education, that itself engenders social education. This is the root of personal, group, community and societal liberation. Such understanding goes beyond education; it is a form of revelation or even a personal and social epiphany.

Can we, the post Thatcherite/Reaganite generation, indulge in political education? Have we the courage, the ingenuity, the revelatory potential for such a project? Perhaps that is the most profound question for the professional who, unavoidably works by and for the rules of the State, through its various formal and informal agencies that it directly and indirectly funds to forward its interests and protect the investment of those who most profit by its continuance.

CHAPTER 11

Assata Shakur
A Voice from the Palenques

Assata Olugbala Shakur was born (JoAnne Deborah Byron Chesimard) on 16th. July, 1947 and for nearly five decades she has been a freedom fighter after escaping the chains of oppression. She made it to the other side. She has, in that time, defied social and political definitions of expected behaviour by black women.

A former political prisoner, Assata's life is the subject of books, movies and poetry. She grew up in racist Wilmington, North Carolina and it was that experience that motivated her to join the Black Panther Party. By 1969 the Panther's had become the number one organization targeted by the FBI's COINTELPRO (Counter Intelligence Program), having marked themselves out as subversive by demanding the total liberation of black people. J. Edgar Hoover, the notoriously corrupt Director of the FBI, called the BPP the greatest threat to the internal security of the country and vowed to destroy it, its leaders and its activists.

However, Assata went even beyond the Panthers when she joined the cause of their more radical offshoot the Black Liberation Army (BLA) that emerged from conditions in black communities; poverty, indecent housing, massive unemployment, poor medical care, and inferior education. The BLA saw that black people were not free or equal; the vast majority of men and women in prison were black; ten-year-old children were being shot down in black neighbourhoods, which had been saturated with drugs with the near collaboration of the white authorities. A situation had been built, many thought with government compliance, which preyed on the disillusionment and frustrations of young blacks. The concept of the BLA arose because of the political, social, and economic oppression of black people - and where there is oppression, there will be resistance. The BLA was part of that resistance movement. The Black Liberation Army stood for freedom and justice for all people.

Assata means (in Yoruba) 'she who struggles' (Shakur means 'the thankful one' or Thankful to God whilst 'Olugbala' is 'for the love of the people'). Her activism with the Panthers and the Black Liberation Army (BLA) and her dissent over the best part of half a century epitomizes her name. Assata as stated that her life wasn't beautiful and creative before she became politically active. But her life was totally changed when she began to struggle.

That struggle started in earnest in 1973 with an incident of what would now be called 'racial profiling' took place on the New Jersey Turnpike. Assata was travelling with Malik Zayad Shakur (no relation) and Sundiata Acoli. State troopers stopped them, reportedly because of a broken headlight. The three were made to exit the car with their hands up.

What happened next changed the course of Assata Shakur's life. Shots were fired and state trooper Werner Foerster and Malik Shakur were killed. Assata and Sundiata Acoli were charged with the murder of state trooper Foerster. The subsequent trial found them both guilty. The verdict was no surprise. But many questioned the justice provided by the all-white jury.

Assata had been shot with her arms in the air. Her wounds could not have happened unless her arms had been in the air. The bullet went in under her arm and travelled past her clavicle. It would have been medically impossible for that to happen if her arms had been down.

Assata was sentenced to life plus 30 years. What she saw in prison was, in her own words: "Wall-to-wall Black flesh in chains."

When she witnessed how women were caged in cells she marvelled at the fact that they, the individuals so harshly penned up, were the labelled terrorists. It made no sense to her. She later said she could not imagine how many sisters had been locked in the cell she occupied (the detention cell) and all the agony they felt and tears they shed. Assata was conscious that was the cell where they put the sisters who were having hard times, kicking habits or who had been driven mad from too much oppression.

Those conditions made her aware how glad she was to be a revolutionary. She was thankful that she knew who the enemy was, but she knew that she could not live peacefully on the same planet with such people. She identified herself as being part of a family of 'field niggas' (using the simile deployed by Malcolm X) and concluded that was something very precious.

It struck her that so many of her sisters were so completely unaware of who the real criminals and dogs are. She saw them blaming themselves for being hungry, hating themselves for surviving the best way they knew how. Seeing so much fear, doubt, hurt, and self hatred was the most painful part of being in what she saw as a 'concentration camp'.

But in spite of all that, she has claimed that she felt 'a breeze' behind her neck transforming into a hurricane and when she now takes a deep breath she has said she can 'smell freedom.'

Assata spent six and a half years in prison, two of those in solitary confinement. During that time she gave birth to her daughter Kakuya. In

1979, she was liberated by comrades in a daring escape. There was a nation-wide search for her. She became a hunted person; posters in police precincts and banks described her as being involved in serious criminal activities. She was highlighted on the FBI's most wanted list; and to police at all levels she became a 'shoot-to-kill' target.

Assata fled to Cuba and was reunited with her daughter. She recalled that when she arrived in Cuba, she expected everyone to look like Fidel Castro. But she saw everything and everyone was different. She saw Black, White, Asians all living and working together. The Cuban women elegantly dressed and groomed and people would just talk to her in the street. Assata found herself wondering why people were so friendly until she realized that they were not afraid of each other. She was used to living where people were afraid to walk the streets. She understood that she "had some healing to do" and that she hadn't known the extent of her "wounds" until she came to Cuba. Shakur began to heal with her work, raising her daughter and being a part of a culture where she felt that she and others were appreciated; appreciated by society, not depreciated by society.

Assata agrees with Angela Davis that the 'prison industrial complex' is a modern incarnation of slavery. Her experience of incarceration enlivened her consciousness of the position of poor people in the face of state power and violence. For her "We've forgotten where we came from." She has pointed out that the Maroons (slaves that fled captivity from the 16th century onwards) escaped from slavery and started their own communities and has said that Cuba might be seen as an example of this. According to Assata everyone needs to identify with their own history. If they know their history, they can construct their future.

Shakur saw the Maroon communities were like the Cubans, in that latter identify with those who fought against slavery not the slave master. Assata claims that those who made the Cuban revolution will not let the people forget what happened to them. Seeing herself as a modern incarnation of Maroon culture she has said that Maroons seriously study history; they have to, else they know they have no future.

For Assata we have to de-Eurocentrize the history we learn, wash away the pollution of those who seek to have power over us as the history given by the slave owner is corrupt. She insists that we have to strive for a more accurate perspective of what happened and create a different society in order to be able to clearly see and so know and remember our history and construct a future for ourselves.

Looking back over her experience Assata believes that she had no idea how ignorant she was, having no knowledge of authors, filmmakers and artists outside of America. She has understood that although we may believe we're free we are not and that our world vision is tainted to the extent that we cannot understand that we are oppressed. The poor have fewer opportunities to be doctors and lawyers as tuition fees increase. Our problem, for Assata is that we want to belong to a society that wants to oppress us. We want to be plantation owners, slave drivers instead of slaves, when the reality is that being one is no better than being the other; they are both inhumane states of being.

Shakur claims: "Where I was born, no matter what we do, no matter what we earn, we're still not appreciated by society. In Maroon societies, like Cuba, people feel like they have power. No matter who they are." In Cuba Assata found that people saw themselves as part of a world, rather than just part of a neighborhood. "Maroon societies identify with oppressed people all over the world. Maroons have a different perspective of outrage and justice." She told of a white Cuban soldier who came back from fighting and expressed his disdain for the whites that were supporting apartheid. She was amazed because in her mind he was as white as the supporters of apartheid, but she began to realise that was not how he saw himself. He couldn't understand how the South Africans could support apartheid.

Assata has developed a deep empathy for those who have suffered and has said that anytime she comes across someone that feels indignant about atrocities, wherever they are, that person has a special place in her heart. For nearly 20 years, she has carved out a life for herself in Cuba. She lives in exile and while many rejoice in her new life, America has not forgotten her alleged crimes. In 1997, the New Jersey State Troopers wrote to the Pope asking for the Pontiff's help in having her extradited.

Former New Jersey Governor Christine Todd-Whitman issued a $100,000 enticement for anyone to assist in the return of Assata Shakur. Congress called on Cuba to send her back, which was supported by most Black congresspersons. In the absence of normalised relations with Cuba, there is no binding extradition treaty between Cuba and the United States.

Assata Shakur sees herself as an escaped slave and because of government persecution, being left with no other choice than to flee from the political repression, racism and violence that dominate the US government's policy towards people of colour. In a poem Assata wrote of: "our duty to fight for our freedom. It is our duty to win. We must love each other and support each other. We have nothing to lose but our chains."

This is a poignant message that might sum up the task she seems to have given herself for the rest of her life; she is part of black history, world history, she has lived through it and can describe it accurately. This is the power of personal narrative, a power that has the potential to shape the future. She has said that at this moment, she is not so concerned about herself and that everybody has to die sometime, but she wants to die with dignity. She is more concerned about the growing poverty, the growing despair that is rife, and about younger generations, who represent our future. She is also concerned that one-third of young blacks are either in prison or under the jurisdiction of the 'criminal in-justice system.' The rise of the prison-industrial complex worries her as she sees it is turning people into slaves again. Repression, the police brutality, violence, the rising wave of covert racism that makes up the political landscape are other aspects of the current milieu that she sees as distressing. According to Assata, young people deserve a future, and she feels that it is the mandate of her ancestors to be part of the struggle to ensure that they have one. She argues that: "they have the right to live free from political repression, but more and more they live in a police state and that fact compels us to fight against political repression." From her exile she has continued to urge people to fight to free all political prisoners because: "the concentration camps of America are turning into death camps."

Assata has claimed that like most poor and oppressed people, she does not have a voice and that poor, oppressed people have no real freedom of speech, no real freedom of expression and very little freedom of the press. For her, the black press and the progressive media have historically played an essential role in the struggle for social justice and we need to continue and to expand that tradition and create media outlets that help to educate people and our children, and not "annihilate their minds". In making this plea she has said:-

"I am only one woman. I own no TV stations, or Radio Stations or Newspapers. But I feel that people need to be educated as to what is going on, and to understand the connection between the news media, White run institutions and the instruments of repression. All I have is my voice, my spirit and the will to tell the truth. But I sincerely ask, those of you in the Black media, those of you in the progressive media, those who struggle in the corrupt educational institutions, those of you who believe in truth and freedom, let people know what is happening. We have no voice, so you must be the voice of the voiceless."

Living in exile is hard. Shakur misses her family, friends, the culture, the music and "how people talk, and their creativity." She also misses "the look of recognition Black women give each other, the understanding we express without saying a word." She sees herself as adjusting by learning to understand what is going on in the world. She learnt of the joys of life by learning about other cultures. For her, living in Cuba has been "a privilege" it being such a rich culture.

She doesn't see herself as that different from those she considers as her sisters who struggle for social justice. Shakur recognises that in the 1960s it was easier to identify racism, that "there were signs that told you where you belonged." She recalls the struggle "to eliminate apartheid in the South". But for Assata, now "we have to know the other, cleverer, more covert forms that exist today. We knew what a token was then. Today young people don't see Condoleezza Rice or Colin Powell as tokens. That's a problem."

When Assata was in the Black Panther Party, she was called a terrorist. Looking back she has said "How dare they call us terrorists when we were being terrorized? Terror was a constant part of my life. I was living under apartheid in North Carolina. We lived under police terror."

The US Senate's 1976 Church Commission report on intelligence operations inside the USA revealed that "The FBI has attempted covertly to influence the public's perception of persons and organizations by disseminating derogatory information to the press, either anonymously or through 'friendly' news contacts." This same policy is evidently still very much in effect today.

The media, if they cover protest at all, ridicule or minimize it; the numbers of the people who attended is halved. The news, publishing in general, is big business and it is owned operated by affluent white men. Unfortunately, they shape the way that many people see the world, and even the way people see themselves. Assata has argued that too often black journalists and other journalists of colour mimic their white counterparts, gearing their reports to reflect the foreign policies and the domestic policies of the same people who are oppressing the people. In the establishment media, the bombing and murder of thousands of innocent women and children in Libya or Iraq or Panama is seen as 'patriotic', while those who fight for freedom, no matter where they are, are seen as 'radicals', 'extremists', or 'terrorists'. For Shakur: "As such it is clear, we have to struggle against a system of organized lies." But there has to be some motivation for this. She recalled:-

> "We had to learn that we're beautiful. We had to relearn something forcefully taken from us. We had to learn about Black power. People have power if we unite. We learned the importance of coming together and being active. That fuelled me."

She realized that she wasn't just a 'Coloured girl' but part of a whole world that wanted a better life. Assata argues that she is part of a majority and not a minority. Her life has been a life of growth; if you're not growing, you are not going to understand real love; if you are not reaching out to help others then you are shrinking. Her life has been active; she is not a spectator and looking at her life she motivates us not just to watch helplessly but realise we can be active. And Shakur argues that we can't afford to be merely spectators while our lives deteriorate: "We have to truly love people and work to make that love stronger. Never in our history has critical resistance to the status quo been more important." From her exile she sends us a poignant but loving message: Free all Political Prisoners. I send you Love and Revolutionary Greetings from Cuba, One of the Largest, Most Resistant and Most Courageous Palenques (Maroon Camps) that has ever existed on the Face of this Planet.

I read these words, not for the first time, on my last visit to Venice, whilst wandering around the Islands in the lagoon. The longest stay I had on any one of the islands was my visit to Torcello. I think it was the idea that it went back so far in the history of colonial Venice that attracted me (5th or 6th century I think). It has only a few dozen people living on it now and it is hard to see where the 20,000 or so population stayed when it was thriving.

The Byzantine cathedral, Santa Fosca is quite astounding. The basilica is over 1,000 years old and anything with that lineage is worth touching or smelling. The marble pulpit has bits that go back to the 7th. century church.

I climbed to the top of the tower and looked out over the lagoon. It was quite a dizzying day and with a little imagination it could have been anytime. I roamed around the church and the central dome and the Museo dell Estuario for hours till the late afternoon then wandered along the canal that runs from the vaporetto stop to the basilica and back. There are a couple of little cafes along the way. As dusk began to fall I got myself something to eat and sat outside a small restaurant. I had spoken to no one all day and that seemed kind of natural. I went back to Santa Fosca and on the edge of a field just past the tower I laid down on my day sack and stared at the sky that seemed full of stars and listened to the night. I guess I must have fallen asleep at about 2am. I dreamt of Assata and the Palenques and the smell of freedom. I awoke as the light broke over the lagoon. It was quite cold but the colours of the island, the sky and the lagoon were fascinating. I wondered if I had ever felt so free or if I ever would again. I walked to the mud shore and looked out towards Venice, sat down and slowly ate a chocolate bar and drank the water and red wine I had brought with me. I then strolled back to the vaporetto stop and took a slow boat back to St Marks.

Later I made my way to San Lazzaro. I liked the idea of Byron going there. One of the monks told me that his great-grand father had met the good Lord. I also loved the idea of a press producing works in 36 languages

200 years ago, words tumbling loosely into the world, little droplets of freedom.

I remember being alone in a police cell...they had turned the lights out...I could hear nothing but the beating of my own heart...I tried to recall when I had been more frightened...I knew they were going to come for me, that I was about to take a mighty beating...the loneliness of that moment can still be felt...how can you tell anyone about it? About how it is to be cut off from the world...the whole world and isolated in your fear...the fear that you might die having done nothing...there is an effort one makes to connect to the world after that and times and tastes like that. What makes the motivation to 'say', to 'speak' to find words and ways of connecting? To find things in your life that might connect you to others and try to say to them...to touch them...make connection more tangible...but it may be those who are cut off are just that...that the attempts at building bridges or crossing the lagoon of loneliness is no more than a kind of insubstantial nonsense...others are more able to do that or they don't have to or something...to be where others stand...I waste my time with these things...I waste the time of others with them...we are not better than we ought to be...maybe fate and destiny should be worshiped...art is not for those not given to the world of art perhaps or certainty. That boy in a cell is the reality - he should be embraced for the truth he is...the night draws in on him as the chatterers chatter about their world and worry about their chatter which is what the world outside loneliness is...there is no connection just the rumour of it...the relief is in the stop…the end of trying...but right now, I'm still trying and that is partly because I've been to Cuba and the echoes of the Maroons urge me to persist.

CHAPTER 12

Clive Michael Charles

The youngest of nine children, Clive was the brother of John Charles,
West Ham United's first black player (they were one of only six sets of
brothers to play League football for West Ham).

Many European players migrated to the USA in the early 1970s, but Clive
Charles was one of the few who stayed after the financial collapse of soccer
in North America. He helped to build a structure from the grass roots to
work with players who went on to play for the national teams of Canada,
Mexico, and the United States, and populate the professional ranks in
America, Europe and Asia. Those he worked with won Olympic gold
medals, and were victorious in World Cup football; many of these people,
touched by Clive's example, went on to become teachers themselves

Clive can be considered one of the real pioneers and champions of the
modern game in America. His biography is a rags to riches story if ever
there was one. If ever one needed to demonstrate that human talent will
overcome adversity, look to Clive Charles. I contacted Clive at his home in
Maine, USA:

"I played my first game for the West Ham first team on 21st. March, 1972.
It was 1-1 draw at Highfield Road. It was on the same night as Frank
Lampard played for England against Yugoslavia, that's why I got a game. I
was lucky enough to help create the goal that gave West Ham the draw.
There was about ten minutes of the first half to go when I crossed to Pat
Holland who headed it down for Clyde (Best) to put it pass Bill Glazier, the
Coventry keeper. I got three more league games that season.

I played in the game against Tottenham Hotspur, on 1st. April,1972. April
fools day! (he laughs). That was first time three black players had played on
the same side in the First Division at that point.   But probably more
significant for us, after Kevin Lock came on as substitute for Johnny Ayris,
Kevin laid on Ade Coker's goal. The average age of the eleven players on
the field was just 21.

I was born in Bow, East London on 3rd. October, 1951 and went straight to
West Ham from School, having been associated with the club from the age
of 12. I'd been going to the Tuesday and Thursday training evenings at the

club. West Ham was always my club. My school days were spent in Canning Town and couple of teachers were helpful. I first noticed that I had some talent for football at the age of 8. Albert Dunlop, a teacher at my first school, Star Lane and David Jones at Pretoria, they were both helpful to me, but they didn't coach you in those days. My first real coach was John Lyall at West Ham. He was a wonderful teacher, a natural. We were very much on the same wave length. He looked at the game intelligently and had a way of reading people. He had a real philosophy and although the club meant everything to him, he always did what he saw as right for a player. I admired him for that and took a lot of his ways into my own coaching. He had a lot of patience but the one thing he didn't like was people who'd suck up to him. He'd sooner people be polite and respectful than give him a load of flannel.

I was good at Cricket. I played for Newham and London Boys, but it was something I played in the summer, it was never going to compete with football. I was approached by some people from Essex to go down to Chelmsford, but I wasn't ever going to take it up. I kind of knew my future would be in football.

I was the last of nine children, all different colours! There was Jessie, Josie, Bon, Len, Bonzo, Marge, Rita and John. Another died. John was the next eldest and seven years older than me. The first four were white, as was Michael who died. Then there was Bonzo and Margie, they were sort of like me: tanned! My mum, Jessie, she was a housewife. I wouldn't say the family was poor, not compared to some others around us. We never went short of anything that mattered, but I suppose we didn't want a lot. But yea, compared to some we didn't have much in the way of material things and you had to work hard to get by in the East End at that time. You had to keep going. As you know, coming from the area yourself, Plaistow, Canning Town and that district have always been thought of as deprived areas, and they were and are. Some people had a hard time of it and yes life was never easy there, but we had a lot of fun as well. But when you think back, from where I am now, you think 'Wow! We did ok!' I certainly think that a lot of people here in America would see Canning Town in the late 1950s and early 1960s as quite a tough place to make something of yourself. But, there are worse places.

When I was still living in my family home in Canning Town Clyde (Best) lived with us, so he was like a brother. I'm still close to my family back in London, John, my brother, his wife Carol and their kids and grand kids. My mum, fifty years ago in Canning Town, could never have dreamed that her sons and grand children would have achieved so much.

My brother John did a good job of not spending any time with me (laughs).

But that probably helped. It allowed me to develop my own style. I was a totally different player to John. He was a hard, tough tackling player. I was more of a footballer. I liked to get forward on the overlap. As such it wasn't too long before I attracted the interest of the England youth set up. I got four youth caps and played alongside John McDowell. Getting into the England Youth side showed that I was good in my own right. It wasn't just about my brother being in the team. We never actually played together in the first team for West Ham, but we did play in the same Football Combination side during most of the 1970-71 season. I think I was a good player, but it wasn't like now. There was not a shortage of left-sided defenders then, at least not to the extent there is in the current English game. I was potentially on a par with most of the people who could play at left back at Upton Park; it was just that they had become established before I matured. I'm not bitter about that, it is the way football is. Like a lot of things in life you have to make the most of what you've got, and that's what I had at West Ham (laughs).

I signed pro forms in 1968. By the time I broke into the first team squad I was a creative left-back, one of the forerunners of today's wingbacks. However, this wasn't always the case. I was originally a left/centre midfielder. West Ham converted me to a left back when I was about 15. Most of my games as a colt had been as a midfielder. The problem was that, at the time, I was one four players fighting for a fullback slot. I was competing against Billy Bonds, Frank Lampard and John McDowell at first. I was close to Frank Lampard. Frank took me under his wing a bit when I came to West Ham. Like me he had been at Star Lane School and was in the fourth year at Pretoria when I was first year.

Later on things got a little less cramped. Bill was pushed into midfield opening up the right back spot for John McDowell. Nevertheless, I was still understudying McDowell and Lampard, two contenders for the English international defence. There's a time when it's right for you to come into the first team, a moment when you can blossom. Miss that and it gets harder to make your mark. John (McDowell) was ready to play and I didn't get a chance to establish myself, but that's the way things go in football. Today, at clubs like West Ham, the likes of Frank Lampard and Billy (Bonds) would maybe move on to bigger clubs, clearing the way for younger players to develop, but then, well players stayed with clubs longer and unless a young player matured really early, they had to go down a division or two to get regular games. But effectively that put you even further down the line in terms of proving yourself. It was a bit of a gamble, but I can't complain. It's a privilege to do something you love for a living and I had a good crack at that in the English League.

I've never forgotten my roots and I have fond memories of being at Upton Park. I was friendly with Paul Grotier, Tony Carr and Patsy Holland; we were all in the same youth team together. I remember when we had been beaten 1-0 at Elland Road. Billy Bonds, Ted MacDougall and myself were the last players left in the bath. Bonzo had fought for the whole of the game. He had run his balls off. Ted had spent most of the time keeping out of trouble. There was an exchange of words then the fists started flying. I was in the middle. I was a young pro and these were big stars! I didn't know what to do. The rest of the team rushed in to pull Bill off of Ted. Of course no one cared about me (laughs). I would be out of the team next week. I could have drowned! (laughs).

I was with West Ham while Bobby Moore was club captain. Bobby was by far and away the best player I ever played with. No one was even near his class. He was a good passer, but was average at every thing else, but put that all together with a unique footballing brain and you got something else.

I wish I had been more dedicated as a player. They are more dedicated now because of the money. They know what dedication can achieve. I always trained hard, and worked at my game, but we didn't earn much more than a dust man in my day. I was lucky though. I played against Bobby Charlton, the great Manchester United and Leeds sides - some good teams. The manager, Ron Greenwood, used to have squads of 24 because we were playing games back to back. One Easter, I got a new car. It was second hand, but it was new to me. I got to the ground late. Normally it wouldn't matter, I'd only have to get ready to watch the game and anyway, on that day I was number 24 on a list of 24. But Frank (Lampard) had gone sick about an hour before the game and Ron told me I was in….against Spurs, in front of a packed ground. We won the match, but I knew I would be out for the next game - that kind of thing was frustrating, it was tough. But I thought, Great! I've got a new car and I get to play against Spurs laughs).

I played 14 times for the West Ham first team, but I only ever got one clear opportunity to break into the side. It was in the first game of the 1973-74 season. The first game I got in my own right, on the strength of my own form, it was against Newcastle at Upton Park (25th. August, 1973). Frank Lampard was playing at right back and John McDowell had been dropped. It was my chance to stake a claim for a regular place. I'd never had a bad game for West Ham, but we lost that game 1-2 and I had a stinker (laughs). I stank the field up. The next game I was out!

I didn't really know Ron Greenwood. I was a bit young; he was a bit aloof. I learnt a lot from him though, but I learnt most from John Lyall. Ron was a great coach. I'm not so sure about him as a man manager though. Not a lot of people got close to Ron. I suppose I was a bit intimidated by him.

John Lyall was the first one to make sense. He had something to say, more than 'get forward' or 'stay back'. He thought about the game and talked about it in an intelligent way. He articulated his ideas.

I don't know if following my brother John to Upton Park was helpful or unhelpful. I think sometimes we expect brothers to be the same, or expect them to be the same way. But everyone was always fair at West Ham. In the past West Ham has been connected with racism; Alf Garnett and all that, but I never experienced any racism at Upton Park. I only really come across it in one game against Manchester United. Ron Greenwood had the balls to take me, Ade Coker and Clyde to Old Trafford. Although Ade didn't play we took some stick that day. I didn't see myself as a paving the way for others when I was playing, but I suppose we must have been. I just didn't think of myself as a black soccer player. I was just earning a living. I've never spoken to today's black players at West Ham so I don't know what they think or how things might have changed. Living 6,000 miles from England I'm not really qualified to say if blacks are discriminated against in terms of management in England, although I don't see too many black managers. But it's a tight knit circle anyway, even in terms of whites. It's the same twenty or so names that get mentioned every time there's a top job going. It's the same in the States in Grid Iron and basketball. If Harry (Redknapp) or George Graham got the sack at one club, they'd move on to another. It's a bit of a closed shop anyway. As far as West Ham being a racist club I can only say that they took me on and I think Ron Greenwood was the first Division One manager to play three black players in the same team. Jimmy Andrews, a former West Ham man took me to Cardiff and Frank O'Farrell, who had also been at Upton Park, made me club captain at Ninian Park. That was the first time I really thought about the fact that I was a black player. The local newspapers made a big thing about me being the first black player to captain a League side. Until that point I had thought about myself purely as a footballer rather than a black footballer.

Yes, problems with race are always a factor and they shouldn't be, but there is a bit of a bandwagon and one or two people make a living out of promoting anti-racism, so it is in their interests to look for and find racism, and, don't get me wrong, it's there. But I'm not sure how far saying 'don't be racist' gets rid of it. It goes deeper than that. People say racism is about ignorance, and that might be true, but it's more about fear. When I was in Canning Town as a kid we didn't get any noticeable racism, because everyone was more or less on the same level; no one had much of anything (laughs). It's when you think you have something to lose to a group of people that you start to dislike that group. That's the bottom line. So if you are afraid of a group and they happen to be black you might express that fear and actually be being racist. But if they were just a different religion you would fear them just as much and discriminate against them just as much. So if you want to get rid of that sort of thing you got to get rid of the fear. And that's not so easy. You can say 'don't be afraid' but that is not going to stop anyone's fear. That won't make them feel less insecure about themselves.

You read some stuff that talks about how bad it was or is, but that's the thing to say now; they can't say anything else really. Just like years ago they said nothing, often the same people, that was the thing then, you didn't say anything 'cause it was seen as an expected thing. So the people who are saying 'this is bad' or 'that was bad', you don't know what they are actually thinking, all you know is that they are saying what they have to say now. Like you are right to stop people shouting out 'you black this or that' but just because you have stopped them shouting it out, expressing it, it don't mean they are ok with race. I suppose it is much harder now to find out who is racist as anyone who was going to say anything has been educated just not to say it. That stops people being offended, but beyond that, who knows? That has to be done, but it goes deeper than just doing that. Can you make it so that no one ever gets offended about anything? I suppose if you did that would have a cost.

That defeat against Spurs was to be my last game for West Ham. I didn't want to leave Upton Park, but I couldn't get in the first team. Keith Coleman came from Sunderland, which was going to further limit any prospects. I had to think of the future. I got married in 1973 to Clarena and we had a family on the way. She was an air hostess. The wedding took place in London but we had met while I was on loan to Montreal Olympics in NASL (1971-72) nearly three years earlier. I'd been playing for four months, alongside Graeme Souness. Graeme and I became great friends. I enjoyed the experience. So I asked Ron Greenwood for a transfer. Greenwood was having a clear out at the time anyway, so a lot of first team players were in the reserves. We were being watched by plenty of scouts.

I went to Cardiff under Jimmy Andrews, at first on loan. Jimmy had been a winger at West Ham in the 1950s. They were in relegation trouble. I played in the last eight games of the season. In the final match we were at Ninian Park playing against Crystal Palace. Thirty thousand people were there for the game; it was between Palace and us for the drop. We got a draw and stayed up. So I signed for them. That was in March 1974. I played just a hundred games, 75 League matches, in three years, scoring 5 goals. I thought the club was going somewhere. They had good support and a good manager. We went down the next season though (laughs). But we did come back up the next year.

I'd had a bad injury at Cardiff and had been having a bit of trouble getting over it. Don Megson, who had been at Bristol Rovers, got the job at Portland and asked me to come over. I really wanted to go to the US. Everybody was going at the time. It was the best thing I ever did. Clyde (Best) was already playing there of course. When the time came to leave Cardiff, I was pleased to take Clarena home."

Clive set up home with Clarena in Portland. They took to Oregon, its climate and people and the seeming appetite for the organised football. Letting it be known he "…could play the piano with his left foot" Clive's dexterous south paw powers had been the engine that had driven his playing career. Indeed he was so 'kak handed' as we say in London's East End that he once played basketball, refusing to leave the left side of the court. But his sense of humour and weakness for practical jokes were the perfect counterpoint to his intelligence and determination. He saw his knowledge of football and wit as the means he used to enhance his formative years growing up in London's Dockland. He deployed the same qualities in his coaching career:-

"My time with the Portland Timbers was very special. It was the start of all the good things to come for me and my family in America. I was with the Timbers from 1978 to 1981. Played around 70 games. In 1982 I was with Montreal. I played for Pittsburgh Spirit in the Major Indoor Soccer League and Los Angeles Lazers in 1982. Football gave me the chance to see lots of America, going to away games and changing clubs. You learn about the place and yourself. I got locked out of my hotel room by accident once…this was in California. I was running round the corridors almost naked, trying hard to look like nothing unusual was happening.

The Timbers are now a good, good organization. It was an honour to have been a Timber. If it were not for the Timbers and the support of people like Harry Merlo (a Portland wood manufacturer and philanthropic supporter of sport in Portland) at that time, the late 1970s, youth soccer in the State if Oregon would not be in the healthy position it is right now. Many of the blokes I played with at Portland are involved with giving chances to our young players. Men like Bill Irwin, Jimmy Conway and Brian Gant have and are making football an attractive and popular game in Oregon. And it all started with the Timbers. I played alongside and against some great players Jimmy Conway, who was a winger with Manchester City, became the Assistant Coach at the Timbers."

I first watched Clive in America at an NASL game at the Robert F.

Kennedy Memorial Stadium, Washington, D.C. and it was clear that he charmed the supporters, many of whom regarded him with the same awe as they might the likes of Pele, with his hybrid Afro/mullet hair do (mullets were the Haute Coiffure of the North American Soccer League at the time) his deep brown eyes and cockney twang. Like his former West Ham skipper, Bobby Moore, Clive always looked immaculate when he run out on the field. His football boots polished, and shirt tucked neatly into his shorts. Watching him with the fans after the game it was clear he had a way of putting them at ease, and he shook my hand when I told him I was from East London and was a West Ham fan. 'You're a long way from home' he said with a mock sternness. 'So are you!' I replied. He laughed and told me I was right. But Oregon was to become as much of a home to him as the London's Docklands had been.

As a player Clive quickly earned a reputation as one of the NASL's best, and hardest, defenders. His quickness on the back line made him an anchor of the Portland defence. He recorded 12 assists and was named three times as an NASL all-star, Clive was selected by Pele as a member of his all-time greatest NASL team.

After 17 years as a player, Charles embarked on 17 years as a coach. Hundreds of players came from Britain, Europe and South America as part of the NASL invasion of the 1970s most came to make a relatively easy, comparatively fast buck, but some made a longer term impact. However none left a legacy in the USA in quite the same as Clive Charles. He became a highly respected and trusted coach who touched the lives of those he worked with and amongst.

He began by driving around the Portland area in an old Volvo, starting up clinics and camps. In 1982 he began his long term relationship with Reynolds High School in Troutdale that gave rise to the successful Reynolds Lancers team and served as Director of Player Development for the Oregon Youth Soccer Association. Thus Clive became a part of Portland, and his work produced the blood for the pumping heart of soccer in the Rose City. He created a strong youth programme that persists to this day. But Charles is best known for the University of Portland teams that after his appointment as 'Soccer Director' in 1986 claimed a place amongst the best in the USA for many of the seasons under Clive's guidance:

"After a pretty successful career I went into coaching and just went from strength to strength I suppose. The Portland Academy has grown from 20 kids when we started; now we have about 400 families involved.

When I was playing for West Ham, even at 20 and 21, I was coaching in schools, doing clinics and so on. So it was a long time ago I realised I had something to say, and thought that it was good enough for people to want to listen. I had the ability to teach, but I didn't know much about much other than football. I probably see myself not so much as a coach but more as a teacher. I'm able to get information over to people in a way that seems to make sense to them and I enjoy sharing that. I am not so much result-oriented as teaching-orientated. If it becomes all about winning all you get is frustrated when you lose. But I tend to ask questions like: 'Why didn't we connect up with that pass? Why did that work and that didn't?' I can't say results were secondary, but they were kind of linked up with everything else. I think you always look to the next game. How are we going to make it better, not perfect, but nearer perfect. I get a lot out of getting players to improve their game but also develop as people. I think the two things can be connected.

My style seemed to work, but I think that Portland University was ready for soccer. After two years we organised our tournament and a thousand people turned up. The previous year there had been about 40. In the first year it was 8-8-3 then it was 13-7-1, but our schedule was not good. In the third year we got Kasey Keller and there was a paying crowd of 3,000 to watch us play Santa Clara. It was then I knew we had something.

By the next week a little press box had been thrown up and we're thinking we needed to construct a stadium! A couple of years before we were lucky to get 500 paying nothing! Next thing a stadium's being built.

I got asked if I would look after our women's programme. I knew nothing about women's football, partly because they were at home when the men were away and I was with the men. But I said I'd do it, but only if the programme was brought up to the same standards that we had with the men. We couldn't get a sniff of the ball when we played UC Santa Barbara and then I knew we'd got a job on our hands.

In the second year I signed Tiffeny Milbrett. She was marvellous. She turned the programme round more or less on her own. It went from something that was just average, and we got a top 10 team. After that I would say to our players: 'You are here because of what Tiffeny did. If she hadn't have come to the University, we would not have won a match and you wouldn't have wanted to come here.'

I don't really have a preference between coaching men and women, probably as I see no difference between what has to be done, although you probably have to approach each of them differently. When women are with women and men are in the company of men we act differently than say when men are with women. That's no secret and it's just how it is. What I would say to any coach, coaching men or women, be as honest as you can with your players."

I don't think I'd come back to England. In fact it is probably true that the best thing I ever did was leave England. Living and working in American has made me a better coach. I think if I'd have stayed in England I'd probably have been quite restricted in what I could have learnt. For every John Lyall there were a dozen who really didn't have much idea what coaching was about and in the 1970s no one in the English game was prepared to learn from other sports or the way things were done in South America or Europe. Look how Malcolm Allison had to struggle at West Ham in the 1950s and 1960s just to try things that had been successful abroad. I know that is changing now, but even at this time, the English game is a bit inward looking. In the United States you sort of get a bigger picture. If I sat down and chatted to people I played with in England and talked to them about coaching they probably wouldn't understand what I was talking about. Harry Redknapp, he's a great guy, but he would have no idea, and he played in the US for a bit. That's not having a go at him; it is just the environment he's in. In England it is getting to be a case of buy, buy, buy and if you get one out of three or four right, that's ok. You can always sell the ones that didn't work, if not for what you paid for them. It's all a bit frantic, almost panicky at times. Players come and go in what seems like no time and there is no time to establish any kind of identity with a club. So you end up with three or four clubs dominating things and then about a dozen or so clubs with nothing to choose between them as all the players are at about the same level; good enough to be where they are but not good enough to be playing for the very top clubs. Look at the game in England now and almost any team of about 15 could end up in forth or fifth place in the League by the end of the season. That, up to a point, is good, but there is practically no chance of the same clubs winning the League or even a major trophy. So success is finishing 10th! Then, when the European or World Cup comes along everyone thinks England are going to win it. But if you are brought up on the idea that coming 10th is good, how are you in the right frame of mind to actually win? Winning is not everything, in fact it is just something, but the ambition, the want to do as well as you can is important, and that has to be based on an idea of what real success is. Young fans, young players who turn out for their schools, can take that sort of thing into their everyday lives. Why should anyone be satisfied by second best? Again, there is nothing wrong with coming second, but that shouldn't stop you from trying to be first or even a better second.

I wouldn't have had the opportunity to coach women in England, certainly not to the highest standard and coaching women has taught me patience and as such made me a better coach. You have to be ready to learn things from your players to be the best possible coach. There comes a point when things are going really well when you are learning as much from each other and it isn't just one way. I'm not sure many coaches in England have a chance to get to that point. Probably there are too many demands to produce performances over night. But you can only teach a player so much, after that your job as a coach is learning as much as you can about them; how you can put them in a place where they can be the best they can be and in a position that is most useful to the team. That is about collaboration, working together and that of course takes trust. Trust is something given and you are honoured when it is given. But to get trust you have to give it. I think that is kind of hard in the game in England right now. That's a shame because without trust there can be no respect; so fear and threat takes over and eventually that gets destructive. Where I coach, at Portland University, we've been lucky to have some good people on the staff and some good people playing. Together we've managed to build something bigger than a soccer programme. It is a bit like West Ham used to be; there's a family atmosphere and people feel a loyalty to the place and each other. That goes beyond football really. In the end that is the biggest thing any sport can do; become the source of something that endures throughout your life.

I've coached Portland University and American national squads, and being with West Ham has a lot to do with that. I think if you learn from your experiences in the game it's all good. Not getting into the side might be seen, over a broader view of things, as being as good for me than say if I have gotten a consistent place in the first team. If you want you can learn as much from the knock backs as anything else. In fact I think we learn more from having to do what is hard. That's what I think a coach can do; help players see the wider implications of what is happening to them because of their involvement with the team. That way football can help you live your life and is not just an end in itself. Why does someone support West Ham? It's not because they keep winning is it? Yes, some people living in East London say they support Liverpool or Manchester United, because they want to be linked with the success of those teams, but when Arsenal start dominating they will just change their shirt from one to the other. That's not really support. No, you support West Ham because they are your team: you are loyal to them: you are committed. That is a fine quality in a person. So shouldn't we reinforce loyalty and commitment and ask questions when people are just fickle? Your dad or mum might not be as successful as some mums and dads, your wife might not be the most beautiful woman in the world, but do you leave them because of that? No, we find things in each other. We learn to love what can't be seen and see other types of success. The Portland players and staff care about the fans who come to watch;

this makes everyone feel part of something and there is reward in success and there is reward in being supportive to each other in failure. We better learn to do that in life because most of us are going to have our fair share of failure; we have to in order to achieve any kind of true success.

Unlike some other sports your place in a soccer squad is reliant on the decisions of others, you can do so much about that, do your best and so on, but at the end of the day you have to learn to deal the best you can with the cards you are dealt. If you can do that, make the most of whatever it is you're given, then you must be successful. At West Ham John Lyall and Bobby Moore showed me that you can make something out of nothing, how much more can you do with a bit more than nothing? We built a soccer tradition in Portland out of some footballs in the back of an old car! A difficulty young people have today (not just young people maybe) is that they always seem to need or want more. It seems harder to make the most of any little opportunity. A place in the side is not enough; it has to be a guarantee of a place. The reality of course is that we mostly just get the one chance and it is up to no one but us to make the most of it. You miss a chance on goal and no one is going to say: 'Shame, why don't you have another pop?' The next chance you get it will be up to you to make the best of it. This, I think is the job of a coach to teach this sort of thing. Sport gives opportunities to learn about this stuff in a very real way. We do that in Portland and I know it works. It's not that young people are just 'bad' or 'spoilt' - that's too easy, although some undoubtedly are - but in the main it's because they haven't had the chance to learn the lessons. We all have to learn these things by experience. No one can just be told and then get it. It's like saying: 'There aren't enough black managers' and that 'someone should do something about it'. Sure 'they' should, but you can't wait for 'them' to help you, you might wait forever! You should do something about it! What's the good of being given something just because of the fact that you 'are' 'something'? A woman, black? That is just as racist as not being given something because you are black. If you want something you got to go out and get it, that's a rule of life no matter what or who you are. You can't expect to be given chances; you got to make the world give you a chance. There's plenty of examples, 'role models', of people doing just that, so it's not just a case of saying it's ok for me to say that.

In the under-23 US national side I've had a midfielder who starts for Ajax. I've had a right back that plays for Hanover. I had Kasey Keller at Portland. It was only because I knew Bruce Rioch, when he was at Millwall, (Bruce had coached at Seattle) that Kasey got his chance in England. I love Harry Redknapp, but when I was assistant manager with the US World Cup team

I told him about a good player we had. He said to me: 'You've been away a long time. Things have changed'. We had just played Brazil and Argentina! People in England still think the US is behind, but Joe Max More scored goals in England and he couldn't even get into the US side. MLS (Major League Soccer) has created a great improvement in young American players, as it puts them in a professional environment; they are better all-around than earlier generations.

But the best thing to come out of my coaching in the US is the F.C. Portland youth club. I'm proud of that. The successes of the players that came out of that; Yari Allnutt for instance. He was a good midfielder for the United States, good enough to go to the 1992 Olympics in Barcelona. He played in the MLS for Kansas City and New England Revolution and Rochester Rhinos in United Soccer Leagues. There was Kasey Keller who'd you know about as well as Steve Cherundolo, Conor Casey and, on the women's side, Shannon MacMillan, Tiffeny Millbret and Michelle French, who played for the US and Washington Freedom. We started the club at the start of the 1990s and I'm the executive director. In 1994 our under-18s won the USYSA (United States Youth Soccer Association) national title.

Portland is now my home. I love it here. My kids are Americans. My son, Michael, he's a golf pro. My daughter Sarah studied for her Masters degree at Oregon State University. She played in defence for Portland in the Collegiate First Division (a very good standard) from 1994 to 1997. Bobby Howe, who was national coach and is now Head Coach with the Timbers, he's a former Hammer too as you'll know. Jimmy Gabriel, who played for Scotland, and myself all say that we are better coaches for being in the US. It's a melting pot here. It's more flexible, you have to adapt, be open to new ideas. You pick up things from Grid Iron football and basketball. All sport in the US starts in the universities, so we get to work with the cream. After turning out for Portland University most of the players go on to become pros. I had three girls from my Portland women's side in the US Women's World Cup winning team. They can earn between $0.5m and $1.5m a year here. Our women get bigger crowds than most lower division matches and some as good as some of the better clubs in England.

I've been offered more money and opportunity to coach in MLS. I've had chances to coach at bigger schools and I can't say I wasn't tempted because it meant bigger office, prestige, better facilities and a much bigger budget. But I didn't really want to leave. I think it's easier to leave a place that was already established when you went there. But after building the place yourself, it's tough to leave. It is a good place for me to be and give a little back. I owe a lot to the game, everything really. I will never be able to repay what it's given me, but Portland has been a good place to give what I can."

Clive always remained true to his West Ham roots as was made obvious when he was asked how the US 2000 Olympic team that he took charge of would play. His answer was short and clear: "The US was going to play an attacking, entertaining style of soccer."

The US were in Group C, along with the Czech Republic, who had just finished second in the European under-21 finals, and Cameroon, an experienced Olympic power that included five players from their World Cup 1998 squad, ten of whom had played in the national team that had been victorious the African Nations Cup during the winter. The Kuwaitis were the other team in the group. They were a young squad but with experience in the Asian Cup. It was clear to Charles that the American's task was neither straightforward or easy, so he made no predictions about medal prospects but instead focused on making the Games an enjoyable experience for his players that would provide a high quality of competition against good opponents. He said:-

"I didn't want to repeat the experience of the World Cup '98. The 'win no matter what' attitude did no good for the team's moral and so their game wasn't as good as it might have been"

But the USA was resolute in wanting to do better than past teams. Only once, in 1924, had America gone into the final stages of the tournament, and that was only out of the preliminary round. Seven Olympic competitions went by before the US got their next win. That was in 1984. After that there were two more victories, over Kuwait in 1992 and Tunisia in 1996.

The US team was the most experienced ever sent to play in the Olympics; thirteen of the players had MLS experience, and four had played for European clubs. Fifteen had been to the FIFA world championships at under-17 or under-20 level. The squad included three overage players: defenders Frank Hedjuk, at the time of writer Blackburn Rovers' goalkeeper, Jeff Agoos and Brad Friedel, a goalkeeper. These three players, together with Ben Olsen and John O'Brien, both midfielders, had substantial experience of international football. Other members of the squad included: defender Chris Albright, who had impressed in the qualifying rounds: Brian Dunseth: Sasha Victorine, the Los Angeles Galaxy striker: Josh Wolff, a forward who played for Chicago Fire: and the highly promising Landon Donovan. Donovan was an adaptable striker, who although just 17 years of age was thought to represent the future of US soccer. The American strike force looked potent, but the defence seemed, for many, to lack steel. It was perhaps telling that two overage players were defenders

The US started with a 2-2 draw against the Czech Republic. On two occasions the US had led the Czechs. Particularly lamentable was the penalty kick conceded after Chad McCarthy had made a late tackle. Conor Casey, Josh Wolff and Chris Albright were unremitting in their efforts against the Czech Republic. Wolff and Albright netted for the US.

Another draw followed, this time the score was 1-1 with the renowned Africans from Cameroon. The match was more one-sided than the game against the Czechs, but again the Americans could not find that vital final touch. Throughout the whole ninety minutes John O'Brien was a thorn in the African's side, continually identifying and blasting through gaps in the Cameroon's defensive carapace. He made an outstanding run, leaving five defenders in his wake, letting off a dangerous drive in the penalty box that was just off target. On the cusp of half-time when Alright Wolff scored. But after Patrick Mboma pulled the Africans level early in the second half, a seemingly clear Conor Casey goal was disallowed. However, even the most biased supporter of the 'Indomitable Lions' would admit that the USA were the dominant force in the game and probably deserved more than a draw. For much of the match, the US threw everything at the Cameroon keeper Daniel Bekono, but could not take full advantage of the pressure applied. Bekono produced the performance of his life (that the fates usually save for visiting goalkeepers at Upton Park!). He denied the US nine chances, producing remarkable saves, some at point-blank range. Josh Wolff had four clear opportunities that should have been converted into goals in the first half alone, and in the second half the Americans had a string of chances. But for all this, a point from the then African Champions, and the eventual Gold medal winners, was a good performance. In fact, as it was clear that Charles' team had bettered their illustrious opponents, the game could be said to have been amongst the best ever produced by a US soccer team on the international stage.

Nevertheless, Charles subsequently received criticism because he chose not to use the then wonder kid Landon Donovan in an attempt to win the game. Charles explained why he didn't bring on Donovan, who warmed up for about ten minutes early in the second half:

"I was thinking about using Landon. We were creating opportunities. He is a very good finisher. It was a matter of where you were going to put him. The team was playing very well. The midfield was playing very well and defensively they were closing people down very well. So, if I put Landon in, it would have been up front. I needed a big man up there in Conor (Casey) as a target. As I was thinking about that, Wolfie scored (actually he set up a penalty kick for Peter Vagenas to score) and two minutes later he made a great near-post run and nearly scored a second one. I thought, you know, I was going to leave things as is. Sometimes you can mess around with things. I just felt that Josh was playing very, very well. I felt we could score another one. I left things alone."

A little later Charles was asked why he didn't make even one substitution. His reply was typically to the point and honest: "You're used to college son. This is the real game." This of course did not endear him to a section of the American soccer press. One particular hack wrote: "Clive Charles doesn't look like much of a genius these days."

The response to the result of the Cameroon game might be seen as an example of the insularity of elements within the soccer scene in the US at the time. The Americans had effectively run all over one of the most dangerous footballing nations in the world, certainly a team worthy of respect as champions of their continent. That Charles managed to get a point from the game and almost took his side to victory against the mighty Cameroon was deserving of praise rather than derision.

A 3-1 trouncing of Kuwait completed the USA's group commitments. The Kuwaitis never looked like getting much from the game although it took a Landon Donovan goal two minutes from the final whistle to make the three points secure for the Americans. Many were surprised when Donovan was left out of the first two group games, but against Kuwait he looked phenomenal. Danny Califf opened the scoring with five minutes of the first half remaining and Allbright got a second for the US. This gave Charles and his team the distinction of going into the last eight as the winners of group C:

Sept. 13th Brisbane 19:00		Sept. 16th Canberra 20:00	
Cameroon 3	**Kuwait 2**	**USA 1**	**Cameroon 1**
Nicolas Alnoudji 37	Khalaf Almutairi 63	Pete Vagenas 64 pen	Patrick Mboma 16 pen
Patrick Mboma 76	Jamal Abdulrahman 88		
Abdulrahman 86 og			

Sept. 13th Canberra 20:00		Sept. 19th Brisbane 19:00	
USA 2	**Czech Rep. 2**	**Czech Rep. 1**	**Cameroon 1**
Chris Albright 21	Marek Jankulovski 28	Lukas Dosek 74	Lauren Etame Mayer 24
Josh Wolff 44	Lukas Dosek 52 pen		

Sept. 16th Brisbane 19:00   Sept. 19th Melbourne 20:00

Czech Rep.2   Kuwait 3   **USA 3   Kuwait 1**

Marek Heinz 2   Khalaf Almutairi 56   Danny Califf 40   Bader Najem 83

Roman Lengyel 91   Faraj Saeid 64, 73   Chris Albright 63

                                            Landon Donovan 88

	P	W	D	L	F	A	Pts
1.**USA**	**3**	**1**	**2**	**0**	**6**	**4**	**5**
2.CAMEROON	3	1	2	0	5	4	5
3.Kuwait	3	1	0	2	6	8	3
4.Czech Republic	3	0	2	1	5	6	2

The games against the Czechs and the Cameroonians were held at Bruce Stadium in Canberra and were both matches demonstrated the exemplary standard of American midfield containment. The US had perturbed the Czech and Cameroon forwards, and laid siege to their defensive ramparts. The effervescent and versatile attack that Charles had crafted had taken command of the opposition by the 25th minute of both games, and it was only a lack of finishing power (a perennial problem for American teams) that stopped the USA from taking full points for their group games.

Japan awaited the USA in the quarter-finals and it was they who scored first. Wolff equalized twenty two minutes before full-time. But Japan regained the lead just four minutes later. Against the run of play Vagenas pulled the Americans back into the game with a last minute penalty. Time not being able to separate the opponents the tie had to be settled via penalty shoot out. The Americans held their collective nerve and won the penalty competition 5-4.

In the end the game was an even match, but the USA had done well to equal a powerful Japanese team and outgun them when the chips were down. They were now one game from a medal and a possible 180 minutes from Olympic Gold. Charles and his boys had surpassed anything done previously by a team from the USA and far exceeded the expectations of most commentators.

America's entry to the Olympic final was blocked by Spain. The talented Iberians lashed at their unsuspecting challengers with a four man strike force that swiftly penetrated the back line. Early in the game a quick brace of goals, that were facilitated by mistakes by Danny Califf, more or less killed the match. Spain's front raiders constantly shuffled and shifted, confusing and confounding the resisting American's, sophisticatedly breaking through from myriad angles, consistently out manoeuvring the USA midfield and defence. Vagenas did score another penalty, but the Spanish never really looked in danger of losing a place in the Olympic Final, although the USA did well to hold the score to 2-1 until three minutes from time when Spain gave themselves a two goal advantage.

It seems the USA must have taken a lot out of the Spanish as they were beaten by Cameroon in the final. The title had to be settled on penalties after a 2-2 stalemate and the African champions added the Olympic Gold to their list of honours winning the penalty competition 5-3.

The USA 'soccerteers' looked at low ebb in the bronze medal match. It seems their morale had suffered and this put them at a psychological and physical disadvantage. They were defeated 2-0 by Chile.

This was a disappointing conclusion to a great display by the USA. Charles and his team had good reason to walk away from the Olympics proud of what they had achieved, and that was, by far and away, America's best Olympics football tournament ever, and the most notable display by a USA men's football team in history. It demonstrated the strength of MLS and its ability to producing quality players.

By making history for US soccer, Charles had not only confounded his critics but made fools of them.

Semi-final results

Sept. 26th Sydney 20:00		Sept. 26th Melbourne 20:00	
Spain 3	**USA 1**	**Chile 1**	**Cameroon 2**
Tamudo 16	Vagenas 42 pen	Patrice Abanda 78 og	Patrick Mbomba 84
Angulo 25			Lauren E.Mayer 89 pen
Jose Mari 87 pen			

Third place match result

Sept. 29th Sydney 20:00
Chile 2   **USA 0**

Inan Zamorano 16 pen, 84

Players

Beyond the accolades involving wins and losses, Clive Charles made a positive and lasting impression on a large majority of players who passed through the soccer programmes at the University of Portland. Clive was a

central character in the soccer community in the Pacific Northwest of the
United States, and the mentor to dozens of American professional players.

As a former professional himself, Charles understood the qualities
needed to reach and survive at that level. While he was an exceptional
coach on the field, he was also gifted in preparing players to make their way
in the MLS, WUSA (the Women's United Soccer Association) or the big
Leagues of Europe. For Charles, a crucial factor was being honest in his
assessment of the player's ability. He knew that only a truthful appraisal
would be authentically helpful in terms of a player making a crucial
judgement about their personal future. As good as his Portland teams were,
it is still a huge leap from varsity soccer to the cut and thrust of the
professional realm. And it not just about being able; it is a question of
timing. For Charles, going to college or playing professionally depended not
only on individual talent but also that ability to be channelled into a
different echelon of the game. So, for Clive it was true that if a player is
good enough, they should play professionally, but at the same time there is
a crucial point, a window in time, when that transfer can be most
successfully made.

Preparation was critical for Charles. There is a long tradition within the
West Ham club that goes back to the 1950s. In effect, part of what has
come to be known in the English game as the 'West Ham Way' includes an
understanding that 'plans go wrong'. A plan is really a belief that people
are able to predict the future. It is a bit of a humbling and disconcerting
fact to admit that this is just human ego and fantasy. The more elaborate a
plan, the more likely it is to fail. In fact, only the most simplistic and short
term plans have much of a chance of working, which begs the question
'Why bother with them?' However, what human beings are good at, what
they do almost by instinct, is prepare and adapt to situations. Looking at the
way Charles worked it is obvious that he had implicated this type of attitude
into his coaching. He would work all week with the men's or women's team
and allow them to play to their potential in games. Gradually, teams would
develop a feeling of fidelity and understanding which gave rise to an aura of
'readiness'. His 2000 Olympic squad had this characteristic as did several
of the other American teams he took responsibility for; it was a kind of
spiritual field effect nurtured through the relationships within squads. It was
almost a physical feeling within his programmes at Portland.

However Charles was more than just a great coach and a capable player.
When his name is mentioned to those he worked with they describe him as
a genuine, honest person. He is a highly respected man and an inspirational
teacher. What Charles' former players remember most about him are the
private moments he shared with them. Times when he would chat with

them in his office or take a late telephone call from them when they needed advice or just a little comfort.

At Portland Clive worked with many fine players who would go on to distinguish themselves in the professional ranks including Scott Benedetti, Nate Jacqua, Ian McLean, Darren Sawatzky, Curtis Spiteri, Davide Xausa and Wade Webber; and with the WUSA Betsy Barr, Justi Baumgardt, Erin Fahey, Tara Koleski, Erin Misaki, Brooke O'Hanley and Lauren Orlandos. A few of his most high achievers are detailed below to give some idea of the former Hammer's contribution to American and World football.

Kasey Keller

Born on 29th. November, 1969 in Olympia, Washington State. Kasey started out with Colonial Meats, North Thurston High School, before finding his way to the University of Portland for whom he played between 1987 and 1990. Before 2006 the 6ft 2in goalkeeper appeared four times in the World Cup and was one of the first American goalkeepers to break into the English FA Premier League.

Keller got his first cap against Colombia on 4th. February,1990. After being a member of the USA National Team in the 1990 World Cup, he was signed by the English club Millwall, becoming a favourite amongst the the south London club's fans between 1992 and 1996. Keller graduated to the Premiership on signing for newly promoted Leicester City and promptly led them to the League Cup glory in 1997. After being overlooked by USA coach Bora Milutinovic for the 1994 World Cup, Kasey made Steve Sampson's squad in 1998, and played two games in World Cup Finals. Keller was an overage selection for the 1996 Olympic team, starting all three matches.

Kasey was named U.S. Soccer Athlete of the Year in 1997 and 1999. In 2000 he signed for Spanish club Rayo Vallecano and played there for two years. He returned to England and the Premier League in 2001 with Spurs. At first he found himself as being little more than cover for Neil Sullivan, but he made himself first choice, and was ever present for Tottenham throughout the 2002-03 and the 2003-04 seasons.

Keller, second choice to Brad Friedel in the 2002 World Cup, has amassed 91 caps for the USA and is his nation's all-time leader in wins and shutouts. Playing in the USA's historic 1998 victory against Brazil, Keller made a number of crucial saves to preserve the Americans' 1-0 lead. His performance prompted the great Brazilian Romario to remark: "That is the best performance by a goalkeeper I have ever seen."

In the 2004-05 Premiership season, Keller fell out of favour at Tottenham as Paul Robinson took the number one shirt. In November

2004, Kasey went on a months' loan to Southampton, a Premiership club ravaged by injuries to its goalkeeping personnel.

On 15th. January 2005, Keller joined Borussia Mönchengladbach on a free transfer during the Bundesliga's winter break. He got off to a good start in Germany, keeping a clean sheet in his first appearance. Keller held on to the 'keeper's jersey throughout the second half of the season, seven times walking away unbeaten and so playing an important part in saving the club from relegation.

Keller crowned his nation's run in the 2005 CONCACAF Gold Cup tournament with a shutout in the final match against Panama and two saves in the penalty shootout gave the USA one of its greatest ever triumphs. Keller started the first seven games of the final round of World Cup qualification in 2005, recording 507 scoreless minutes in a five match shutout run. This lead the USA to qualification for the 2006 World Cup Finals in Germany. He then became the first male player in USA history to win his third Athlete of the Year award. On 2nd May 2006, Keller and team-mate Claudio Reyna became the first two Americans named to four World Cup Rosters. Kasey Keller's professional appearance career record is:

1992 - 1996 Millwall F.C. 176
1996 - 1999 Leicester City F.C 99
1999 - 2001 Rayo Vallecano 51
2001 - 2004 Tottenham Hotspur F.C 85
2005 Southampton F.C. 4
2005 Borussia Mönchengladbach 43
1990 - United States

Keller said of Charles: "Clive was more than a mentor; he was the person that I took so much out of. To me, he was family." Keller was one of Charles' first players to go to Europe in 1990, and he believes his choice of Portland for school changed his life: "It was the smartest career move I ever made. Clive and (assistant coach) Bill (Irwin) really set me up perfectly to be the first American kid to go over (to England). I owe a lot to Clive and Bill for preparing me very well to go over and not be surprised by anything that was thrown at me."

Chris Brown
Chris Brown grew up in Portland, Oregon. His parents introduced him to football when he was five-years old, and he was coached by his father in the first couple of years of his childhood playing career. By the time he was eight Brown had begun to be involved in competitive games with FC

Portland where he played until he went to college. He led FC Portland to an under-18 National Championship.

Brown represented the USA at under-17, under-18, under-20, under-23 and Olympic levels. This being the case, Chris was a strong college prospect. But his ambition since the age of ten had been to work with Clive Charles, his club coach during his time at Jesuit High School. As a freshman at Portland University, Brown's team got to the Final Four.

Brown scored 33 goals in his Portland career, and was named in the All-West Coast Conference First Team in his senior year. After four years at Portland, Chris left to train with the USA under-23 squad and caught the eye of Kansas City Wizards' head coach, who told Brown he was going to select him. Chris was selected in the First Round (sixth Overall) of the 1999 MLS College Draft. With the Wizards Chris' goal scoring talent put him ahead of all the rookies.

In 2000 Brown was part of the Wizards' squad that won the MLS Cup. During the 2003 season Chris was transferred to New England. He endeared himself to Revolution fans by scoring a hat trick in his first game at Gillette Stadium during a 5-1 win over the Chicago Fire. That was the first and only hat trick of Brown's career and the fourth in Revolution's history.

On 8th. April, 2004 Brown moved to San Jose Earthquakes. Although only playing a total of 561 minutes in eleven games for the Earthquakes (seven starts), Brown demonstrated he continued to be a dangerous striker, netting twice on 8th. May 2004 against MetroStars and grabbing another on 4th. September against New England.

Following the 2004 season, Brown joined Real Salt Lake. He played twenty nine games for RSL, making twenty five starts as a utility player, covering three different positions: forward, midfield and defender. On 16th. July Chris scored his first goal for Real in the 10th minute of a match at Kansas City.

Looking back at his time at Portland Brown recalled: "When you go to Portland Clive is pretty much a father figure to the girls and the boys. He takes you almost as his son or daughter. I knew I'd have my best chance to be a pro with a coach like Clive. He told me that if I came to Portland, I would leave a better player. If I wanted to be a professional, I would be a professional. And he did just that. Charles doesn't separate his men's and women's teams; they hang out together every night, every day."

Paradis Ariazand had joined the women's team during Chris Brown's senior season at Portland and they started a relationship; they were married a year later. Ariazand played one season for Charles, then joined Brown with Kansas City with her coach's blessing. According to Brown: "She had a long talk with Clive and he told her to do what she needed to do. I owe a lot to him."

Kelly Gray

Kelly Gray was born on 7th. April, 1981 in Palo Alto, California. He is currently a defender with Houston Dynamo in the MLS. Gray played forward and midfielder at the University of Portland from 1999 to 2001. He scored thirty two goals in his three years for the Pilots and was voted a second-team All-American and first-team All-WCC (West Coast Conference) as a junior.

In 2001 Gray played for the USA under-20s in the World Youth Championship in Argentina. By that time he was beginning to attract interest from European clubs and the MLS. When Kelly talked about his options he said: "I'm going to go back home (after the tournament) and talk to Clive. Whatever Clive thinks is best for me, that's what I'm going to do."

Gray played one more season at Portland before turning professional and having a very solid rookie year. Apparently Clive knew when Gray was ready to leave. Gray's trust and confidence in Charles was the norm, not the exception.

After his junior season, Gray signed a Project-40 contract (Nike Project 40 allows younger players to compete at professional levels while still attending college) with MLS, and was selected fifth overall in the 2002 MLS SuperDraft by the Chicago Fire. Gray made an immediate impact with the Fire, starting twenty games as a rookie while scoring two goals and five assists. He appeared in twenty games in 2003, again starting twenty, while scoring two goals and one assist. On 20th. January the same year he captained the American under-23 team. While playing more defensively in 2004, he started twenty three games for the Fire, scoring one goal.

Gray's versatility has not been entirely advantageous in terms of his development. Three years into his career with the Fire it was still unclear what his position should be. Although a consistent starter, Kelly wanted to return to his hometown and subsequently joined the San Jose Earthquakes in June 2005. Along with the rest of his Earthquakes team mates, he moved to Houston for the 2006 season.

Steve Cherundolo

A USA National Team player Steve is small but swift, with good man-marking ability and passing skills. A defender for both club and country, Cherundolo has become a consistent presence on the right side of the USA defence. Cherundolo's goal against Germany on 22nd. March, 2006, from seventy yards is considered to be the longest strike in USA soccer history.

Steve was the West Coast Conference Freshman of the Year following his first year at the University of Portland in 1997. He left after his sophomore season to begin his professional career in January 1999 with Hanover 96. After helping Hanover gain promotion to Germany's top division in 2003, he became a regular fixture in their line-up at right-back. In 2005 Hanover reached fourth in the table, their best position ever. Steve was voted Vice-Captain by the players for the 2004-2005 season. After starting Hannover's first four games, he travelled to Jamaica to make his USA international debut on 8th. September 1999.

A member of the 2005 CONCACAF Gold Cup-winning side, Steve trained with the full USA Men's National Team in San Diego prior to the 1998 World Cup and has been a regular in the American national side ever since 1999 (apart from when prevented by injury). He made his debut in the under-23 side as an 18 year-old against Canada on 28th. March, 1998. With the experience gained in all four of the USA under-18 National Team's international matches in 1997 Steve 'co-captained' the USA under-20 Men's National Team to an 11th place finish at the 1999 FIFA World Youth Championship in Nigeria. Cherundolo recalled the guidance Clive gave him when he was trying to make up his mind about turning professional: "He told me, 'When you're ready, I'll send you on your way. Until then, I need all your efforts.'"

Charles told him it was time to go following his sophomore season. Steve also gave an insight into Clive's approach to the game: "When Clive wins, it's great for him, but I don't think it's on top of his list. Players becoming complete living up to their abilities. That, I think, makes him most happy. He definitely left his mark. Some of the things he tried to instil in his players were to take care of the little things and the big things would take care of themselves. He tried to teach you to be a good person. He taught me how to grow up. You get that right, and everything else is easy. Even though he wanted me to become a good player, he was more concerned with me as a person and how I developed into a better man as opposed to a better player. He was just a class act. If people remember him as that and try to continue those ways, then I think he will certainly have left his mark."

Conor Casey
Casey led the USA 2000 Olympic men's football team to their historic fourth place finish. He started all of America's half a dozen games in Sydney. After returning to the University of Portland where his twenty three goals had led the nation's scoring charts, he had a choice to stay with the Pilots or move on to Germany with the opportunity to play for Borussia Dortmund as well as offers from a number of other leading clubs. The

choice was not a hard one for the boy from Denver.

Casey, who had played for the USA under-18 National Team recalled: "After one year with Clive, my game just doubled and tripled under him. It was really amazing how quickly I improved under him. Clive is the man responsible for preparing me as a player for the professional game. He showed me how the make that step. I benefited from him being a professional"

On completion of his sophomore year in Oregon, Casey left Portland in 1997 with Charles' blessings. For a while he was a team mate of Steve Cherundolo's at Hanover. He moved to Karlsruher SC, a former First Division club, looking to help them get back to the top flight. He once said of Clive Charles: "As a person, what was different about him was just pure honesty. He meant everything he did, and he wanted to be that way even if other people did not agree with him. Alongside my parents, he always reminded me that there were more important things to life than soccer."

Tiffeny Carleen Milbrett

Tiffeny Milbrett was born on 23rd. October, 1972 in Portland and grew up in Hillsboro, Oregon with her mum and older brother Mark. She was a two-time Parade Magazine All-American while attending Hillsboro High School in Portland and holds the Oregon high school goal scoring record, having netted fifty four times in her High School career.

In 1990 Milbrett enrolled at the University of Portland. That same year, she was named Soccer America's National Freshman of the Year, being her team's top goal scorer with eighteen and Portland's MVP (Most Valued Player). The following year at the Women's World Cup she led the team with twenty five goals and six assists. She was invited to join the Olympic Development Programme. She did so well that a scout invited her to train with National Team when she was sixteen. She missed her high school graduation to travel to Bulgaria with the under-20 National Team and was a member of the under-20 team that won the 1993 International Women's Tournament in Montricoux, France. She was also in the USA Team that won the silver medal at the 1993 World University Games in Buffalo, NY.

In 1994 Milbrett topped the American charts with thirty goals and eight assists. She was tied with Mia Hamm as the National Collegiate Athletic Association's leading goal scorer in Division I colleges.

Tiffeny is a three-time participant of the USA Olympic Festival, playing for the West in 1990, 1993 and 1994, winning a gold medal in 1993, a silver in 1994 and she was a three-time (1991, 1992, and 1994) NSCAA (National Soccer Coaches Association of America) All-American. She was also West Coast Conference Offensive Player of the Year in 1992 and 1994.

Milbrett was part of the USA team that won the title at the 1994 CONCACAF Qualifying Championship in Montreal and she helped the team qualify for the 1995 FIFA Women's World Championship in Sweden where the USA finished third. Tiffeny, then 22, was summoned off the bench to replace Michelle Akers, the first superstar of women's football. Milbrett scored, so finishing that tournament with three goals to her credit, equalling Kristine Lilly and Tisha Venturini for top goal scorer for her team in that tournament.

Tiffeny was a member of the Gold Medal winning USA Women's National Team at the 1996 Centennial Olympics. She scored two goals during the Games, including the match-winner against China to capture the gold medal

In 1995 and 1996 Milbrett turned out for Shiroki Serena in the women's J-League in Japan.

Tiffeny was top USA goal scorer during the historic 1999 FIFA Women's World Cup. In the 2000 Olympic Games in Australia she helped lead her team to the Silver Medal. Milbrett scored twice in the gold medal game, including a dramatic equalizer in stoppage time. In the 2000 CONCACAF Women's Gold Cup, Milbrett scored seven goals and was named MVP.

In 2001 Milbrett finished a controversial third in voting behind USA team mate Mia Hamm and Chinese superstar Sun Wen for the FIFA Women's World Player of the Year.

Tiffeny went on to play for the WUSA with eight teams, the last of which was New York Power.

Milbrett, whose blunt remarks have earned her the nickname "No Tact Tiff" from her team mates was, as a player, able to combine sizzling speed with outstanding technical ability. A diminutive but explosive striker, she was recognised as one of the world's best when running with the ball at her feet and creating dangerous scoring opportunities.

WUSA Commissioner and former USA Coach Tony DiCicco said of Tiffeny: "I remember watching highlights of how Ronaldo would make world-class defenders look like they were running in sand. Tiffeny has that same quality. When she puts it into gear, she just freezes people. She has to be the most exciting player to watch in the world."

Milbrett moved into third place on the USA all-time scoring list, and will likely become just the fifth player in football history to score 100 international goals.

The all-time leading scorer in WUSA history, Tiffeny, almost single-handedly carried the New York Power to the play-off semi-finals in the first season of the WUSA and was named MVP and Offensive Player of the Year. She scored more goals than all the rest of her team mates put together, which is an unprecedented achievement at the game's highest level.

When asked who had been the most influential person in her life Milbrett named Clive Charles. When questioned about which coach was most influential in her career again she named Clive Charles. It was the same response when she was called upon to name who she saw as the best coach in the world.

Tiffeny grew up watching the Portland Timbers and attending the team's summer camps. Charles, a defender by instinct and practice, was among the players who worked with her. She joined his FC Portland women's team when she was 15 and as such, going to Portland was something of a taken for granted course of action for Milbrett. She joined the Pilots in Clive's second year as women's coach. According to Tiffeny: "I never would have thought to go anywhere else, and I wouldn't have gone there if not for him. I didn't go for the school and I didn't go for the education. I went because Clive asked me to. When he asked, I said yes within a half-second, without any thought."

Charles became the father in Milbrett's life. She said: "I didn't have a father in my life. He filled that void. I don't know if he'd like me saying that but it's true. When you talk about guidance, support, trust and love, those are things you get from your parents."

For Tiffeny Charles provided: "everything you'd want from a family, to feel respected and understood and trusted. There's a real, real close bond, very tight-knit, very special. If you didn't go to Portland, you'd never understand it."

According to Milbrett Portland soccer means as much to her now as it did when she was at the University. In fact, on reflection she says: "It might be more important to me now. I understand things more. I have a better perspective. My blood's purple (Portland's colours). I think everyone else would say that, too."

Shannon Ann MacMillan

Shannon is able to play in midfield or attack. A skilful dribbler, MacMillan also has one of the hardest shots in the women's game; she is tremendously strong and fast and able to wear down defenders.

Shannon was the youngest member of the USA Women's National Team that won the silver medal at the 1993 World University Games in Buffalo, N.Y., where she made her debut as an international player. In that same year she was part of the USA Women's under-20 National Team that won an International Women's Tournament in Montricoux, France.

Shannon, who was named as the Soccer America Player of the Year in

1995, was originally left off the roster for the residential training camp leading up to the 1996 Olympics. But having been brought into the squad at a relatively late stage she scored in both the semi-final (against Norway) and gold medal game (against Sweden) to help the USA to the gold medal. MacMillan walked away from the Games as her nation's top scorer with three goals in five matches, including the match-winners against Sweden and Norway. Her 'Golden Goal' against Norway was one of the most important in USA football history, pushing America into the Olympic final and avenging the loss at the 1995 FIFA Women's World Cup.

Shannon was member of the USA's gold medal team at the 1998 Goodwill Games and the following year at the Women's World Cup, She played in all six matches, but started just one, against North Korea. However, her influential part in the match was noted and she recorded one of the most important assists in USA football history, providing the corner-kick for Joy Fawcett to head home the winning goal in the quarterfinal against Germany just seconds after entering the match. She took to the field in the 57th minute of the final against China, replacing Cindy Parlow so proving herself more than worthy of her winner's medal.

MacMillan played in twenty six games for the USA in 1999, scoring eight goals with fourteen assists and became just the 12th player in USA history with twenty or more career goals. In 2000 Shannon was one of the USA team to claim Olympic silver.

At club level Shannon played for the La Jolla Nomads, who won the state club championship for two consecutive years (1991 and 1992), winning the Western Regionals in 1991 before going on to finish second at the national championships. In the 1996 and 1997 seasons MacMillan appeared in the Japanese women's professional league with Shiroki Serena alongside college and national team mate Tiffeny Milbrett.

As assistant womens football coach at Portland in her first year in the role Shannon helped the team make the 1998 NCAA Final Four. But she continued to be an active player, and was elected to the All-WUSA First Team in 2001 and was San Diego Spirit's MVP. She was named as the 2002 Chevy Female Player of the Year. On 26th. April, 2003 she scored four goals in the USA's win over Canada.

When asked about the effect Clive Charles had on her career Shannon, who left an abusive, shattered home life as "a shy, quiet, timid individual," to join Charles at Portland said: "I definitely owe my career and where I am today to that man. He basically turned my life around. When I took that Greyhound bus (from San Diego) to Portland, I got off a weak, timid, unconfident little girl who didn't know her potential or how to achieve it. Really, through his teaching, friendship and love, he became the father figure I'd never had. I didn't really have a lot of confidence when I came to Portland, and he helped me become a happy, confident person. Hands down, I owe everything I have achieved in soccer and where I am with the national team to him."

MacMillan had never met Charles until her recruiting trip to Portland. Before introducing himself, Charles watched how Shannon interacted with the players and coaching staff. He concluded that she would be a good fit into the team and at the school. MacMillan quickly found out that Charles cared about her as a person. She arrived at Portland in 1992 to immediately find her troubles exacerbated when, during her fist week at college, she learnt that her best friend from high school had died of heat stroke. She recalled: "I remember being blown away and wanting to give up and not knowing what to do." Clive took her aside and asked, "Do I think you should be on the field? Yes. But at the same time, it has to be your decision. If you decide never to touch a ball for me, I will still honour your scholarship. We are here for you.

"I was just blown away by that," MacMillan recollected almost a decade later. "This guy actually cared about me as a person first. I literally bit my tongue from saying, "Where do I sign? He saw something in me that I never knew was there. He helped me believe in myself and gave me the tools to achieve every dream I set. There is this utter sincerity about him and he truly cares more about his players off the field than he does on the field."

Shannon went to Clive with her troubles, "always bawling my head off." He kept a box of tissues in his desk, he told her, just for her. She asserted: "He's truly an incredible and special man. I am where I am as a person and a player because of Clive. I love him. I owe every step of my career and who I am as a person to that man."

As an assistant coach of the women's team at Portland Shannon got to see Charles from another perspective: "He just had a profound knowledge of the game. Just to see the way he handled the men's team differently than he did the women's team. He knew how to deal with women. He could go after the men, and that was going to motivate them. Gameday, he sat back and became a fan. He did his work all week, and when game day came, it was our turn to shine and be the individuals we are. You didn't hear him yell during a game. Just being in there and seeing how much time and effort he put into preparing for a session and how worried about people if they were not doing well in school or if they had personal issues; how genuinely he cared about people. He was such a great guy. He could make anyone comfortable and feel like they they could conquer the world.

When I was on the coaching staff, every morning he would ask for an update on someone; 'how she is doing?' He really had his finger on the pulse of all the teams and every individual. I think he did great in the way he empowered people to empower themselves. People that, maybe if they went to another school, might not be in the league (WUSA). Because they went to Portland, they became a great soccer player with a great brain under Clive Charles. That's how they are able to go out in this league and survive."

Wynne McIntosh
Born 17th. October, 1975 in Billings, Montana, Whynne helped the Pilots to four-straight NCAA Tournaments between 1994 and 1997, including three consecutive semi-final appearances and a trip to the 1995 championship game. That same year she was ranked eighth nationally with six game-winning goals, She finished her career as Portland's third all time leading scorer (42 goals). McIntosh first met Charles at the age of thirteen at a soccer academy in Seattle: "I distinctly remember some of those sessions. You meet him, and he demands respect. He has a really great way of dealing with players."

A member of the under-20 National Team pool from 1993 to 1995, McIntosh has represented her country at under-18, under-17 and under-16 levels. She also made the West Regional under-16 and under-19 teams.

Wynne spent the 1998 season playing professionally in Germany but was back in America in the role of player-coach for the W-League Denver Diamonds in 1999 and 2000. Wynne spent the 2001 season with California Storm of the WPSL (Women's Premier Soccer League) before signing for New York Power as a free agent in March 2002 and promptly earned a place as a defender. She moved to San Diego Spirit in September of 2002. Wynne played the 2003 season with the W-League Seattle Sounders.

McIntosh, who has a United States Soccer Federation 'B' coaching license, served as an assistant coach at San Jose State University in 2001, helping the Spartans to their first WAC Championship and first NCAA play-off berth. She moved on to coach for the Colorado Rush Soccer Club, as well as Emerald City FC in Seattle.

Hired as an assistant coach in June, 2002 by Portland University, McIntosh entered her fourth season on the combined staff, sharing recruiting and player development responsibilities. Pilot teams have never missed an NCAA tournament throughout McIntosh's coaching tenure while posting a combined record of 92-39-11. She currently resides in Portland with husband James Tanner and pet dogs Daisy, Roscoe and Copa. The couple were expecting their first child in 2005.

One of Charles' assistants in 2002, McIntosh recalled: "I always felt so bad that we didn't win (the Championship) for the school and for Clive. I am so blessed to have him in my life"

McIntosh, who lost her father when she was thirteen, said: "I would definitely say that Clive plays a fatherly role. I'm not around him that often, but his presence in my life is definitely as a father figure. I feel like I can go talk to him about anything. Clive simplifies everything. He is just a really, really good teacher. He has such a wealth of knowledge."

Wynne said that some of her closest friends in college were members of the men's soccer team: "The guys were playing Central Florida, and all the girls were out there screaming and stuff. Clive kind of encourages that."

Her abiding memory of her coach is very much akin to most of the other players who were influenced by him: "He cares about all of us as people. He cares about what's going on in your life, about how your mom's doing, about how your dog is doing.'"

Justi Baumgardt-Yamada

A left-footed midfielder, clever play-maker, fine long passer, and skilled in possession, Justi started her football triumphs at a young age. In 1992 she was named Parade High School All-American Player of the Year and the nation's No. 1 high school recruit She was selected as National Player of the Year in 1993 and in the same year was named Seattle Times Athlete of the Year. The House of Representatives in the State of Washington passed a resolution in her name in honour of her election as the Player of the Year in leading Federal Way to two state championships.

Baumgardt-Yamada was Portland's MVP as a sophomore in 1995. Justi scored five goals and registered twelve assists as a sophomore to help the University of Portland advance to the Final Four in Chapel Hill, N.C. She scored a goal twelve seconds into a match against San Diego State, the fastest goal in WCC history. Justi started all twenty one games for Portland in her freshman season. Her seven goals and twelve assists placed her amongst the University's top players and helped her earn WCC Freshman of the Year honours.

Elected WCC Player of the Year in 1996, Baugardt-Yamada led the league as a goal scorer. That same year she was ranked fifth nationally with eight game-winning goals and was the Pilots MVP.

Justi is a Three-year NSCAA All-American and Two-time NCAA Final Four All-Tournament Team member. In 1997 she scored eleven goals and provided thirteen assists to help the Pilots to the West Coast Conference title. She finished her college career as Pilots fourth highest goal scorer with thirty seven and first in assists with fifty. Justi started eighty four of eighty five games in her College career.

Making her debut with the USA Women's National Team against

Canada on 12th. June 1993 as an 18-year old. Justi did not appear as a full-international again until 28th. February, 1997, against Australia in Melbourne. Her debut international goal was the first of the game against Australia in Bathurst 3rd. March,1997. She played for the USA on the 1997 Nike Victory Tour, scoring against South Korea in St. Charles, Illinois.

However, between Baumgardt-Yamada's first and second appearances in the senior team she was member of the under-20 National Team and competed at the Nordic Cup in Denmark in August 1993, and again in Germany in August 1994. In April 1993 she was a member of the squad that won the international tournament in Montricoux, France and participated in the 1997 Nike Victory Tour and USA Cup and travelled with the team to Australia, China and Portugal in 1998.

Baumgardt-Yamada played for New York Power and was with the Sacramento Storm in 2000 but was drafted in 2001 by the Washington Freedom.

Although Clive worked with both the men's and the women's teams at Portland, as well as giving a huge commitment to the various national sides, according to Justi: "It was never a problem. He may have missed one or two games at the absolute most."

Recalling her relationship with Clive Justi said: "After I graduated and I was training with the national team, I would go back to Portland and train with the men's team. He coaches differently. It's amazing to be able to see the differences."

She had known Clive since she was 13 years old and wanted to play for him at Portland: "As soon as I had been coached by him for a few sessions, I knew he was an amazing coach. He knows the game. He understands the game. And the way he can teach the game; he's so good at understanding the different personalities of players. I have spoken to players that have been around Clive that are from other schools, and I've never met anyone that doesn't love the man."

When former Pilots are asked about their experience of working with Charles they consistently refer to the intense learning environment he fostered; it was focused, pragmatic and challenging but for all this, great fun. However, it seems beyond all the coaching and teaching skills, the root of Charles' impact on the people he worked with was his kindness. Indeed those who knew Clive best consistently state that there wasn't anyone who had a negative word to say about him. Joe Etzel, Portland's long serving athletics director, who claimed Charles was the "best hire" he ever made once said: "Clive was a person you never heard somebody badmouth. All the success he had....he didn't seem to have people who were jealous of what he'd accomplished. He was just a great individual."

Portland senior Imani Dorsey was a member of the 2002 Women's College
Cup national championship team as well as the 2000 and 2001 NCAA
Division I National Championship semi-final teams. She was Four-Time,
All-Conference selection and 2003 Conference defender of the year. Imani
was Buzz Freshman of the Year, 2000 and team captain in 2003. In terms
of her achievements she could be seen as personifying Charles' ability as a
coach, but the other side of Clive seemed to be the seed of Dorsey's
motivation. She recalled: "When I first met him I knew I wanted to play for
him. He just commanded your attention and your respect every time he
spoke to you. He was pretty much a father figure to almost all of his
players." Imani's reaction and development are indicative of the response
of many who worked with Clive.

A chronicle of achievement
Clive started the process of creating Portland University's internationally
recognized soccer programme in1986. When he took up the post he was
part of a fairly anonymous athletic department that had very little soccer
tradition that existed within a small (2,800 enrolment) Catholic university in
Oregon's largest city. He was the third head soccer coach for men in the
history of the University. However, at the end of the 1987 season Portland
were third in the WCC. A 3-1 victory over Notre Dame was among the
team's thirteen wins.

The following year, Clive's men were ranked as high as number two
nationally and challenged for the NCAA title, winning their first twenty one
games. In the Final Four they were defeated by the eventual champions
Indiana, but Portland had begun the development of dozens of athletes
who would play professionally and for varied national teams. The playoff
appearance was the University's first in soccer. Portland won the first of
three straight WCC championships and four in a six-year period.

In 1989 Charles was appointed as Portland University's director of
soccer, and took over as head women's coach. He led the Pilots to a 10-6-0
season. The men's team again climbed to number two in the polls and
earned the second of six consecutive NCAA berths, reaching the second
round. The team finished at 18-2-4, the second-best record in school history.

By 1990 Portland's Harry A. Merlo Field was one of the nation's best
soccer facilities. Clive's men won the WCC title, but lost in the first round of
the NCAA play-offs

The Pilot women won the first of two straight Northwest Collegiate
Soccer Conference Championships and appeared in the national top twenty
for the first time, reaching number twelve. Tiffeny Milbrett was named the
NCSC Player of the Year and was the Soccer America Freshman of the

Year. The following season Milbrett achieved All-America honours and her second NCSC Player of the Year award while establishing a school record with twenty five goals.

The three-year supremacy of the Conference Crown by the Portland men came to an end in 1991, but they reached the post season's second round. The women produced a 13-2-2 record which made a powerful case for its first-ever NCAA play-off berth, but were obliged to wait for that distinction.

In 1992 Charles led two teams to the NCAA play-offs in the same year, an achievement with little precedent. His women made history, winning a school-record eighteen games and earning the University's first women's NCAA playoff berth and the first of seven successive postseason bids. Portland's men achieved number one national ranking, while the women reached number three in the USA, with Tiffeny Milbrett scoring thirty goals and providing a twelve assists. The women joined the WCC and both programmes claimed league championships. The then biggest crowd in the history USA women's soccer, 5,596, crammed in to Merlo Field for the first-ever meeting between Portland and North Carolina, recognised as one of the best teams in the country.

Portland's next campaign, with Charles named as head coach of the USA under-20 women's team (a post he would hold for three years), saw both the women and men simultaneously earn NCAA playoff berths for the second year in succession. Shannon MacMillan and freshman sensation Justi Baumgardt led the Pilots to their first-ever NCAA Playoff win, a 2-0 first round defeat of conference rival Santa Clara. Portland lost in the quarter-finals at Stanford by the only goal of the game.

The men concluded their schedule 9-3-6, losing to St. Louis on penalty kicks, in the first round of the play-offs.

The Pilot women recaptured the WCC title in 1994 with a 7-0-0 record and reached the NCAA Final Four, staged at Merlo Field. The highly successful, but injury-plagued season came to a conclusion with a 1-0 defeat to Notre Dame. The Pilots placed a record five players on the all WCC first team.

The run of six consecutive play-off berths achieved by the Pilot men ended, but the team boasted the programme's eighth winning season under Clive's nine years at the helm.

Charles provided commentary and expert analysis for ESPN's (Entertainment and Sports Programming Network) coverage of the 1994 World Cup and received high ratings.

On consecutive weekends in 1995 Charles took both the men's and the women's programmes to their respective Final Fours, making him only the second collegiate soccer coach in history to lead two teams to the NCAA semi-finals in the same year (UNC's Anson Dorrance was the first in 1987). The men's team were defeated in the semi-finals by the only goal of the game. Wisconsin, the team that would be NCAA champions, were their nemesis at Richmond, Virginia. But Clive's boys collected sixteen wins for the third best win total in school history.

The women's side lost 1-0 in extra-time to Notre Dame in the national championship game at Chapel Hill, N.C., finishing the year with a school-record twenty wins.

Charles was named assistant coach of the USA Men's National Team. The Portland men produced an 8-2-1 record over their last eleven games of 1996, but failed to gain an NCAA play-off berth for just the second time in nine years. The Pilots' average home attendance of 2,554 was the best in the country.

The Pilot women reached their third consecutive NCAA Final Four, but lost 3-2 to Notre Dame in the semi-finals. Portland finished the season with nineteen wins and a third consecutive WCC title. The 1996 Pilot women posted a tweny one game unbeaten streak, including an undefeated conference run, before falling to Notre Dame.

Justi Baumgardt became the fifth consecutive Pilot to be named the WCC Player of the Year after Portland's second undefeated conference season and the following season she earned her fourth all-WCC first team honour, becoming just the fourth female WCC player to achieve this. Baumgardt left as the University of Portland's all time assists leader (50), and third highest ever goal scorer. She led the Pilots to a fourth straight WCC title and sixth consecutive NCAA appearance, but a first-round loss at home to UCLA ended a 14-5-0 season. With crowds averaging 1,834, the Pilot women attracted the second highest home attendance in the country.

Early in the season, with the Portland men and women winning on the same day, head coach Clive Charles recorded his 300th career collegiate win, making him just the 11th coach in NCAA history to amass that many wins.

The Pilot men lost four of their last six games and missed the NCAA tournament for the second year running; it was the first time since 1988 that the programme failed to take part in post season play in back-to-back seasons.

The Pilot men finished the 1998 season with two victories and a 10-5-3 record, but failed to achieve a third straight NCAA play-off berth. Despite a roster decimated by injuries, the Pilot women advanced to their fourth NCAA semi-final in five years, but lost 1-0 in four overtimes to number one

North Carolina in what would be the longest game in play-off history. Portland had a 19-3-2 final record.

In 1999 the Pilot men, led by all-American freshman forward Conor Casey, ended a three-year play-off drought. Although Portland were at home to Washington, they lost 3-2. However, Casey was the nation's top scorer. Six Pilots were named to the all-WCC team, headed by co-Player of the Year and Freshman of the Year Conor Casey.

The Pilot women concluded their season with an atypical 12-7-1 record, but still tied for second in the WCC. Portland missed out on its first NCAA tournament in eight seasons. Seven players earned all-WCC honours

The following season Clive's women advanced to their fifth NCAA semi-final in seven years, only to lose 1-0 to UCLA. Portland finished with an 18-4-0 record and won the WCC title with 6-1-0.

Charles directed the men to a number three ranking, but they missed the play-offs with a 10-7-2 record after losing six of the final eight games. Portland won their first four games by a 15-1 margin, before falling 2-1 to North Carolina in the last four. The Pilots equalled a school record with twenty wins (20-4-0), and tied for second place in the WCC at 5-2-0.

Freshman scoring sensation Christine Sinclair was named national Freshman of the Year, and was joined on several all-America teams by junior defender Lauren Orlandos.

In 2002 the Pilots claimed their first WCC title since 1992 finishing 13-6-1 overall, and 5-1-0 in the WCC. Portland went on to beat NCAA first round opponent Oregon State 2-0 before falling to Stanford for the second year in a row; the shootout score was 10-9. Nate Jaqua was named an all-America for the second consecutive year. Curtis Spiteri was also named an all-America, while Alejandro Salazar earned WCC Freshman of the Year honours.

The Pilots made history recording the school's first ever National Championship by defeating Santa Clara 2-1 in double overtime in the College Cup Final. Portland tied the school record with twenty wins for the second consecutive season. Sophomore striker Christine Sinclair confirmed that she was one of the premier collegiate soccer athletes, leading the nation with twenty six goals. She was named the WCC Player of the Year, won the Honda Award for best woman collegiate soccer player, and was joined on various all-America teams by senior defender Lauren Orlandos. Freshman midfielder Lindsey Huie was selected the WCC Freshman of the Year and a first-team freshman all-American.

Clive amassed a combined 439-144-44 record for his men's and women's teams, which included thirteen conference titles, (losing only 25 league games) twenty NCAA tournament berths (including six Final Four appearances), taking in nine College Cup appearances and seven Final Four appearances as coach of both the men's and women's teams in a combined thirty one seasons. He was one of just five men in NCAA coaching history to win more than 400 College soccer games.

Clive put in seventeen seasons as coach of Portland's men's teams and fourteen seasons with its women's teams. Twenty-three Pilots earned All-America status during Charles' tenure.

The women's programme has claimed seven consecutive post-season berths, advancing to the Final Four in 1994, 1995, 1996 and 1998. The men's team made eight NCAA appearances in the last twelve years of Clive's reign, advancing to the semi-finals in 1988 and 1995.

Charles ranks fifth all time and was fifth among active NCAA Division I women's soccer coaches in all time winning percentage (.792).

Clive also spent eight years as a USA Soccer staff coach. Late in 1995, Steve Sampson his former West Coast Conference coaching rival with Santa Clara, named him his top assistant to the men's national team. The USSF (United States Soccer Federation) had budgeted for a full-time assistant coach and Charles could have stepped down from his post at Portland University but his loyalty to his players, and the programme he had built, kept him from resigning and instead he moonlighted with the national team. It wasn't the only time Charles turned down an offer to move away from Portland. He could have succeeded Tony DiCicco as coach of the women's national team in 1999 and the University of Connecticut approached him to replace Joe Morrone in 1996. Several MLS teams also courted him to no avail.

Clive successfully guided the Americans through the qualification games to the 1998 World Cup Finals in France. In 1997 Charles had been named as coach of the USA under-23 men's Olympic team for the 2000 Olympics in Australia by Sampson. In his first year in the job his record included two victories over Germany, a 1-0 triumph over Argentina, and a come-from-behind win over Chile.

In Sydney, Charles' tactics and player selections were often questioned by media and fans - not to mention a rather tasteless public display by the father of one of the team's younger players - but in the end it was Charles who had the last laugh as the United States shocked both football fans and football observers throughout the world by reaching the medal round (semi-finals), a best ever performance for the USA, before falling to a powerful Spanish side.

Clive led a young squad to a third place finish at the 1997 World University Games in Italy and in 1999 his under-23 players achieved third place at the FIFA Confederations Cup in Mexico. In the same year the team won a bronze medal at the Pan American Games in Winnipeg, Canada. At the time Charles commented: "We're in great shape...US Soccer has never been in as good shape as it is right now."

Illness

Clive found out that he had prostrate cancer on 11th. August, 2000, just before departing for the Sydney Olympic Games with the USA under-23 team. He went home that day and told his family and together they experienced the kind of numbness not uncommonly felt by families on receiving such information. But for Clive, Australia provided him as he said "with another focus" and this helped.

Charles talked with Tom King, the USA national team general manager, and Dan Flynn, the USA Soccer Secretary General, and told them he had been diagnosed with cancer. The three agreed take a week or so to review the situation, but King and Flynn said that Clive was the best person to judge his condition. According to Clive he felt okay enough to continue his role with the American team, his only concern at that point being not wanting to go to the Olympics with more or less attention to his cancer because "...whatever press we were going to get, I wanted it to be about soccer. I didn't want my illness to get in the way of that." This attitude was typical of Charles; putting others ahead of himself, but acting as the consummate professional.

Probably the worst time for Clive was when he came back from the Olympics; in the doctor's office after the results of a CT scan had come through, showing that the cancer had gone from the soft tissue to the bones.

However, hormonal therapy had an effect. The cancer stopped growing in the bones for a year. Clive told how he understood the gravity of his situation at the 2001 women's Final Four. He started to lose his appetite and experience back and hip pain. He was sleeping a lot and the pain was intensified. It was clear that the hormonal therapy wasn't working. He recalled: "Deep down, I knew I was in a battle."

By January 2002 it was clear the cancer was back in Clive's bones. Radiation therapy followed and Clive suffered some intense pain. However, it dealt with hot spots, his right shoulder and left hip, but it wasn't killing the cancer. It was just helping with the pain. He struggled to get out of bed at points. There were prolonged bouts of vomiting and Clive was spending twenty hours a day in bed; he simply couldn't get out. Clarena tried to get him to eat biscuits, but he just couldn't eat or drink. But Clive made myself get up. Some days he'd just get up, walk around the living room, and go back to bed.

For some time Clive didn't talk to anybody outside his family; he couldn't take any phone calls. He spent time only with his family. But he received hundreds of the cards and e-mails and they helped a lot. He got cards from all over the world, from people he didn't even know he knew.

Subsequently, in the spring of 2002, Clive was given chemo-therapy, and within a week, he was feeling better. Although he was vomiting every day, CT scans indicated that the cancer was shrinking in the bones. It was like a light at the end of the tunnel. He started to get up, walk around the garden, walk up and down the street, walk in the park. He told of how he "...hadn't laughed for so long. And then in June something happened and I had a big belly laugh. I can't remember what it was, but I laughed. I knew I was on my way back." However, Clive was quite aware that there was no cure for his condition.

A private man, Charles did not publicly disclose his illness until March 2002. By this time the chemo-therapy had seemingly given him a new lease on life, and he was strong enough to coach both Portland teams. However, looking back on his the first day back at work Clive admitted to being a little scared meeting people again: "They didn't know what to say; I didn't know what to say." He started to go in once a week, then twice a week. The first day he spent all day at school was the next big event. "I actually went in and did a day's work" he recalled with some amusement.

Pre-season training arrived and Clive didn't know what he would be able to do. He sat and watched training the first day, but within a week, he was coaching. And he coached every day thereafter. But every week, whilst still coaching, Clive was undergoing the chemo-therapy. He told of the character of his treatment: "You just sit there with a drip 'til you're done. I sit there a couple hours, and sometimes I'm sick, and sometimes I'm not. With radiation, I was sick every single day." It seemed that six months into the treatment, all reports on Clive were positive.

At the end of what was to be his last season Clive said he had enjoyed the campaign that took Portland to the NCAA championship. He said that it had been emotionally no different than any other year aside from the fact that he'd been tired. The treatments had been rough, but apart from that he said things had been fine. He had coached both the men's and women's teams at Portland. He had achieved something that in the spring of 2003 he hadn't thought possible and overall he had been able to do pretty much what he would have normally done.

In the late summer of 2002 Clive confessed that part of him would have liked to have taken on another role with the USA national team, given the joy his work at that level had brought him, and that if his heath allowed him it was a possibility. However he admitted that another part of him said to "...keep taking the treatment, wake up in the morning, and keep smelling the roses."

At that point he had felt his treatment had gone well, although some days he felt better than others. Seemingly calling on his coaching acumen, Clive saw knowing what to do, learning how to live with that and knowing when to take breaks is important. He said that he had a good staff team, and that they had done a good job of making him stay away sometimes when that was the best thing to do.

Clive reflected on how his illness had raised his consciousness of "A real deep love of family." He said that "...more than anything. I thought I loved my family, but my goodness!"

Prior to Charles' announcement about his condition his assistant coaches called several alumni, and urged them to return to Portland. Wynne McIntosh told how, "We were in pre-season in Virginia...Garrett (Smith - then assistant coach at Portland) called and said that we should come back to Portland if we could. So we knew something was going on."

At the time, McIntosh was a non-roster player battling for a spot in the New York Power first team. But she felt compelled to make the cross-country trip to be by Charles' side in his time of need. McIntosh and Tiffeny Milbrett flew from Virginia to Portland. They met up with Smith, Shannon MacMillan, and former Portland player, Cindy Griffith. McIntosh recalled: "Garrett told us that Clive didn't know we had flown back and we hadn't seen him yet. He walked in and we were all sobbing our brains out. I haven't cried that hard in a long time. His wife Clarena has been unbelievable." McIntosh said that Clive said he had felt the best he had felt in nine years. McIntosh, who was closest in proximity to Charles through her role as assistant coach at the University, told how Clive looked well, although he tended to get tired easier than usual.

However, at the time Justi Baumgardt-Yamada sadly told how: "The way Garrett says it is... he will eventually die of cancer...but all of us have gotten to tell him exactly how we feel about him. I think it's good that he knows that. We just want to be really encouraging.

American stars Kasey Keller, Tiffeny Milbrett and Shannon MacMillan were some of Clive's earliest successes at Portland. The seeds he planted in his final classes grow with vigour. Players like Canadian international Christine Sinclair and young MLS players like Nate Jaqua and Kelly Gray show his memory will not soon be forgotten.

When the players who went through Portland are asked about Charles, there's an enormous outpouring of love. In the last months of his life Clive said that this meant "everything" to him and that was the reason he had stayed at Portland. He said that the love was reciprocated and that everyday he told his players that he loved them. He confessed it was something he couldn't hide.

The current and former players that made up Charles' extended family have demonstrated how they felt about their former coach in no uncertain terms. Most of them were in attendance on 18th. September, 2002 when Charles was honoured with his lifetime achievement award.

Champion Pilots

Clive was named the women's soccer Coach of the Year in 2002 by Soccer Buzz, an online magazine covering the sport of Women's College Soccer and that specializes in promoting the game of women's college soccer. Charles won the Far West Region Coach of the Year four times, and was West Coast Conference Coach of the Year seven times. Twenty-eight of his players have been named All-American.

On 8th. December, 2002 the Pilot women steamrolled through the NCAA play-offs and, in Texas, during a violent downpour, claimed the first NCAA Championship, the pinnacle of collegiate soccer in the United States. For the first time in the school's history they beat West Coast Conference rival, Santa Clara, 2-1 in a sudden-death double extra-time. It was the University's first NCAA Division I title in any sport and the Pilots' first triumph in seven final four appearances.

Many men and women who had played for and worked with Clive had travelled from around the world to be part of the greatest moment of Clive's collegiate coaching career. The stands at that championship field in Texas were like a human history of Charles' time at Portland. They had come to see their alma mater win national athletic glory, but they viewed it as the masterpiece and finale of their teacher's work, so in effect they were there for him.

According to Wynne McIntosh: "Winning lifted a weight from our shoulders" and Tiffeny Milbrett called Portland's triumph "the best day of my life, hands down." Shannon MacMillan agreed: "That was one of the most emotional weekends of my life…Hands down, it's the highlight of my career. I don't think there's a man, a programme or a team more deserving than Clive and Portland. There was nothing better than seeing Clive's face." After Christine Sinclair's golden goal, Kelly Gray said: "His face said it all."

The Cup final victory was the highlight of Clive's career at Portland. He accepted a lift home in the private jet of Harry Merlo and the coach apparently sat the whole journey with a wide smile on his thinning face, the trophy clamped by his arms.

Portland finished the year 19-4-3 and sophomore striker Christine Sinclair was recognized as one of the premier collegiate soccer athletes, leading the nation with twenty six goals. Sinclair was named the WCC Player of the Year, and won the Honda Award for the best woman's collegiate soccer player. She was joined on various All-America teams by senior defender Lauren Orlandos. Midfielder Lindsey Huie was named the WCC Freshman of the Year and a first team Soccer America Freshman All-American. It had been a fantastic year for the Pilots and the best ever in soccer terms for Clive Charles, but he deflected all praise on to his current and former players crediting them for building the programme.

Anson Dorrance, head women's soccer coach at the University of North Carolina, Chapel Hill said after the Pilot's victory: "Him winning that national championship....there wasn't a coach out there who didn't want him to win."

Jerry Smith, head coach of the Santa Clara University women's soccer team, had been one of the first people to congratulate Clive Charles after the Pilots had beaten Pennsylvania State University in the semi-finals. He recollected with some amusement: "I said, 'Clive, I could not be happier for you and your team making it to the championship game. We're about to defeat North Carolina in the semi-finals and, when we do, we're going to kick your butt in the finals."

"The moment the ball went into the goal against Santa Clara, I was really disappointed for my team, I was disappointed for my players, I was really heartbroken for my seniors, and one moment after that I couldn't have been happier for Clive Charles. He and I shared a nice embrace and a moment and brief conversation within fifteen seconds of that ball going into that goal. If Santa Clara wasn't going to win the national championship, I would want Portland to win it because of my good friend Clive Charles and everything that he's been though."

In 2002 Charles was honoured with a Lifetime Achievement Award from the WUSA and awarded an honorary degree from Portland University. In mid-August 2003 he was inducted into the Oregon Sports Hall of Fame for his lifetime achievements as a player and a coach, but had been unable to attend the induction.

Portland's triumph did not escape the notice of Oregon's political élite who, on 14th. February, 2002, brought Charles' achievement to national attention.

In Washington, a resolution was sponsored by US Senators Ron Wyden (the Democratic representative for Oregon) and Gordon Smith (Wyden's Republican colleague) congratulating the Pilots for winning the school's first NCAA championship in any sport, by way of victory in the 2002 NCAA Division I national championship. The resolution won unanimous approval from the Senate.

Wyden announced that: "Not only is the women's soccer team the first to bring home a national championship in any sport for the University of Portland, but it overcame steep odds to do it. Climbing from the eighth seeded team to defeat seven nationally ranked opponents, including the reigning champs, and win the national championship, these women deserve our congratulations and pride for their tremendous accomplishment."

"Oregon takes pride in the team's impressive accomplishment," said Smith. "Their success on the field is the culmination of determination and sheer talent combined with the outstanding leadership of soccer legend Clive Charles."

As well as praising the Pilots accomplishment, Wyden recognized that the 'Title IX' law had laid the basis for equal opportunity in collegiate sports. The Title IX law states that: "No person in the United States shall, on the basis of sex, be excluded from participation in, be denied the benefits of, or be subjected to discrimination under any education programme or activity receiving Federal financial assistance."

"In this day when Title IX of the Education Amendments is under challenge, we cannot forget...before Title IX was enacted in 1972, only one in seventeen high school girls played team sports. Now that number is one in 2.5. Title IX has helped our nation develop fantastic athletes like the young women I am here to congratulate. We must continue to encourage these athletes, and provide them with our full support."

The resolution passed by the Senate not only highlighted the exploits of the women's soccer team, the leadership of head coach Clive Charles, but the indispensable role of each player, coach, trainer and manager, and the commitment and pride of the University of Portland's students, alumni, faculty and supporters. The coaches and members of the 2002 women's soccer team received a copy of the official resolution from the Senate.

Subsequently Charles was invited, with the team, to the White House by President George Bush. Clive's response was typically disarming: "It'll be the Queen of England asking us to Buckingham Palace next!"

Clive's love for the Pilots programme he built never got in the way of what he saw as his players' best interest. Unlike many college coaches, Charles didn't falter in his guidance of his best players when the professional ranks called. Keller, Steve Cherundolo, Casey, Gray and Nate Jaqua all left after their sophomore or junior years, under the council and tutelage of Charles.

Charles was named Grand Marshal of the Grand Floral Parade in the Rose Festival, along with the 2002 national champion women's soccer team. This event is an awe-inspiring occasion with all-floral floats bringing fantasy to life for a half million viewers over a 4.3 mile parade route. Occuring in

June of each year, the Festival is Oregon's largest single-day spectator event. The parade boasts the country's largest permanent marching band, beautifully decorated equestrian units, and culturally rich performances in grand style. Captivating generations since 1907, this internationally distinguished parade has been recognized by the International Festival & Events Association and *USA Today* as one of the top five parades in America. Every year the Rose Festival president designates an individual or individuals as Grand Marshal of the Grand Floral Parade. Former honourees include film maker Will Vinton, Senator Mark O. Hatfield, retired Oregon Symphony conductor James dePriest, golfer Peter Jacobsen and the Portland Police department.

I was given a video film by Clive's family showing him and Clarena heading the parade in the back of a bright red, open toped Cadillac bedecked in flowers. He looked thin and weak, but the smile never left his face.

Number 3

Weeks before Clive's induction into the Oregon Sports Hall of Fame, his former club Portland Timbers had announced that they were going to retire his number 3 uniform at the final match of the season on Friday 29th. August, 2003, in a half time ceremony. However, on Tuesday 26th. August, surrounded by family at his home in North West Portland, Oregon, Clive Charles passed away at the age of 51.

Although he wasn't to see his old number 'raised to glory', when he heard of the intention he said: "To know that the number three will hang from the rafters permanently is unbelievable to me. To this date, I can remember what it felt like to put that jersey on before every game. I sincerely wish my friend Bobby Howe all the best, and my sincere thanks go out to the Timbers and the Portland soccer community."

Clive's son Michael, 28, who lettered in golf at the University of Portland (he tutored the game in the Portland area) and his daughter Sarah, 25, a child psychologist and school counsellor, attended the event and heard the huge expressions of goodwill felt for their father.

For the first time in their short A-League history, the Portland Timbers were playing a match that began with the Timbers already eliminated from the play-off race. They had been eliminated by the El Paso Patriots beating them 3-1 the previous weekend in Texas. However, it was that same El Paso team that were visiting PGE Park on what was Clive's evening; his spirit breathed through the atmosphere and the Timbers Army supporters had spelled out "CHARLO" (Clive carried the same nickname into American soccer that was given to his brother John in England) in scarves on the dugout in front of section 107, the domain of those diehard Timbers' supporters.

The number '3' had been painted in the middle of the park. The board that everyone knew held Clive's number 3 was hanging in the northeast corner of the stadium, just under the roof, but it was still covered at this point. The Timbers wore black armbands on their left sleeves, and before the match kicked off, both teams stood silently on the pitch in a moment of silence.

At half-time, Timbers General Manager Jim Taylor stepped up to the podium to start the ceremony. Most of the members of the current Timbers squad had remained on the field for the ceremony, sitting quietly behind the touchline beyond the advertising boards.

Jim Taylor spoke about what Clive had been to and done for the Timbers franchise. This was followed by Timber's captain and former Portland Pilot Brian Winters reflecting on the impact Clive had made on his life. He expressed his thanks to Clive on behalf of all of the Pilots players he had coached over the years.

Former Portland Timber Bill Irwin, who like Clive had played for Cardiff City in the English Football League, and had been Clive's assistant almost as long as Clive had been the Pilots coach, spoke of his former team mate and good friend. After Bill had concluded, Timbers Head Coach Bobby Howe spoke of what Clive had meant to the team, and the city saying: "The retiring of Clive's jersey is a fitting testament to not only an outstanding player and true professional, but also to a colleague and a great friend. He has been an inspiration to all players that have had the privilege of playing for him, not only at the University of Portland, but also at club and national team levels."

During the speeches, Clive's son Michael was also on the field, appearing understandably sombre and after completing their contribution each speaker embraced him.

After Bobby Howe had spoken, Jim Taylor announced the official retirement of Clive's number 3; the gesture was the first of its kind in the nearly eighty year history of PGE Park, and as the five men turned to the northeast corner of the stadium, a white banner slowly fell and Clive's number 3 uniform was unveiled, along with the years that he had played for the Timbers: 1978 to 1981. The crowd rose as one in a standing ovation which lasted for the best part of a minute. Taylor said: "It only seems fitting that the first-ever retired jersey to hang in the rafters of PGE Park belongs to Clive."

In the same year Clive joined the Timbers, the team also hired Jim Serrill, better known to all Timbers fans as 'Timber Jim', who continued to act as the Timbers mascot and one of their biggest fans twenty five years later. Timber Jim, at the age of 49, was still climbing the pole and sawing off pieces of the log after each Timbers' goal.

A few weeks previously, on 16th. August, while the world was watching news of the major blackouts that affected the Northeast, an article quietly slipped out on *Oregon Live's* website (largely disabled by the blackout), and in the *Oregonian*, stating that Timber Jim was retiring. It was also announced that Timber Jim would not be returning for the final three home games, as Jim had taken a job in Seattle that would only allow him to return for the weekends.

But the evening of 29th. August, 2003 at PGE Park would not have been complete without Timber Jim being there. As the game began he proudly led the cheers of the crowd, firing up his chainsaw, just as he had done in the days when Clive Charles played in defence of the Timbers.

After Clive's retired jersey had been unveiled, Jim Taylor announced that Timber Jim would be sawing a piece off the log in Clive's honour, and just as he had done hundreds of times before, Timber Jim sawed the last few inches off a log that was set up behind the north goal and brought the piece out to midfield and presented it to Michael Charles, who held the piece aloft as the crowd once again rose to their feet in applause. Michael himself then went to the podium and spoke of his father, but the emotion of the evening seemed to be overwhelming him by this point, and he spoke only briefly. But his love for his father was very apparent, and it was evident from the moist eyes of those around him and throughout the stadium that many thousands of Portlanders and people throughout the football world felt like they had just lost a family member.

The match kicked off and El Paso were caught off guard by Bryn Ritchie, who put the Timbers 1-0 up at the end of the first half. In the second 45 minutes, former Portland Pilot Scott Benedetti fittingly scored the second goal of the evening for the Timbers. With six minutes of the match remaining, Jake Sagare netted for Portland, creating a fitting 3-0 to be emblazoned on the scoreboard. The '3' shone out like a beacon of meaning over the park.

The Timbers Army and other Timbers fans presented Timber Jim with a number of mementos, including a trophy fashioned from a cut log with Jim proudly standing on a pole atop the trophy (with the log having been signed by most of the regular Timbers' Army supporters) and a handmade green and yellow Timbers' axe, together with a photo of Timber Jim signed once more by the Timbers' Army supporters.

For many Timbers' fans saying goodbye to the two most enduring symbols of the Portland Timbers', and of soccer in the Rose City could have been an instance of great sadness. But instead, the moment defined itself as a time of joyful memories for many Timbers' fans. Afterwards, many of the Timbers' Army supporters remained to meet the players, the coaches, and Timber Jim. The atmosphere was one of great appreciation for Clive Charles who was a central figure in making Portland into 'Soccer City USA', through his playing career, his school soccer academy work (where he oversaw all team and player education and development) and as a coach at the City's University. He had poured his heart and soul into the beautiful game, and made it thrive in his adopted home. Portland has some of the most loyal soccer supporters in America, and this had much to do with the spark Clive lit to create an ember that grew to the flame which continues to burn to this day.

On 29th. August, 2003, the Portland Timbers' broke their A-League single-game attendance record with a crowd of 13,351. It was also the largest crowd the A-League had seen that season. When the crowd had melted away Clive's number 3 shirt fluttered gently in the breeze, a reminder of a legendary football player, coach and a lifetime of achievement.

It was not only in Portland that Clive's life was remembered and celebrated that day. The following was read before the Clemson-South Carolina women's soccer match: "One of the most influential coaches in our country lost a two year battle with cancer last week. Please stand and join as we pause for a moment of silence, in honour and memory of Clive Charles. Clive Charles was an inspiration to players, coaches, and educators alike. Although his legacy will live on, we will miss him dearly."

Hammers never die

Just before he died Clive quietly returned to England and his native roots in the East End of London. He was there to say his final goodbyes to family and close friends. Among visitors to his sister Rita's home in Collier Row, on the West Essex border of London's Docklands, no more than a dozen miles from where Clive and his brothers and sisters were born and grew up, to see Clive were former West Ham team-mates Frank Lampard, Harry Redknapp and Brian Dear. It had been a sad twelve months for the Charles family. A year and six days before Clive died his elder brother and fellow former Hammer, John (see Belton 2003) the first Black professional to play for West Ham, also died of cancer.

John, his wife Carol, and their family made some visits to Clive and his family in America. Carol and John told me about the last occasions they had spent with John's 'little brother'.

"Our Clive had this beautiful beach house on Cannon Beach in the

States....we stayed there. Anyway, we went out one day after dinner." John interrupted Carol's flow: "Clive always walks his dinner off." Carol continued the story: "Well we walked for about two minutes and John had to sit on a bench. We walked for about an hour and half, about four miles." John made a light-hearted excuse: "Well it was that sand weren't it?! You needed stamina to walk on that!" Carol went on: "When we came back he was still sitting on the bench. Clive said he looked like Forest Gump." They both giggled.

Clive's nephew Keith, John's oldest son, recalled finding out about his uncle's plight: "We heard about Clivey. Clivey was first to have the cancer identified. That was kept schtom (secret). It was a big shock."

Mitchell, Keith's younger brother told me: "When we found out about Clive it shook dad up. He told me Clive was ill, with cancer. He seemed very quiet about it. He kept a lot of his emotions to himself. But you could see it affected him. They were alike in different ways. They both liked good food. Their ways were very alike. They even looked alike."

For a time both John and Clive knew they were each fighting, like the East End boys they were, against cancer simultaneously. Clive was able to be at John's bedside just days before his brother passed on. He left John with this message: "These last few months have been difficult for both of our families and us. It would be so easy to feel sorry for ourselves, to say 'why us?' To give in, to stop trying, but that is not our way. We both have so much to live for. John, I think of you every day. I've never told you this before, but when I was young you were my hero. I love you very much. Keep your chin up. Keep a smile on your face. Your little brother, Clive." John died peacefully on 17th. August, 2002

After Clive had passed away his long time assistants Bill Irwin and Garrett Smith respectively took charge of the University of Portland's men and women teams. Both retained their titles as 'assistant' coaches. The University had not determined whether the programmes would continue to have one head coach or a different coach for each team, but there was poetry in the irony; no one could replace Clive.

Of course, condolences flooded in. The famed Head Mentor of the University of North Carolina women's soccer programme Anson Dorrance spoke for many involved in soccer when he remembered: "He was always very gracious after every match, regardless of the outcome. He didn't change his demeanour. He wasn't catatonic if he lost a game and arrogant when he won one. He was just a very gracious man and that's the way you win respect in our profession, the way you handle yourself in triumph and defeat."

Dorrance described Charles' work with the men's Olympic team as inspiring: "I was just so impressed with the job that he did with our Olympic team in Australia. They played some of the most attractive soccer I've ever seen an American team play."

USA Soccer President Dr. S. Robert Contiguglia said: "Clive will be remembered as much for what he accomplished on the field, as what he did off the field. He was a man who developed the game in every significant way possible in this country, from his playing days in the NASL straight through to the development of young athletes on both the men's and women's side of the sport. More importantly, he was a friend, a guide and a mentor to all of those who were touched by his kindness and generosity. While his presence will be truly missed, his spirit will continue to echo throughout the lives of those who knew him."

For U.S. Men's National Team Manager, Bruce Arena: "Clive Charles was instrumental in the progress of soccer in the United States on both the men's and women's side of the game. His contributions at both the collegiate and national team levels speak for themselves. He will be sorely missed, and we express our deepest sympathies to his family."

According to Portland's director of athletics Joe Etzel, Clive would: "never be replaced. We're just going to have to do the best we can in his absence."

For Portland Timbers' general manager Jim Taylor: "No one in soccer has touched and enriched more lives in Portland than Clive Charles. He was a tenacious defender on the pitch, a world-class mentor and coach and as kind and giving a man as you'll ever know. He has done more for the sport of soccer in Oregon than anyone ever has or ever will. He is the consummate professional, a first-class human being and a person that we all owe a huge debt of gratitude to. He is truly an inspiration to us all."

Jerry Smith, head coach of the Santa Clara University women's soccer team admitted it would be odd to play against Portland and not see Charles across the field from him: "The number of times we would look over at each other and just have a smile, or a shrug of the shoulders or a raise of the eyebrows, I will really miss that because I don't have that with many of my colleagues. Portland will always remain my second favourite women's college team, and it always will be because of Clive."

Kasey Keller said: "Clive was probably one of the closest people that I had in my life. For me, it's hard for me to believe that he is no longer here to be a part of it. Him not being here anymore is very difficult."

Shannon MacMillan lamented: "He said his form of cancer was treatable but not curable. He was such an incredible person that it didn't change him at all. It only helped us see what an incredible fighter he was."

Loren Wohlgemuth, a former sports information director at Portland who worked with Charles for seven years recollected how off the soccer field Clive was not adverse to enlivening the day with some humour: "He would walk into your office and if you weren't there, he would grab a sticky note and draw a little cartoon, and it was usually off colour, and hide it somewhere so a couple of days later you would find it. You knew it was him. He was the practical joker in the building." Wohlgemuth said Charles was always making side bets with people; for instance, wagering a quarter that he could spit his gum into a garbage can twenty five feet away, or betting a milkshake that he could kick a ball into a goal from a far distance. "There was always somebody who would take him up on it and they would always lose," Wohlgemuth said.

But perhaps one of the most telling of remembrances of Clive came by way of the work of Alberto Salazar, one of the all time great marathon runners. His son Alejandro was mentored and guided by Charles through university soccer and Alberto started a website where admirers of Clive shared stories. One told of the 1988 men's Final Four game between Portland and Indiana. The game was deadlocked and scoreless at half-time. In the Pilots' locker room, Coach Charles called for silence. For fifteen minutes he and his players eavesdropped on the tirade of Indiana's coach in the next room. Finally, Charles told his team: "Go out and keep doing what you're doing and have fun."

Clive's family held a private funeral service for the great husband and father who died far too young. Unlike his brother John, he was never to be compensated with the joy of grandchildren; like John he would have been a good granddad.

For Clive Charles the University of Portland organised a memorial service at 3 pm. on 8th. September, 2003 that was held in Chiles Center, part of the University's Campus and sporting facilities. At the latter Bill Irwin said: "We grieve for Clive's family and his thousands of friends at the University and around the world who have lost a generous and sensitive friend. He loved the game...the game was his passion. He really cared about his players and tried to help them in any way he could. No problem was too trivial. He wanted to make them better players and people."

The University's senior vice president, Rev. E. William Beauchamp, said in a prepared statement: "Clive's life and work were gifts of extraordinary worth, and his impact as teacher and coach, friend and mentor, will be felt for many years to come."

Clive's contribution to soccer in the USA was massive. The impact he had on both the US men's and women's national team, MLS, WUSA and countless University of Portland players was arguably the greatest legacy left to world football by any player or coach that has gone through the West

Ham system. He is certainly up there with John Lyall, Ron Greenwood, Malcolm Allison, Noel Cantwell and Bobby Moore. Yet he has hardly received the credit he deserves. It is hard to think of any British Black player who has achieved so much over such a long period of time and as such it is hard to understand why his contribution is not more widely understood and celebrated.

Many people who knew or met Clive were convinced that he was going to beat cancer. For most Portland soccer fans and former players the announcement of his death didn't seem real. It did not seem possible. Wynne McIntosh expressed such a perception: "We've always thought of Clive as sort of invincible. Then you start to think; what if it got to the point where we have to lose Clive? We can't lose Clive!"

And Justi Baumgardt-Yamada recalled: "The last time I talked to him he sounded good. I spoke to his daughter (Sarah) the other day. She said he has such a great attitude."

It just didn't seem that Clive was a person who could or should be taken from this world. In many ways the future was to prove he wasn't. While cancer has taken his physical presence from the sidelines, it's clear from what his former players say about him that he will always be a part of their lives. The day Clive passed Tiffeny Milbrett and Shannon MacMillan were selected for the USA roster for the 20th. September-12th. October Women's World Cup

Clive's continued influence has also been assured by the Charles family establishing the Clive Charles Foundation to help fund cancer research. For them of course football was always a background. Clive was a good, caring, loving husband and father. A giver of bear hugs and laughter, with boundless generosity.

With infectious enthusiasm, Clive fought his way through his three-year campaign against multiple cancers, while defying the prognosis that his cancer would kill him within months. In his un-American language and in his Cockney accent, he professed that winning wasn't everything. He was always gracious, articulate and honest. These qualities are why he was so beloved by his players and why his death is such a loss for football. This is perhaps Clive Charles' most fitting epitaph: football yes, but played and taught with love.

Charles was a great ambassador for the game of football at all levels for both men and women and he had a deep understanding of the game, its gifts and possibilities. He was considered one of the finest people in American soccer, loved by his players, revered by his peers, and respected for his gentle demeanour and intense passion for the sport.

It was in 1995 that Charles, by then recognised as an eloquent speaker, addressed the men's championship banquet. Knowing how moments of glory can merge into the mists of time, he asked student-athletes from all four participating teams to consciously consign the moment they took to the field to long term memory.

Following Clive's passing the Portland University decided to build the Clive Charles Soccer Complex, in memory of their greatest ever coach, but also to continue the work he started. It was estimated that the cost of the development would be around $1.8 million. In 2004 one of the first initiatives of the project was completed. Flood lights were installed at Merlo Field (now designated as part of the Clive Charles Soccer Complex) allowing night games to be played for the first time in school history. A crowd of 4,070 showed up at the inaugural night match, a 4-0 victory over Weber State on 10th. September. It seems fitting the one of the first developments at Portland since Clive's death involved the bringing of light into darkness.

Charles was a surprising challenging and at times uproariously funny man. He could be stubbornly insistent in a motivational way. The edge of his almost impatient energetic keenness was tempered by his inherent patience as a teacher. He was capable of being blunt and even abrupt in his honesty, but could wrap the same in his endearing wit, that sometimes ran at the speed of light. He was a friend to many and he made relationships with those who made up the teams he tended that endured long past playing days. I have followed Clive's career from afar, and have modelled much of my own teaching style and attitude on his example. I know it to have brought quality to my life and those I have had the honour of working with as a teacher and tutor.

Jeff Gadawski played for and coached with Clive and went on to become President of the FC Portland Academy, the community programme inspired by Clive Charles. He remembered Clive as: "a teacher who used soccer to teach life".

This is perhaps the greatest tribute a coach can have. The moment the game moves beyond the pitch, it has its reason to be. Other than that it is 'just' a game. Although the United States 2006 World Cup squad is studded with names of men who honed their skills under the coaching of Charles, the likes of Steve Cherundolo, Josh Wolff, Landon Donovan and Kasey Keller, Clive used football to help people make themselves 'better' as human beings, he used 'soccer' to enhance humanity. That was his great gift and the greatest gift football can bestow. It is no accident that football tournaments are quests for 'cups'. Of course, most people never get to so much as touch these trophies; some never even see them, except perhaps as images on television or in magazines. The competition for the 'cup' is an echo of the ancient quests for the Holy Grail, the outcome of which was never to actually find that object, but to learn and grow from the trials and tribulations undergone during the endless search. The point of questing for the Grail was not the getting of it, but how one went about trying to get it; it was a finding of self. In Clive's time, Portland became Camelot to his King Arthur and his teams were the Knights of the Round Table. All were ostensibly involved in the quest for the material glory of championships by winning games, but at base their shared project was what the great American psychologist Carl Rogers called 'becoming'; the 'united' process of being all we can be. As a youth worker in the East End of London and across the world I have tried to implicate this into my own work. Hardly ever is what we are doing really totally about just that which we are ostensibly doing: singing, playing football or even going down the pub. It also involves us 'becoming', making our selves in the process of living. These days, as a lecturer involved in training what we now call 'informal educators', I find that it is more and more difficult to put over this point to those involved in what is increasingly an instrumental educational system, heavily focused on 'skilling-up' and certification. But taking inspiration from the likes of Clive Charles helps. He might be pleased to think his influence has gone full circle and is still working in the place where he grew up and learnt his football. I hope so.

The boy from Canning Town was the greatest coach in more than a century of University of Portland athletics, but Clive Michael Charles was a man who prized development over victory, yet he was one of America's most successful coaches. He was not only amongst the most talented and creative individuals in the history of soccer in the United States, he was also the most loved of teachers and coaches. In August 2003 the American and world football community lost a great coach and teacher, but it gained a legend and an exemplary role model who rose above all the scandal and silliness of the modern game to demonstrate the way a person can develop and grow in dignity and integrity through the sport that Clive, growing up in the same place and time as I did, just a mile or so down the road from West Ham United's Upton Park home, knew as football.

CHAPTER 13

The Culture of Stuart Hall

A profound contributor to the field of cultural studies. His work has made a huge impact on issues relating to culture, race and ethnicity.

Stuart Hall was born on 3rd. February,1932, the son of an accountant, in Kingston, Jamaica. Television-viewers in Britain know him for his gentle, thoughtful explanations of issues surrounding multi-cultural society and as a widely-respected social commentator, but he has been a leading figure of the British left for more than thirty years and a visionary race theorist.

As a cultural theorist, Hall has been prolific and he has contributed to key works on culture and media studies, as well as to political debate. Arguably, no one else has had the same influence in the shaping of the field. In the 1980s Hall was part of the vanguard of criticism against Thatcherism and Reaganism. His passionate, principled attack on the New Right in the 1980s and his critique of authoritarian populism reached a readership well beyond the confines of the academy. His later work has moved on to the terrain of hybridity, identity, Occidentalism, race relations, multiculturalism and the politics of difference and diversity.

Throughout his career Hall has remained faithful to a Marxist, democratic tradition, and is committed to investigating a constantly changing British social landscape. His criticism of New Labour for what he perceived to be their lack of principle has been unrelenting for more than a decade.

It was in 1951 that Stuart moved to England with his mother. They lived in Bristol before Hall took his place at Oxford University where he studied as a Rhodes Scholar at Merton College and gained his Masters degree. He started his PhD on American literature, but it was his informal education at Oxford that introduced Hall to nationalist West Indian thought, left-wing British History, international socialist politics, and continental philosophy. Stuart never finished his doctorate, although he has seventeen honorary doctorates, fourteen in Britain, two in the United States, and one European. He never read sociology at university, but became a professor of sociology in the Open University. He enjoys the irony of all this, seeing the situation as 'fun'. He has never thought of calling himself an academic at all. He describes himself as an intellectual, seeing that he takes ideas and the life of the mind very seriously. This echoes the view on intellectualism held by great Palestinian thinker, Edward Said. For Said, we are increasingly living in a time dominated by the 'expert', the person who knows a lot about one thing but not much beyond that. Edward saw himself as an intellectual in that he wanted to pursue the connectedness of experience and reality and the interrelated nature of world, history and current issues. This of course requires a very different perspective to that of the expert, who like everything in the capitalist environment, becomes increasing specialised and imprisoned in their 'field' (like slaves on the plantation). But Hall does not understand himself as a scholar. This is not because he fails to appreciate scholarship; it is not what he feels he does. Hall defines himself as a 'public intellectual', a person committed to ideas, and to serious work of the mind. For Hall there is no question that some of the places that have offered him an honorary doctorate in Britain have done so because they have substantial numbers of black students, and they wanted to have somebody, who could speak to them and who they would feel they might identify with.

Following the increasing politicization of his thought and his identification with emancipatory socialist politics, Hall became a committed socialist in the early 1950s. He joined forces with Charles Taylor, Raphael Samuel, and Gabriel Pearson to launch and edit the journal *Universities and Left Review*, later merging with E. P. Thompson, Raymond Williams, Ralph Miliband and John Saville to produce a radical socialist journal, *The New Reasoner* which became the *New Left Review*, in the wake of the 1956 Soviet invasion of Hungary, which saw many thousands of members leave the Communist Party of Great Britain (CPGB) and look for alternatives to previous orthodoxies.

When Hall left Oxford in 1957 he was the only one of the original group who had the time to do the arduous editorial work. So Stuart was the full-time editor in London. The *New Left Review* office was situated in Soho, above a coffee bar which financed the publication. In the same year Stuart joined the Campaign for Nuclear Disarmament (CND). Other members included J. B. Priestley, Bertrand Russell, E. P. Thompson, Fenner Brockway, Frank Allaun, Donald Soper, Vera Brittain, Sydney Silverman, James Cameron, Jennie Lee, Victor Gollancz, Konni Zilliacus, Richard Acland, Frank Cousins, A. J. P. Taylor, Canon John Collins and Michael Foot; a veritable troop of the British intellectual Left.

Hall worked as a supply teacher in a secondary modern school on the edge of Brixton, near the Oval, but continued to edit the *New Left Review*. The school was so challenging that there was always at least one teacher who failed to turn up for work, few being able to cope more than four days week with the teaching conditions. It was the first school Hall was sent to and he spent about three years there. It was the first time he had taught a mixed class of black and white children. He would leave school at 4.30pm in the evening and take the tube to the journal office and edit it to around midnight, take the night bus back to the Oval, and turn up at the school the next day. At the same time Stuart was lecturing part-time in adult education, working once a week in Bexley Heath for around seven years teaching Russian literature and translation; he says he had a wonderful time. He also lectured for the Film Institute. That is when his connection with film deepened.

In 1959 Hall gave up the school work but he continued to lecture part-time and during 1961 he moved to Chelsea College, part of London University, and taught complementary studies. He saw it as his job to "civilise the scientists". He was appointed as the first lecturer with the designation 'Lecturer in Film and Allied Media'. The course did well, and his was the first higher education appointment to teach film. He taught film and television to pharmacists, chemists, and engineers.

In 1964 Stuart co-wrote *The Popular Arts*. This resulted in him being invited by Richard Hoggart to join the Centre for Contemporary Cultural Studies at Birmingham University. His career blossomed and Hall became one of those who defined 'Cultural Studies' as an academic discipline. In 1968 he was appoinyed as Research Fellow and then Director of the seminal Centre for Cultural Studies, creating a genuinely collaborative approach to the study of culture. He produced a series of dazzling publications in the 1970s and the Birmingham Centre changed the way in which social scientists think about culture. In November 1971 Hall, then a fellow at the CCS, told a visibly shocked BBC television audience: "there is something radically wrong with the way Black immigrants, West Indians, Asians, Africans are handled by and presented on the mass media.

This, over three decades ago, marked the beginning of the critique of how TV, radio, newspapers, magazines and now the internet are prejudiced in covering Black communities and maintain closed doors to black and minority ethnic journalists. As such, Hall might quite correctly be called a pioneer within a whole range of cultural issues. For him, the media exist in an intimate, sympathetic relationship to power and established values, favouring a consensus view of any problem. As such, the media overwhelmingly reflect middle class attitudes and experience. This makes the media unfit in terms of producing a genuine portrayal of the black community and the challenges it faces. For Hall, the media are particularly defensive about the sacred institutions of society, while Black people are most likely to encounter problems in the sensitive power-areas of: employment, public discrimination, housing, parliamentary legislation, local government, law and order, and the police.

Hall, more than any other individual, has so compellingly and carefully dissected how the British media's acclaimed freedoms mask its powers to hurt and deprive defenceless Black people. Understanding the conflict of interest between the media and Black people is fundamental. For Hall the mass media play a crucial role in defining the problems and issues of public concern being the main channels of public discourse in our segregated society. The media transmits stereotypes of one group to other groups and attach feelings and emotions to problems. It is the media that set the terms in which problems are defined as 'central' or 'marginal.' As a result, the media ignores the real issues with which Black people must contend. For Hall, this is because the media, on the whole, naturally gravitate to the liberal middle-ground; they find conflict and oppression, the real conditions of Black existence, difficult and awkward. They tend to redefine all problems as failures in communication. This analysis is particularly relevant in the current period that is rife with Islamaphobia and slanted portrayals of those from Muslim backgrounds.

Hall's influential articles of the 1970s included: *Situating Marx: Evaluations and Departures* (1972), *Encoding and Decoding in the Television Discourse* (1973), *Reading of Marx's 1857 Introduction to the Grundrisse* (1973). He also contributed to the book *Policing the Crisis* (1978). In 1979, he was appointed as Professor of Sociology at the Open University. After this he published further influential books, including: *Culture, Media, Language* (1980), *The Hard Road to Renewal* (1988), *New Ethnicities* (1988), *Resistance Through Rituals* (1989), *New Times* (1989), *Modernity and Its Future* (1992), *The Formation of Modernity* (1992), *What is Black in Popular Culture?* (1992), *Cultural Identity and Diaspora* (1994), *Questions of Cultural Identity* (1996), *Critical Dialogues in Cultural Studies* (1996), and *Representation: Cultural Representations and Signifying Practices* (1997).

Hall retired from the Open University in 1997 to sit on the Runnymede Trust's Commission on the Future of Multi-Ethnic Britain, host *Politically Incorrect* on Consumer News and Business Channel (CNBC), serve as emeritus at The Open University and Visiting Professor, Goldsmith College, Milton Keynes. His research interests continue to be in the fields of cultural theory and cultural studies, race, ethnicity and cultural identity. He published *Visual Cultural: A Reader* in 1999.

In the realm of identity formation Hall has suggested that there are two kinds of identity: identity as 'being' (which offers a sense of unity and commonality) and identity as 'becoming' (or a process of identification, which shows the discontinuity in our identity formation.) He uses the Caribbean identities, including his own, to explain how the first one is necessary, but the second one is truer to their/our post-colonial conditions. To explain the process of identity formation, Hall has used Derrida's theory of difference as support, and argues that the temporary positioning of identity is 'strategic' and arbitrary. This has challenged traditional notions of fixed identity through nationality and/or ethnicity and shown the part of psychological and social psychological considerations as well as obliging a deeper sociological analysis of identity. The certainties of former times about identity are now clearly seen to be in reality in a state of constant flux and reassessment. It no longer tells us much to say 'I'm British' or 'Jamaican' as these categories are so diverse in themselves and mean different things to different people. They are also in a constant and increasingly swift state of change in terms of personal and public perception; for example, the term 'Black British' had no real meaning at the time of Windrush. Indeed, for the greater part of the history of black people in Britain such an expression would constitute a contradiction in terms for both black and white people living in the UK.

But Hall is interested in identification more than identity. He sees the product of identification to be identities, and the outcome of identifying in any stable way is to take up a position, not necessarily forever, but to hold a position stable enough to be able to say "I own it". In that sense, for Hall, our lives consist of taking up of a series of 'positionalities'. This does not mean that identity is something you can choose. A white person can't choose to be black (Ali G, Eminem and Vanilla Ice notwithstanding) but that white person can choose to be white in many different ways. So a biographical narrative of life lived might be thought of a series unfolding positionalities, each of them constituting an identification which is of some substance, some significance. However, it may be that very little is fixed and hardly anything static in terms of the base lines of identity. Again, this seems increasingly important in a world that often appears to be at the point of tearing itself apart on the basis of very concrete notions of identity.

Hall's 'political' influence on the politics of New Labour is tangible, although he might recoil at the thought. He wrote many influential articles in the CPGB's (Communist Party of Great Britain) theoretical journal, *Marxism Today* (MT), which challenged the left's views of markets and general organisational and political conservatism. This discourse had a profound impact on the Labour Party under both Neil Kinnock and Tony Blair, especially as many of the people around both leaders came to political maturity at the highest point of *Marxism Today's* influence. However, Hall regards himself as unreconciled with the Labour Party.

CHAPTER 14

The Farrakhan Phenomenon

Minister Louis Farrakhan is villain to some, a champion to others. If you
only know him through media accounts and sound bites, he may sound
like a cross between a lunatic, a terrorist and a tyrant.

Many African Americans who've grown up without fathers (or mothers), feel
Louis Farrakhan to be something of a patriarchal figure and a mentor who
has provided confirmation that what they do has consequences and that as
human beings they have responsibilities, to themselves and society but also
to the Minister himself and his God.

Farrakhan, although for a long time a notorious figure in America, came
to international attention on 16th. October, 1995. This was when he called
for the Million Man March and a million men heeded his summons. In spite
of the huge commotion and controversy this event provoked, there are
many who see themselves as indebted to Farrakhan in both a personal and
social sense, having been provided with some definite direction by the often
seemingly eccentric Muslim leader.

Whatever your take on this, Farrakhan succeeded where other leaders,
White and Black, had failed. During a period of intense Black-on-Black
violence, a million African Americans stood together and demonstrated
their mutual trust in each other. Following that seminal event, the Minister
has completed a series of "friendship tours," making whistle-stop visits to
nearly one hundred countries where he was often welcomed as if he were a
head of state in nations that the USA saw as their enemies. For all the
criticism of him, Farrakhan has become the leading Black spokesman in the
USA and his influence has spread beyond the Black constituency.

Following the Million Man March, *Time* magazine included Farrakhan
as one of the one hundred most influential people in America, a distinction
just a handful of Black people have achieved. *Vanity Fair* listed him amongst
sixty five international states-people who "shape and rule the world." He
was cordially received by Philadelphia's Jewish Mayor Ed Rendel, and he
met with Richard Daily, Chicago's Mayor. The Minister gave the keynote
address at the Congressional Black Caucus' annual convention and the likes
of the former Ghanaian President Jerry Rawlings, Fidel Castro, Yasser
Arafat, Saddam Hussein and Muamar Qaddafi have bestowed their
nations' honours on Farrakhan. Within seven days Farrakhan had

discussions with Nelson Mandela and Edgar Bronfman of the World Jewish Congress. The following week he hosted a Rap summit, featuring Snoop Doggy Dog, Ice Cube and Doug E. Fresh. He is admired by Black youth and held in esteem by world leaders.

Prior to the Million Man March being announced, a *Time* survey showed that more than seventy percent of black Americans admired the Minister and almost fifty percent felt he represented them. Farrakhan filled a void in Black leadership, but more significantly, his message is unequivocal and uncomplicated; he directs people to become moral and make commitment to God. The biggest movements of the last decade, the Million Man March and the Promise Keepers, have brought huge numbers of men to the US capitol, not to petition government, but to bring people back to God.

Black America still endures what Malcolm X called in the 1960s 'political oppression, economic exploitation, and social degradation'. However, for many this is premised and feeds on a spiritual and moral deficit in the Black community. It has been claimed that this is why the Million Man March reverberated in the hearts and minds of a vast section of black people. Although the subject of reparations was broached, that was not the prime motivation; economic improvement was a major principle, but it was not a central factor. Although political movement was on the schedule, it was not the main rationale why a million men came at Farrakhan's behest. Atonement and self-improvement were the topics that brought together Black men from every sphere of existence at the strident invitation of a man vilified by the popular media.

Farrakhan had been demonised following a 1985 speech. He was quoted as calling Judaism a "gutter religion", an accusation he fervently refutes, and answering indictments that he hated Jews he has said, "I am not now nor have I ever been anti-Semitic."

The incumbent President Bush has replicated his antecedent's official response to Farrakhan. At the time of the Million Man March President Clinton worked hard to circumvent the Minister and he is still not welcome at the White House. However, given his authority and reputation Farrakhan has obliged the world to acknowledge him.

A dozen years after the Million Man March, hundreds of thousands of young men that went to Washington that day have made incredible efforts to be positive role models in their neighbourhoods. They believe that the most effective action they could take was to develop their communities. This represents powerful political activism through the drive for self-improvement. It is the enduring influence of Farrakhan and the reason that his contribution to society should be seen as illustrious rather than held up to various brands of ridicule and so undermined.

This said, he was been banned from entering Britain. In the relatively recent past the UK has welcomed former Klansman, David Duke, former Apartheid leader, P.W. Botha and a selection of the world's most contemptuous, right wing tyrants. As such, the Home Office ban of Louis Farrakhan appears akin to shameful. Of course there are many, Black and White, who would disagree with or be frightened of his political position and his contention that racial equality continues to be denied to African Americans and that there needs to a separation of races, and the setting up of a Black state within the Union. His confrontational, allegedly anti-Semitic remarks still echo around the Jewish community, provoking anxiety and censure.

However, the opposition to Farrakhan's entry into Britain is an extreme reaction. He is not a criminal or an ex-offender; his talks and speeches have not been linked with any violence against any racial groups. Indeed, his ideas and words are understood by many to have a 'crime-dampening' consequence, putting forth the proposal that people abide by the law in troubled urban areas.

The last decade has witnessed Farrakhan repeatedly express his regret for offending Jewish people and others. He has withdrawn many of the statements that provoked offence. In fact, his position on many issues, including Black Nationalism, which was central of his philosophy, has considerably mellowed.

Native Americans, Hispanics, and poor Whites are frequently cited as having common cause with African-Americans and many of Farrakhan's speeches have in recent times attracted a cross section of the American population. Considerable numbers of white people listen to him and respond positively to his message. Amongst his friends Farrakhan includes White, former Reagan economics adviser, Jude Wanniski, and Father Micahel Pfleger, a White, Catholic priest, tending to his flock in the South Side of Chicago.

Farrakhan is swiftly being understood as a voice that is not talking or referring to any single section of the population, but like Martin Luther King and Malcolm X before him, the Minister is moving towards a position that perceives the issues relating to black people as being the consequence of deep and profound deficiencies in the way that the USA and international economics work and the character of capitalist society.

The Minister has accepted responsibility for what he has said and done. It is unfortunate that his critics cannot accept or forgive him given the alteration in his stance on so many issues. But this of course would be too much to expect in a world fuelled by blame and guilt. However, those who condemn him cannot ignore how his message has become much more refined and lucid. But, the British establishment is probably made even more anxious about him because of this. If he was addressing or focussing on an entirely black audience, it's a good bet that he would have had few problems getting into the UK. The predicament for those who seek to deny Farrakhan a voice (and of course they can't, he has spoken to Britain via satellite) is that his position has progressed on personal and political fronts. In the UK, Farrakhan has been depicted by the media in a crude way. He has been called names, like the 'Black Hitler', the 'Minister of Hate', and the 'Prophet of Rage'. However, in the USA, where racial segregation was made unlawful less than half-a-century ago and religion is the most segregated aspect of life, it is obvious that his role is far more complicated than the UK media seem to understand.

Any critic of Farrakhan can not overlook his credibility within the black communities. However he also has much wider currency because, particularly following the floods that so badly hit New Orleans in 2005, it is becoming increasingly plain that so long as the political structure and economic system of America excludes great sections of the population; this is Farrakhan's basic credo and clearly the source of mass alienation in the USA.

Like an increasing number of Americans (and British), the Minister is an outsider and this is crucial in understanding his profile and his status. With his self-styled brand of Islam he represents a religious community that at the present time is under siege; this has become much more obvious post September 11th. Farrakhan's militant racial rhetoric transforms him into a target for the Right. At the same time, his own social conservatism in terms of welfare, the family, homosexuals, crime, and women distances him from progressive mainstream forces. But many in the USA and the UK have sympathy with the Minister. His ideas are founded on a very basic notion of decency, something that can be attained by practically anyone who makes the effort. This provides individuals and communities with the belief that they can do something. People find a truth in the notion that they, taking on Farrakhan's directives, can and do make a discernable impact on the quality of life.

Farrakhan is a difficult political figure to deal with and comprehend. However, this is not enough to preclude him from visiting British shores. It is his ideas that have locked our doors to him, but unlike many political philosophies the Minister's have substantial and concrete effects. His vision runs against the stream of liberalism and is premised on straight-forward discipline. This seems to diverge from what many in the UK might understand as being essential to a free or democratic society. Farrakhan's way includes censorship and ridged rules of conduct, founded on a severe morality and the need to lead life ethically.

The Minister is not a threat to public order and by banning him the British government is in reality banning his ideas. But, the prohibition of ideas has no history of lasting success anywhere nor at anytime; as soon as a society overtly censors ideas those same ideas are soon related to belief systems and develop into a much more influential force that can be understood by anyone. Not everyone has the political and ethical intelligence of Farrakhan and few have the inherent spiritual morality he has cultivated for the best part fifty years and that was tempered during the heady era of the struggle for civil-rights in the USA.

Let's be clear. The State prevents Farrakhan from entering Britain because he poses a critique of the State that the State is unable to answer. If that was not the case Farrakhan would have been chatting to Parkinson on national television twenty years ago. It is the fear that Government has of Farrakhan that tells us more about the nature of that Government than it does about the good Minister.

CHAPTER 15

Joe Slovo - African Revolutionary

Nelson Mandela pointed out that Joe Slovo was more than just his colour,
as we all are. Slovo played an important part in a contemporary phase of
the long history of Black people's struggle for freedom and justice.

After it was announced that the South African Minister of Housing had
passed away in his sleep early on Friday 6th. January, 1995 tributes flooded
in from all over South Africa and from around the world. At the age of 68,
Joe Slovo had lost an extended battle against cancer. A prominent member
of the African National Congress he was also the leader of the South
African Communist Party (SACP).

Joe had taken up the struggle to end apartheid and bring democracy to
his country early in life. He was a revolutionary political tactician with and
took a leading role in the negotiations that resulted in South Africa's
Government of National Unity, and the first democratic elections held in
the country in 1994.

Months before that fateful January morning Slovo's public appearances
had caused South Africa to share in his fight for life. The world watched as
his strength failed him, but Joe carried on his work as Housing Minister with
the same concentration and commitment he had shown in his almost life
long endeavour to rid his country of the cruelty of segregation. Just before
his death he was well on the road to creating a new national housing scheme
to benefit the country's impoverished majority.

Joe was born in Lithuania, in the small Village of Obelai, on 23rd. May,
1926 to Ann and Woolf Slovo. The later birth of his sister Reina completed
the family. In the climate of anti-Semitism then rampant in the Baltic
States, the Slovos' emigrated to South Africa. Joe was just eight years old.
Woolf found work as a truck driver in Johannesburg.

Joe Slovo started his African education in 1935 at the Jewish
Government School in Johannesburg. In 1940 he entered Observatory
Junior High School. There he was influenced by the militant Irish teacher,
John O'Meara. Young Joe's favourite school subject was history but he also
loved the debating and athletics.

In 1941 Slovo entered the world of work as a dispatch clerk at South
African Druggists Ltd., wasting no time joining the National Union of
Distributive Workers. As a shop steward, he was soon involved in organising

a strike. He joined the South African Communist Party in 1942.

Influenced by Red Army heroism, he left his Doornfontein boarding house and volunteered to fight for the allies in World War II. He later became very active in the Springbok Legion, a radical ex servicemen's league.

Between 1946 and 1950 Joe completed a B.A. and started to study for a qualification in law at Wits University. He was politically active as a student, involving himself in all the many campaigns of the 1950's. This enthusiasm carried on into his first career as an advocate at the Johannesburg Bar. He became well known for his work as a defence lawyer in political trials. He also took up membership of the African National Congress (ANC). Joe marked his intentions to be an active rather than a mere voting member when at a very early stage in the history of the movement he affiliated with its military wing, Unikhonto we Sizwe, and regularly attended meetings of its high command at Lilliesleaf Farm, Rivonia

In 1949 Slovo married Ruth, the daughter of South African Communist Party Treasurer, Julius First. They were to have three daughters together, Shawn, Gillian and Robyn. Shawn Slovo's account of her childhood has been translated into the successful Hollywood movie *A World Apart*.

The Slovos' were among the first six hundred people 'named' and listed as communists under the South African Suppression of Communism Act of 1954. This meant that they could not be quoted or attend public gatherings, but they continued their political activities covertly. Joe contributed to the drafting of the *Freedom Charter*, an important document in the development of South African resistance to racism, and although he was unable to attend the 'Congress of the People' in Kliptown, where the *Freedom Charter* was introduced, he watched the proceedings through binoculars from a nearby rooftop.

In December 1956 Slovo, together with other Congress activists, was charged with treason. He was detained for two months during the infamous Treason Trial of that year. Despite being one of the accused Joe acted as a member of the defence team. During the preparatory examination of the Trial he was charged with contempt of court when objecting to the magistrate's handling of the examination, but he was acquitted on appeal. Treason charges against him were dropped late in 1958.

Joe was later detained for six months during the State of Emergency declared after the Sharpeville shootings in 1960, wherein the police shot and killed sixty-seven people, and injured over one hundred and eighty more. But Slovo was not deterred. He became chief of staff of the Umkhonto we Sizwe in 1961. He maintained this role up to April 1987. At the same time he was a member of the Central Committee of the SACP and at the ANC consultative conference held in Zambia in 1985 Joe became the first white member of the ANC's National Executive.

Joe left South Africa in June 1963 on an 'external mission'. A month later police captured the remaining key figures of the high command of Unikhonto we Sizwe, including Walter Sisulu and Govan Mbeki. A month after these arrests his wife Ruth was detained for almost four months. On her release she left the country, together with her three daughters. The whole Slovo family were now effectively in exile on instructions from the SACP and ANC, travelling to the UK (in 1966 Joe finished his Law studies at London School of Economics), Angola, Mozambique and Zambia.

This peripatetic life style didn't prevent Joe from taking a full part in the continued struggle for his country's freedom. He served on the revolutionary council of the ANC from 1969 until its dissolution in 1983 and in 1977 moved to Maputo, Mozambique, where he established an operational centre for the ANC. It was there in 1982, that Ruth First was killed by a parcel bomb explosion at her office. This was believed to have been the work of the South African apartheid regime. Two years later Slovo was forced to leave Mozambique following the signing of the Nkomati Accord between that country and South Africa. In January 1986, a British court awarded Slovo substantial damages against a South African newspaper group over a report in *The Star* newspaper that he had orchestrated the murder of his wife.

Following the death of Moses Mabhida in 1986, Slovo was elected General Secretary of the SACP whilst retaining his position on the ANC National Executive and its political military council.

In June 1989, the SACP congress adopted a new programme of action to replace its 1962 guidelines. It was accepted that the strategies of armed struggled did not rule out the possibilities of negotiations and compromise. In January 1990, Slovo circulated his paper *Has Socialism Failed?* Always portrayed as an arch Stalinist by the former South African government this document surprised his critics as it acknowledged the weaknesses of socialism and excesses of Stalinism. *Has Socialism Failed* also indicated that the SACP would commit itself to a multi party, post apartheid democracy, freedom of organisation, speech, thought, press, movement, residence, conscience and religion; full trade union rights for all workers including the right to strike; and one person, one vote in free and democratic elections. A month later the SACP and ANC were given legal status in South Africa. In February Slovo was named as the General Secretary of the Party and returned to South Africa to participate in the early 'talks about talks' between the government and the ANC.

In December 1991 Joe was elected Chair of the SACP. During that year

Slovo served as the Party's representative on the National Peace Committee and was re elected to the National Executive Committee of the ANC. He also served on the ANC's National Working Committee. In 1992 an adapted form of his 'Sunset Clause' document, allowing for a form of power sharing with the government, was adopted. So, even though Joe Slovo was a leading theoretician in both the South African Communist Party and the ANC, writing numerous articles for the *African Communist* (he had been an editor this journal) as well as countless pamphlets and contributed to several books such as *No Middle Road*, he perhaps should be remembered first and foremost as one of the main architects of South Africa's agenda for freedom.

Despite his consistent and focused revolutionary stance Joe was a sensitive person who loved classical music, particularly the work of Mahler. His favourite book was *Gogol's Dead Souls*. At the time of his death he was married to agricultural economist Helena Dolny and lived in Johannesburg. It was tragic that he saw so little of his country's joy at the freedom he had done so much to bring about following the 1994 elections. After this momentous event Joe had been given a seat on the cabinet where he served as Minister of Housing until his death less than a year later. Just eight months before his he died Joe said that he had to keep pinching himself to believe democracy and freedom had finally come to South Africa.

A Justification

The above account of Joe Slovo's life was written in response to questions about my academic concentration on important figures from the world wide Diaspora of Black people. In common with all the subjects of this book I wrote it to exemplify that Black History is not something separate or segregated from all other history. It tells us something about the past and the present that all of us share, regardless of colour.

I hope, from the perspective of Joe Slovo's life I have demonstrated that our hope lies not in the acceptance of limitations placed on us by way of 'colour distinction' but in joint action to question all such restrictions, their logic and their meaning within a society that is plagued by institutional forms of prejudice and discrimination. With this in mind I will conclude the book with the words of Nelson Mandela and his goodbye to his fellow African freedom fighter, Joe Slovo.

Nelson Mandela's Address at Joe Slovo's Funeral, 15th. January 1995.

Comrade Chairperson:
Dear Helena, Shawn, Gillian and Robyn; Mrs Rene Ephron, Comrade Joe's sister and other relatives; Deputy President Thabo Mbeki, Ministers, leaders

of the Tri partite Alliance; Dear comrades; Fellow South Africans.

We are assembled to mourn the passing of a leader, a patriot, a father, a fighter, a negotiator, an internationalist, a theoretician and an organiser. Indeed, it is the combination of all these qualities so splendidly in one individual, which made Comrade Joe Slovo the great African revolutionary that he was. Men and women of rare qualities are few and hard to come by. And when they depart, the sense of loss is made the more profound and the more difficult to manage.

Yet we do draw comfort, Comrade Joe, from the knowledge that the greater part of the journey that was the passion of your life has been traversed. From the knowledge that you left a legacy which we shall all strive to emulate. From the knowledge, Comrade Joe, that you continue to live in each one of us through your force of example, vitality of spirit and passion for justice.

Today, as the nation bids you final farewell, we are at the same time celebrating a life lived to the full; the richness of which touched the hearts of millions and made an indelible mark on the history of our country.

When future generations look back on the 1994 breakthrough, they will be justified in saying: Uncle Joe was central in making it happen.

When the working people start enjoying, as a right, a roof over their heads, affordable medical care, quality education and a rising standard of living, they will be right to say, Comrade Joe was a chief architect who helped lay the foundation for a better life.

When those yet to be born marvel at how South Africans of our times managed a delicate transition, they will be within their right to sing, as we did during the years of armed struggle: u'Slovo, ikoniando, a commando of reconstruction and development, a warrior of peace and reconciliation, a builder par excellence.

Comrade Joe Slovo was one of those who taught us that individuals do not make history. Yet, in each generation there are a few individuals who are endowed with the acumen and personal bearing which enable them to direct the course of events.

Comrade Joe Slovo, Isithwalandwe Seaparankoe, belonged in that category. In that sense he was a rare species, an institution. To reflect on Joe's contribution is, therefore, to retrace the evolution of South African politics in the past half century.

Such is the life we celebrate today; a life not so much of white generosity to the black people of our country; for JS did not see himself as a white South African but as a South African. He was a full part of the democratic majority, acting together with them for a just and democratic order.

Comrade Joe Slovo lived the life not merely of a theoretician, confined to the boardroom and library. He was at all stages of struggle there at the forefront, generating ideas, and there too, in their implementation.

Comrade Chairperson; When, in 1934, the village of Obelkei in Lithuania, bequeathed to South Africa an eight year old Yossel Mashel Slovo, there was no predetermined course that his life would follow.

Forced to leave school at an early age because of poverty; part of the passionate political debates of that period among immigrants in Johannesburg; a poor Jewish family upbringing in the period when Nazism was rearing its ugly head; all these factors helped mould one of the greatest South African and African revolutionaries of our times.

Joe Slovo was among the few white workers who understood their class interest and sought common cause with their class brother and sisters irrespective of race.

In this sense, Comrade Joe Slovo leaves the South African working class black and white, a challenge, particularly now that the walls of racial division are finally collapsing: the time for unity has come!

The young Joe could have late chosen a lucrative life, after returning from service in the Second World War, and acquiring the opportunities accorded white veterans. He could have elected, as many in his position did, to part ways with his black colleagues as they rode into oblivion on the bicycles given them as the thankless reward for their service in the War.

But Joe Slovo was a full human being at heart. And he possessed the passion and natural intellect to see reality for what it was. He had, at the age of sixteen joined the Communist Party of South Africa. To use his own words, he had decided that in his life there was only one target, and that target was to remove the racist régime and obtain power for the people.

Those of us who had the honour to be closely associated with Comrade Joe, know that he lived true to his dedication. He knew fully well that he would walk again and again through the valley of the shadow of death to reach the mountaintops of his desires.

I was fortunate to meet him in our younger days at Wits University. With his future wife, Ruth First, Ismail Meer, Harold Wolpe, Jules Browde, J.N. Singh and others, we would debate many issues well into the wee hours of the morning. His sharp intellect and incisive mind were apparent then.

But Joe was a well rounded human being. Up to his last days, he lived life to the full. He never claimed to be a saint. He was a good organiser of enjoyable parties. He liked to eat and dress well. He had humour in abundance.

It is this passion for happiness in his life and the lives of others that we saw in his contribution to the campaigns of the working people; in court as a devastating human rights lawyer; in the underground; and in the formation of Umkhonto we Sizwe in 1961. When we were on Robben Island, we managed on a few occasions to exchange correspondence. But if there is any form of intimate contact that one could point at, it was the glowing praise from the young cadres who joined us and who had developed both politically and militarily under his guidance.

Comrade Chairperson. It is precisely because of his seminal contribution to the liberation struggle that Comrade JS was loved by those struggling for freedom.

Though the defenders of apartheid sought to obliterate his memory, the struggling people knew that he was an effective and skilful MK Chief of Operations; they knew that he was a loved and respected MK Chief of Staff; they knew that he planned and inspired many special operations of the people's army that shook the foundations of the apartheid establishment. They knew too that he was at the core of collectives that drafted many strategy and tactics documents of the movement.

The most central factor in his approach to struggle on any front was the understanding of the political situation, the balance of forces and thus the approaches necessary to advance that struggle. Thus he was able to appreciate changes in the objective conditions and initiate discussions on changes to the tactics to be applied.

He knew when to compromise. Yet he never compromised his principles. He was a militant. Yet a militant who knew how to plan, assess concrete situations and emerge with rational solutions to problems.

We shall forever remember Slovo, as one of the embodiments of the alliance between the ANC and the SACP. Joe knew that the interests of the working class in our country were intimately bound up with those of the rest of the oppressed majority in pursuit of democracy and a better life. He knew too that, for the working class to realise these interests, it had to play an active role in the liberation struggle and the liberation movement.

Joe appreciated that the Alliance between the ANC, the SACP and the progressive trade union movement was premised on concrete democratic and social tasks. He appreciated the need to strengthen this Alliance especially now when we are reconstructing and developing South Africa.

More than in theory, his own practical life demonstrated his profound understanding of the nature of the relationship between the ANC and the SACP: the leading role of the ANC; the principles of consultation, consensus and criticism within disciplined structures of the allies.

The advocates of racial superiority could not understand how Slovo could be part of the liberation struggle and operate under the leadership of the hapless inferiors they despised. But Joe took part in struggle as an equal, as part of the people.

The defenders of national oppression could not understand why Slovo would seek to end the dominance of his racial kith and kin. But Joe's kin was all humanity, especially the very poor.

The champions of privilege and concentration of wealth could not fathom why Slovo identified with the wretched of the earth. But Joe knew that these were the creators of wealth and they deserved their fare share.

It is the tragedy of South Africa that his humanity, pragmatism and industriousness were realised by many, particularly among the white community, only after close on to fourty years of an artificial silence imposed on him by constant banning. And it is a tragedy still, that these qualities are extolled by some as if they were new. Let it be said loud and clear today that the qualities Slovo demonstrated in abundance in the past few years were the same attributes that spurred him to struggle; the qualities that drove him to join the liberation movement and the qualities that he helped engender in these organisations.

We in the Government of National Unity know intimately what vacuum Minister Joe Slovo's departure has left in our midst. We shall miss not only his incisiveness, experience and verve. We are conscious that it is given to a few to so ably combine theory and practice as Joe demonstrated in his portfolio.

But we know too that he has left us a legacy which will continue to guide our approach. And that is to mobilise all the role players in any area of work for joint efforts to build a better life for all. The depth of it all is captured in the profound messages that we have received from the civics movement, mortgage tending institutions, the construction industry, property owners' associations, the banks and many others.

Contained in all of them is the appreciation of Joe's central theme that all of us have a responsibility to ensure that the RDP succeeds. Those with resources have a crucial role to play. The government should discharge its responsibility. But, above all, ordinary people themselves should guide policy formulation and implementation. Among the last issues he was working on with a passion only typical of him was the launch of a campaign to ensure delivery of houses and services and at the same time, to mobilise communities to pay their bonds, rents and service charges.

I wish on behalf of Government to reiterate that the course Joe Slovo had charted will continue to guide us in fulfilling the housing programme. His firmness in dealing with obstacles to this programme will remain one of the central features of our work. Comrade Chairperson; If we have taken liberty to claim Comrade Joe as ours today, this merely underlines that there are those to whom he was more than just a revolutionary and a friend. There were times when our demands on him, indeed the demands of struggle, made it difficult for him to play fully the role of father and brother. There were times when his commitment and that of Ruth First, who was murdered in cold blood in 1982, created a world apart, where full family life, as with most other revolutionaries, became an ephemeral dream.

We know, dear Helena, Shawn, Gillian, Robin and Rene that you feel this pain more deeply. We cannot fully grasp the magnitude of your grief, particularly the bond that was cemented in the normal life that he could live only in the last few years, no longer a fugitive. Please be comforted by the fact that the nation shares your grief; and we shall always be at your side.

Like you, our sorrow is made the more intense because we have lost not just one of our leaders; we have lost a veteran whose qualities are in many respects unequalled. He is irreplaceable.

The irony that Joe so succinctly captured, that life is after all a terminal illness, is the tragedy of the natural order that we can do nothing to change. But like him, we can so live that, when we depart, we shall have made life that much more bearable for others.

Comrade Joe, in our grief, we do remember that you enjoined us not to mourn but to celebrate the achievements you humbly helped realise. If you see tears welling in our eyes, it is because we cannot bear saying: Farewell dear comrade, dear brother, dear friend!

Bibliography

Ashrawi, H. (1995) *This Side of Peace: A Personal Account:* Simon & Schuster Ltd.

Ashrawi, H. (2002) *Birthing the Nation*: University of California Press.

Belton, B. (1997) *Bubbles, Hammers and Dreams*: Breedon Books.

Belton, B. (1998) *The First and Last Englishmen*: Breedon Books.

Belton, B. (1999) *Days of Iron*: Breedon Books.

Belton, B. (2003) *Founded on Iron*: Tempus.

Belton, B. (2003) *Johnnie the One*: Tempus.

Belton, B. (2004) *Gypsy and Traveller Ethnicity: The Social Generation of an Ethnic Phenomenon*: Routledge, an imprint of Taylor & Francis Books Ltd.

Belton, B. (2004) *Questioning Gypsy Identity: Ethnic Narratives in Britain and America:* AltaMira.

Belton, B. (2004) *Burn Johnny Byrne - Football Inferno*: Breedon Books.

Belton, B. (2005) *The Men of '64, Gloucestershire*: Tempus.

Belton, B. (2006) *West Ham United Miscellany*: Pennant Books.

Belton, B. (2006) *Black Hammers: The Voices of West Ham's Ebony Heroes* Pennant Book.

Biko, S. (1987) *I Write What I Like*. London: Heinemann.

Blackstock, N. (1976) *COINTELPRO: The FBI's Secret War on Political Freedom:* Vintage Books.

Breitman, G. (Ed.). (1970). *By any means necessary: Speeches, interviews and a letter by Malcolm X*: Pathfinder Press.

Breitman, G.(1965) *Malcolm X: The Man and His Ideas*:Pioneer Publishers.

Breitman, G. (1967) *The Last Year of Malcolm X: The Evolution of a Revolutionary:* Merit Publishers.

Brooks, G. (1996) *Report from Part Two*: Third World (Reprint edition).

Brooks, G. (2006) *Maud Martha*: Third World Press, U.S (Reprint edition). by Gwendolyn Brooks.

Brooks, G. (2006) *Selected Poems*: HarperCollins Publishers.

Carmichael, S. (1992) *Black Power: the Politics of Liberation in America*: Vintage Books (Vintage Ed edition).

Carmichael, S. (2005) *Ready for Revolution: The Life and Struggles of Stokely Carmichael (Kwame Ture)*: Scribner (Reprint edition).

Carson, C. (1991). *Malcolm X: The FBI file*: Carroll & Graf, Inc.

Carson, C. (2003) *The Black Panthers Speak*: Da Capo Press (New Ed edition).

Caute, D. (1970) *Fanon*. London: Fontana Press Ltd.

Cleaver, E. (1996) *Soul on Ice*: Bantam Doubleday Dell Books for Young Readers (Reprint edition).

Cleaver, E., (Cleaver, K.ed) (1996) *Target Zero: A Life in Writing:* Palgrave MacMillan

Cleaver, K. Katsiaficas, G. (eds) (2001) *Liberation, Imagination and the Black Panther Party: A New Look at the Black Panthers and Their Legacy:* Routledge,an imprint of Taylor & Francis Books Ltd.

Chapman, B. (1970) *Police State*: Pall Mall Press.

Chomsky, N. (1987) *On Power and Ideology*: South End Press.

Chomsky, N. (1989) *Necessary Illusions:* South End Press.

Chomsky, N. (1996) *Class Warfare*: Common Courage Press.

Chomsky, N and Macedo, D. (Ed) (2000) *Chomsky on MisEducation*: Rowman and Littlefield.

Couzens Hoy, D. (1986) *Foucault: A Critical Reader:*Blackwell Publishers.

Curtis, M. (1998) *The Great Deception: Anglo-American Power and World Order:* Pluto Press.

Davis, L. G. (1984). *Malcolm X: A selected bibliography.* (First ed.):Greenwood Press.

DeCaro Jr., L. A. (1996). *On the side of my people: A religious life of Malcolm X.* (First ed.): New York University Press.

De Man, P. (1984) *The Rhetoric of Reconstruction*: Columbia University Press.

DuBois, W. E. B. (1903). *The Souls of Black Folk*: A.C. McClurg.

El Saadawi, N (1980) *The Hidden Face of Eve - Women in the Arab World*: Zed Books Ltd

El Saadawi, N (1983) *Women at Point Zero*: Zed Books Ltd.

El Saadawi, N (1985) *God Dies by the Nile*: Zed Books Ltd.

El Saadawi, N (1989) *The Circling Song:* Zed Books Ltd.

El Saadawi, N (1991) *Searching:* Zed Books Ltd,

El Saadawi, N (1997) *The Nawal El Saadawi Reader*: Zed Books Ltd.

El Saadawi, N (1999) *A Daughter of Isis* : The Autobiography of Nawal El Saadawi: Zed Books.

Falzon, C. (1998) *Foucault and Social Dialogue:* Routledge.

Fanon F (1952) *The Wretched of the Earth:* Macgibbon and Kee/Penguin Books Ltd.

Fanon F (1961) *Black Skins, White Masks.* London: Pluto Press.

Farrakhan, L. (1993) *Independent Black Leadership*: Castillo International (1st. July,1993).

Farrakhan, L. (1993) *A Torchlight for America:* F. C. N. Publishing Co.

Foucault, M. (1977) *Discipline and Punish*: Penguin Books Ltd.

Foucault, M. (1967) *Madness and Civilization*: Tavistock Publications Ltd.

Gabriel, J. (1994) *Racism, Culture, Markets*: Routledge.

Gilroy, P. (2000) *Between Camps. Race, Identity and Nationalism at the End of the Colour Line*: Allen Lane The Penguin Press

Goldman, P. (1979). *The death and life of Malcolm X.* (2d ed.): University of Illinois Press.

Grant, E.A. (2006) *Dawn to Dusk:* A Biography of Bernie Grant MP: ITUNI Books

Hacker, A. (1992). *Two Nations*: black and white, separate, hostile, unequal. (First ed.): Macmillan.

Hadden, P. (1980) *Divide and Rule*: Militant.

Hall, S. Du Gay, P. (1996) *Questions of Cultural Identity*: SAGE Publications Ltd; (Reprint edition).

Hall, S. (1991) '*The Local and the Global*', in King, A.D. (ed.). *Culture, Globalisation and the World System*. London: Macmillan.

Hall, S.(1997) *Representation: Cultural Representations and Signifying Practices*: SAGE Publications Ltd.

Hall, S. (2004) *Critical Dialogues in Cultural Studies*: Routledge,an imprint of Taylor & Francis Books Ltd.

Illich, I (1976) *Deschooling Society*: Penguin Books Ltd.

Illich, I.(1977) *Disabling Professions*: Boyars.

Jinadu A.L. (1986) *Fanon: In Search of the African Revolution:* KPI Limited.

Johnson,T.V. (1986). *Malcolm X: A comprehensive annotated bibliography*: Garland.

Jones, P. Baruch, R (2002) *Black Panthers:* Greybull Press, US.

Loomba, A. (1998) *Colonialism/Post Colonialism*: Routledge.

Marcuse, H. (1968) *Reason and Revolution*: Beacon Press.

Perry, B. (1991). Malcolm: *The life of a man who changed Black America*. (First ed.): Station Hill Press.

Perry, T. I. (Ed.). (1995). *Teaching Malcolm X*: Routledge.

Pico Della Mirandola, G. (1965) *On the Dignity of Man, On Being and the One Heptaplus*: The Bobbs-Merrill Company, Inc.

Pilger, J. (1998) *Hidden Agendas*: Vintage Books.

Pilger, J. (2002) *The New Rulers of the World*: Verso.

Rampersad, A. (1992). *The Color of His Eyes: Bruce Perry's Malcolm and Malcolm's Malcolm*. In J. Wood (Ed.)., *Malcolm X: In our own image*, (pp. 117-134): St. Martin's Press

Rosak, T. (1970) *The Making of a Counter Culture: Reflections on the Technocratic Society and Its Youthful Opposition*: Routledge.

Sales Jr., W. W. (1994). *From civil rights to black liberation: Malcolm X and the organization of Afro-American unity*: South End Press.

Schopenhauer, A. (1883) *A World as Will and Idea*: Routledge and Kegan Paul.

Sennett, R. (1970) *Uses of Disorder*: Alfred A.Knopf.

Shakur, A., Davis, A., Hinds, L.S. (1987) *Assata: An Autobiography*: Chicago Review Press (New Ed edition).

Shakur, A., Buck, M.M. (1999) *Sparks Fly: Women Political Prisoners and the Prison Industrial Complex*: Agit P.

Singh, R. (1997) *The Farrakhan Phenomenon: Race, Reaction and the Paranoid Style in American Politics*: Georgetown University Press.

Slovo. J. (1997) *Slovo: The Unfinished Autobiography of ANC Leader Joe Slovo*: Ocean Press.

Squires, J. (ed.). (1995) *Michael Foucault: J'Accuse*. New Formations (25) Summer

1995, London: Lawrence and Wishart.

Stone, I. F. *The Pilgrimage of Malcolm X* in I. F. Stone (1967) *In a Time of Torment*: Random House).

Strickland, W. (1994). *Malcolm X: Make it plain.* (First ed.): Blackstone, Inc.

Thomas, W. I. (1971) *Old World Traits Transplanted*: Patterson Smith.

Wiley, R. (1993) *What Black People Should Do Now*: Ballantine Books.

Witt, A. (2007) *The Black Panthers in the Midwest: The Community Programs and Services of the Black Panther Party in Milwaukee, 1966-1977*: Routledge,an imprint of Taylor & Francis Books Ltd.

Wittgenstein, L. (1973) *Philosophical Investigations*: Blackwell Publishers (New edition).

Wittgenstein, L. (2001) *Tractatus Logico-philosophicus*: Routledge,an imprint of Taylor & Francis Books Ltd. (New Ed edition).

Wolfenstein, E. V. (1989). *The Victims of Democracy: Malcolm X and the black revolution*: Free Association Books.

Woodson, C. G. (1990). *The Mis-education of the Negro*: Africa World Press, Inc.

Malcolm X (1965) *The Autobiography of Malcolm X*: Grove Press

Malcolm X, (1965) *Malcolm X Speaks: Selected Speeches and Statements*: Merit Publishers

Malcolm X, (1991) *Malcolm X: Speeches at Harvard*: Paragon House

Malcolm X, (1989) *Malcolm X: The Last Speeches*: Pathfinder Press

Websites

See article by Jennifer McBride: www.webster.edu/~woolflm/saadawi.html

Life and Experience in inter War Britain:

www.connectionsexhibition.org/index.php?xml=histories/black/interwaryears.xml

See Youth for Socialist Action website:

http://geocities.com/youth4sa/malcolm.html.

Index